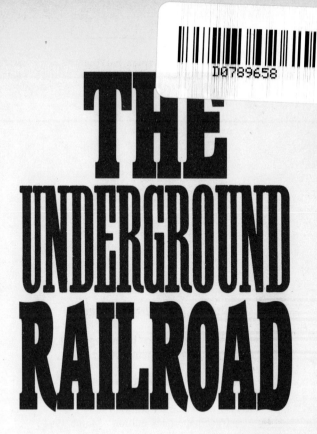

THE UNDERGROUND RAILROAD

CHARLES L. BLOCKSON

B

BERKLEY BOOKS, NEW YORK

THE UNDERGROUND RAILROAD

A Berkley Book / published by arrangement with
Simon & Schuster

PRINTING HISTORY
Prentice Hall Press edition published 1987
Berkley mass market edition / May 1989
Berkley trade paperback edition / March 1994

ISBN: 0-425-14136-5

BERKLEY®
Berkley Books are published by The Berkley Publishing Group,
200 Madison Avenue, New York, New York 10016.
BERKLEY and the "B" design are
trademarks belonging to Berkley Publishing Corporation.

PRINTED IN THE UNITED STATES OF AMERICA

10 9 8 7 6 5 4

CONTENTS

PREFACE

My great-grandfather James escaped out of slavery from Seaford, Delaware, in 1856. My talks with him were a source of numerous imaginative flights in which I accompanied my ancestors through the frightening perils of the trip north. This led me at an early age to begin collecting information on Afro-Americans in general and the Underground Railroad in particular.

Later in my life, I decided to research the stories that my grandfather used to tell me in Chestnut Hollow, Norristown, Pennsylvania, and I was able to verify them through William Still's classic work, *Underground Railroad*, which recorded the narratives of escaped slaves who made their way to the Philadelphia area, many of them unassisted. Among these narratives were the stories and names of several of my relations, including my great-grandfather James Blockson.

I began researching the Underground Railroad by corresponding with and sometimes traveling to visit historical societies throughout the country. No matter where I went in my travels, people pointed out some home, barn, church, or cave that allegedly was part of the Underground Railroad system. These sites need preservation. They are a major part of our national heritage, reminders of the sacrifices of whites and blacks together.

Because of my commitment to the topic, Wilbur Garrett commissioned me to do an article on the Underground Railroad for the National Geographic Society. Aided and supported by the great photographer Louis Psihoyos and the editorial and cartographic staff, I began my research and the travels that took me to the deep South, to the Midwest, and to Canada.

My original plan was to start at Harriet Tubman's birth-place at Bucktown, Maryland, in Dorchester County, and follow her freedom route into Canada. I prepared for a trip that I estimated would take me three months; however, it took three years to complete. This gave me a broader opportunity than any earlier historian of the topic. I met many descendants of slaves and their helpers, black and white, who delved deeply into their memories in order to help me.

The most emotional experience of my travels occurred when I visited the grave of Harriet Tubman in Auburn, New York. This courageous woman, whom her peers called "Moses," is buried in a grove of trees, as is her friend in life, Frederick Douglass. The trees seem to comfort her and shield her from unwanted notice. After I touched the tombstone, read the inscription, and knelt beside the grave, my emotional armor deteriorated. I cried because of my recollections of her nineteen mosquito-plagued and frostbitten journeys leading others to freedom. It had been a long trip for me, even with shelter, modern food, and conveniences, and this woman of steel, without complaining, had made the same trip many times by any means available to her, including boat, horse-back, and foot. Standing there beneath those tall evergreen trees, I reflected on her arduous journey from Bucktown, Maryland, to become an international symbol of strength. Her profound influence seemed to guide me through the rest of my journey just as she herself was directed by her beloved and trusted God.

During the decades of my study of the Underground Rail-road, leading most recently to my article in the *National Geographic* in July of 1984 and to this book of first-person narratives, I have encountered many willing helpers. Custodians of the records of the past in libraries, historical societies, and private collections in the United States and in Canada have been open-handed in their generosity with time and information. They have demonstrated a happy combination of high professional standards and selfless dedication. I also am grateful to donors and dealers who have helped me to build my collection of Afro-American materials and to the descendants of slaves and conductors alike who have passed on their personal and family recollections.

I have been particularly blessed by the dedication of a good staff. Joan Hankins, my secretary, who, with her sister, Jackie Hankins, typed the many versions of the text on typewriter and word processor, has been extraordinarily helpful. Sharon Hollie, a student at Temple University Law School, was an energetic and capable research assistant.

Among the many original manuscripts in the Blockson Collection housed at Temple University are a number of letters from William Still that have not yet been transcribed and published. In one to his daughter dated August 13,1867, he writes that he is "reading Macaulay's History of England with great interest," and that he intends "to write the History of the U.G.R.R. I must do a good deal of reading and thinking in order to be able to write well. I may commence my book this fall some time." His book was published in 1872. His book was a major inspiration for this collection of fugitive slave narratives, which like his presents the stories of escaping slaves and their helpers in their own words.

I have been fortunate in having again the helpful editorial advice and experience of James E. Mooney, with whom I have worked often over the years on books and exhibitions. I have come to depend upon the sense and skill of Laurie Marks in matters cartographical.

The patience of publishers and editors is too rarely acknowledged but I do so here, in proper gratitude for their goodwill.

INTRODUCTION

Over the last century, numerous books have been written about the Underground Railroad, that secret avenue to freedom taken by an increasingly large number of daring runaways from the beginning of the nineteenth century through the frenzied rush in the decades between the Fugitive Slave Act and the outbreak of the Civil War. Rarely, though, has the story been told from the viewpoint of the central characters, the fugitive slaves. Why did they risk death for freedom, and how did they make their way out of bondage? The answers are indispensable to an understanding of the real Underground.

By law, slaves were to be kept illiterate, and those few who could write were generally afraid to record their experiences. Nevertheless, against great odds, many did learn to write and set down an account of their lives. In the pages of this book the reader will meet and come to know the major personalities in this dramatic and too-little-known chapter in American history: Harriet Tubman, as the Moses of her people, struggles steadfastly to achieve her heaven-directed goals. Frederick Douglass escapes from slavery in Maryland to become the most eloquent spokesman for freedom in print and on platform here and abroad. Sojourner Truth, near penniless, still manages to get the funds to continue her unremitting rescue work. Thomas Garrett, a white Delaware Quaker, refuses to budge an inch from his abolition principles while living and working in a slave state. "Box" Brown ships himself to freedom from Richmond crouched painfully in a packing crate finally opened in the Philadelphia office of William Still, a black agent on the line to liberty. William

1

and Ellen Craft, a married couple, escape slavery by traveling openly through the public highways of the antebellum South in that most convincing of disguises—master and slave. The wealthy and well-born Charlotte Forten is here, recording riots in Boston, along with that most piteous and desperate black mother Margaret Garner, ready to sacrifice her child rather than see her returned to slavery.

The discontented and daring hoped that the North Star would guide them to stations on the burgeoning Underground Railroad, which by the early 1830s still didn't have a name. The word spread from plantation to plantation, first in whispers and then in outright talk: there was a railroad to freedom. It was a moment of great trepidation when the runaways met up with a conductor in the dark who whispered "follow me" and then proceeded to guide them on an arduous journey where they were constantly admonished to keep quiet.

Fugitives slaves had first to find a safe place. Some found it in rugged woodland while others slipped into the relative anonymity of towns and cities. Those runaways who could not feel truly safe in the northern states passed on into Canada.

Free-Soil Party members, free blacks, and others in each community worked to provide food, clothing, and shelter for fugitives. Women's antislavery societies organized sewing circles to provide clothing and raise money. There were many dedicated women like the Grimke sisters and Laura Haviland who did much more on their own and against the wishes of their families.

Fugitives were hidden in livery stables, attics, and storerooms, under feather beds, in secret passages, and in all sorts of out-of-the-way places. They were disguised in various ways. They were nursed and nursed themselves through long and serious illnesses. They moved on to the next station at night by wagon, by boat, and by train. Routes of travel were changed at a moment's notice. When fugitives settled down in the free states it was along the Underground Railroad routes, so as to get away quickly when necessary.

All over the South, overseers blowing their horns to rouse the slaves found that the number reporting to the fields was dwindling. The slaves were running from the humiliations and heartbreak of slavery, which had stripped them of dignity and reduced them to a level lower than the dogs that were trained to hunt them.

For over a century we have been led to believe that white abolitionists generally and Quakers specifically extended all aid to runaway slaves. This involvement, however, has been grossly exaggerated. Only a minority of this religious community raised its voice against slavery and participated in the struggle to transport slaves to freedom. True, a few Quakers in the North and South were earnestly involved in the Underground network, and Lucretia Mott, Thomas Garrett, Susan B. Anthony, and John Greenleaf Whittier were four of the most important. Overemphasis on the Quakers' role has led to ignorance about the participation of other religious groups, however. The Wesleyan Methodists, the Jews, the Dunkers, the Unitarians, the Covenanters, and the Roman Catholics probably have as legitimate a claim to consistent Railroad activity as the Quakers.

The history of the Underground Railroad has had an uneven history itself. The most often cited early study of the network is Wilburg H. Siebert's *The Underground Railroad: From Slavery to Freedom,* published in 1898. The bulk of his field work over forty years was conducted in Ohio and Massachusetts, where he resided. Thus the celebrated Underground Railroad chronicler accorded a minor role to the efforts of blacks on the Freedom Train. On the other hand, William Still, a black historian with great narrative skills, published his famous *Underground Railroad Records* in 1872. He interviewed every slave sent to him, and his knowledge of fugitives was immense. A serious distortion has been an overemphasis on the amount of assistance rendered by white abolitionists, who wrote a great deal on the subject. This tended to make the people whom the Railroad was designed to aid—the fugitive slaves—seem either invisible or passive and helpless without aid from others. Slaves did not sit passively waiting to be led out of slavery, however. Once free, they often reached back to help others escape to freedom. Black courage and perseverance, along with the spirited and sympathetic help of whites, brought many men, women, and children out of slavery.

It is one of the strong assertions of this book that the most assiduous organizers of networks to freedom were black freemen, especially in the period of greatest activity from 1850 throughout 1860. These black conductors and agents had escaped earlier or had been born free in the North. They organized their own network quietly and well and were settled and ready for the surge of the 1850s. Many black ministers, in particular, felt that organized assistance to fugitives was necessary to challenge the prevailing religious dogma of many white churches that a truly religious person was patient, in passive acceptance of the will of God.

These narratives demonstrate the relationship between the Underground Railroad and the larger antislavery movement. The abolitionists were dedicated to wiping out slavery in America by a number of methods, from disunion with the South, as proposed by William Lloyd Garrison and his followers; through gradual emancipation, as proposed by lecturers, sewing circles, colonization societies, and other moderates; to undeclared and later declared war upon the slave states, as begun by John Brown. All of these methods had in common the aim of abolishing slavery in the nation. The Underground Railroad was different in that it was a pragmatic case-by-case resolution of the problems of fugitives. It was without a theory or a throng of lecturers, and no national conventions were needed to make the Underground Railroad work efficiently. Yet all were closely allied in their ultimate purpose.

ALABAMA

Forty-five percent of Alabama's population was in slavery, and it was potentially a more onerous form of slavery than in the upper South, because Alabama, alone with Mississippi, continued to enforce the penalty of "burning in the hand" for felonies not punishable by death. State law also permitted up to one hundred lashes on the bare back for such crimes as forging a pass or engaging in "riots, routs, unlawful assemblies, trespasses, and seditious speeches," as Kenneth Stampp points out in *Peculiar Institution* (page 210). The earlier historian Wilbur Siebert wrote in his history of the Underground Railroad (page 195) that, while most of the fugitives had come from the border slave states, some few "favored by rare good fortune and possessed of more than ordinary sagacity or aided by some venturesome friend, had made their way from the far South."

Narrative of Peter Still

This narrative appears in Still's *Underground Railroad Records,* (pages 36 to 38). The dramatic narrative of his brother, Peter Still, is one of the great documents of the Underground Railroad.

The life, struggles, and success of Peter and his family were ably brought before the public in "The Kidnapped and the Ransomed," being the personal recollections of Peter Still and his wife "Vina," after forty years of slavery, by Mrs. Kate E. R. Pickard; with an introduction by Rev. Samuel J. May, and an appendix by William H. Furness, D.D., in 1856. But, of course, it was not prudent or safe, in the day of Slavery, to publish such facts as are now brought to light; all such had to be kept concealed in the breasts of the fugitives and their friends.

The following brief sketch, touching the separation of Peter and his mother, will fitly illustrate this point, and at the same time explain certain mysteries which have been hitherto kept hidden.

With regard to Peter's separation from his mother, when a little boy, in few words, the facts were these: His parents, Levin and Sidney, were both slaves on the Eastern Shore of Maryland. "I will die before I submit to the yoke," was the declaration of his father to his young master before either was twenty-one years of age. Consequently he was allowed to buy himself at a very low figure, and he paid the required sum and obtained his "free papers" when quite a young man—the young wife and mother remaining in slavery under Saunders Griffin, as also her children, the latter having increased to the number of four, two little boys and two little girls. But to escape from chains, stripes, and bondage, she took her four little children and fled to a place near Greenwich, New Jersey. Not a great while, however, did she remain there in a state of freedom before the slave-hunters pursued her, and one night they pounced upon the whole family, and, without judge or jury, hurried them all back to slavery. Whether this was kidnapping or not is for the reader to decide for himself.

Safe back in the hands of her owner, to prevent her from escaping a second time, every night for about three months she was cautiously "kept locked up in the garret," until, as they supposed, she was fully "cured of the desire to do so again." But she was incurable. She had been a witness to the fact that her own father's brains had been blown out by the discharge of a heavily loaded gun, deliberately aimed at his head by his drunken master. She only needed half a chance to make still greater struggles than ever for freedom.

She had great faith in God, and found much solace in

singing some of the good old Methodist tunes, by day and night. Her owner, observing this apparently tranquil state of mind, indicating that she "seemed better contented than ever," concluded that it was safe to let the garret door remain unlocked at night. Not many weeks were allowed to pass before she resolved to again make a bold strike for freedom. This time she had to leave the two little boys, Levin and Peter, behind.

On the night she started she went to the bed where they were sleeping, kissed them, and, consigning them into the hands of God, bade her mother good-bye, and with her two little girls wended her way again to Burlington County, New Jersey, but to a different neighborhood from that where she had been seized. She changed her name to Charity, and succeeded in again joining her husband, but, alas, with the heartbreaking thought that she had been compelled to leave her two little boys in slavery and one of the little girls on the road for the father to go back after. Thus she began life in freedom anew.

Levin and Peter, eight and six years of age respectively, were now left at the mercy of the enraged owner, and were soon hurried off to a Southern market and sold, while their mother, for whom they were daily weeping, was they knew not where. They were too young to know that they were slaves, or to understand the nature of the afflicting separation. Sixteen years before Peter's return, his older brother, Levin, died a slave in the State of Alabama, and was buried by his surviving brother, Peter.

No idea other than that they had been "kidnapped" from their mother ever entered their minds; nor had they any knowledge of the State from whence they supposed they had been taken, the last names of their mother and father, or where they were born. On the other hand, the mother was aware that the safety of herself and her rescued children depended on keeping the whole transaction a strict family secret. During the forty years of separation, except two or three Quaker friends, including the devoted friend of the slave, Benjamin Lundy, it is doubtful whether any other individuals were let into the secret of her slave life. And when the account given of Peter's return, etc., was published in 1850, it led some of the family to apprehend serious danger from the partial revelation of the early condition of the mother, especially as it was about the time that the Fugitive Slave law was passed.

Hence, the author of "The Kidnapped and the Ransomed" was compelled to omit these dangerous facts, and had to confine herself strictly to the "personal recollections of Peter Still" with regard to his being "kidnapped." Likewise, in the sketch of Seth Concklin's eventful life, written by Dr. W. H. Furness, for similar reasons he felt obliged to make but bare reference to his wonderful agency in relation to Peter's family, although he was fully aware of all the facts in the case.

GEORGIA
AND
FLORIDA

At Georgia's forming, slavery was prohibited by law. Judge Leon A. Higginbotham, Jr., wrote in his book, *In the Matter of Color,* that this law was not passed for humanitarian reasons, nor did it move Georgia courts to a more sympathetic view of their responsibilities toward black Georgians. Rather, a gross contradiction became evident. This colony's economy had failed until Eli Whitney's cotton gin stimulated prosperous land owners to smuggle large numbers of slaves from South Carolina and the West Indies for the cultivation of cotton especially but also rice and sugar cane.

By the 1830s, proslavery propagandists had destroyed most of the antislavery sentiment, and cotton became king. Wealthy planters continued to participate in the illegal slave trade, and the idea of emancipation and its implementation seldom occurred in the minds of slaveholders. Hence, a great many runaway slaves took matters into their own hands and made good their escape from southern Georgia into the everglades of Florida and remained in these swamps for many years with the Seminole Indians. Others found security among the Creek Indians in Georgia and eastern Alabama.

Seminole Chief Osceola was one of those who welcomed fugitives. He married a black woman, and his interpreter and guide was a black man born among the

Seminoles and known as Chief Abraham, who had great influence as a negotiator with the American government. Abraham was also the principal counselor to Chief Micanopy, another important Seminole warrior. To a large degree motivated by the desire to eliminate this refuge of runaway slaves, the U.S. government waged the Seminole Wars, ultimately costing forty million dollars.

Daniel Littlefield, an authority on blacks among the American Indians, stated that, "during the period of removal of Seminoles from Florida to Oklahoma, the Trail of Tears, about 450 to 500 blacks went out to Oklahoma with the Seminoles. This was about twenty percent of the entire Seminole population." Dr. Joseph A. Opala, a scholar of authority on the Seminole freemen, wrote in 1980 that about 800 freemen lived in Seminole County, Oklahoma, still cherishing their Indian tradition and their heritage of resistance to slavery.

Narrative of William and Ellen Craft

This narrative of audacious escape appears in Nichols' *Many Thousand Gone* (page 115). It was originally published in *Running a Thousand Miles for Freedom; or The Escape of William and Ellen Craft from Slavery,* London, 1860 (pages 46 and 47).

A quarter of a century ago, William and Ellen Craft were slaves in the State of Georgia. With them, as with thousands of others, the desire to be free was very strong. For this jewel, they were willing to make any sacrifice, or to endure any amount of suffering. In this state of mind they commenced planning. After thinking of various ways that might be tried, it occurred to William and Ellen, that one might act the part of master and the other the part of servant.

Ellen being fair enough to pass for white, of necessity would have to be transformed into a young planter for the time being. All that was needed, however, to make this important change was that she should be dressed elegantly in a fashionable suit of male attire, and have her hair cut in the style usually worn by young planters. Her profusion of dark hair offered a fine opportunity for the change. So far this plan looked very tempting. But it occurred to them that Ellen was beardless. After some mature reflection, they came to the conclusion that this difficulty could be very readily obviated by having the face muffled up as though the young planter was suffering badly with the face or toothache; thus they got rid of this trouble. Straightway, upon further reflection, several other very serious difficulties stared them in the face. For instance, in traveling, they knew that they would be under the necessity of stopping repeatedly at hotels, and that the custom of registering would have to be conformed to, unless some very good excuse could be given for not doing so.

Here they again thought much over matters, and wisely concluded that the young man had better assume the attitude of a gentleman very much indisposed. He must have his right arm placed carefully in a sling; that would be a sufficient excuse for not registering, etc. Then he must be a little lame, with a nice cane in the left hand; he must have large green spectacles over his eyes, and withal he must be very hard of hearing and dependent on his faithful servant (as was no uncommon thing with slave-holders), to look after all his wants.

William was just the man to act this part. To begin with, he was very "likely looking"; smart, active and exceedingly attentive to his young master—indeed he was almost eyes, ears, hands, and feet for him. William knew that this would please the slave-holders. The young planter would have nothing to do but hold himself subject to his ailments and put on a bold air of superiority; he was not to deign to notice anybody. If, while traveling, gentlemen, either politely or rudely, should venture to scrape acquaintance with the young planter, in his deafness he was to remain mute; the servant was to explain.

William Craft would later reveal many of the conversations that took place during their highly adventuresome trip. Once on a steamer between Savannah and

Charleston, while eating dinner, Ellen sat beside the
captain, who, together with the passengers inquired very
kindly after Ellen's health.

"As my master had one hand in a sling it was my duty to
carve his food. But when I went out the captain said, 'You
have a very attentive boy, sir; but you had better watch him
like a hawk when you get on to the North. He seems all very
well here, but he may act quite differently there. I know
several gentlemen who have lost their valuable niggers among
d——d cut-throat abolitionists.' "

They stopped at a first-class hotel in Charleston, where the
young planter and his body servant were treated as the house
was wont to treat the chivalry. They stopped also at a similar
hotel in Richmond, and with like results.

They knew that they must pass through Baltimore, but they
did not know the obstacles that they would have to surmount
in the Monumental City. They proceeded to the depot in the
usual manner, and the servant asked for tickets for his master
and self. Of course the master could have a ticket, but
"bonds will have to be entered before you can get a ticket,"
said the ticket master. "It is the rule of this office to require
bonds for all negroes applying for tickets to go North, and
none but gentlemen of well-known responsibility will be taken,"
further explained the ticket master.

The servant replied, that he knew "nothing about that"
—that he was "simply traveling with his young master to
take care of him—he being in a very delicate state of health,
so much so, that fears were entertained that he might not be
able to hold out to reach Philadelphia, where he was hasten-
ing for medical treatment," and ended his reply by saying,
"My master can't be detained." Without further parley, the
ticket master very obligingly waived the old "rule," and
furnished the requisite tickets. The mountain being thus removed, the young planter and his faithful servant were safely
in the cars for the "city of Brotherly Love."

Scarcely had they arrived on free soil when the rheumatism
departed—the right arm was unslung—the toothache was
gone—the beardless face was unmuffled—the deaf heard and
spoke—the blind saw—and the lame leaped as an hart, and in
the presence of a few astonished friends of the slave, the facts

of this unparalleled Underground Railroad feat were fully established by the most unquestionable evidence.

The constant strain and pressure on Ellen's nerves, however, had tried her severely, so much so, that for days afterwards, she was physically very much prostrated, although joy and gladness beamed from her eyes, which bespoke inexpressible delight within.

Never can the writer forget the impression made by their arrival. Even now, after a lapse of nearly a quarter of a century, it is easy to picture them in a private room, surrounded by a few friends—Ellen in her fine suit of black, with her cloak and high-heeled boots, looking in every respect like a young gentleman; in an hour after, having dropped her male attire, and assumed the habiliments of her sex, the feminine only was visible in every line and feature of her structure.

Her husband, William, was thoroughly colored, but was a man of marked natural abilities, of good manners, and full of pluck, and possessed of perceptive faculties very large.

It was necessary, however, in those days, that they should seek a permanent residence, where their freedom would be more secure than in Philadelphia; therefore they were advised to go to headquarters, directly to Boston. There they would be safe, it was supposed, as it had been about a generation since a fugitive had been taken back from the old Bay State, and through the incessant labors of William Lloyd Garrison, the great pioneer, and his faithful coadjutors, it was conceded that another fugitive slave case would never be tolerated on the free soil of Massachusetts. So to Boston they went.

On arriving, the warm hearts of abolitionists welcomed them heartily, and greeted and cheered them without let or hindrance. They did not pretend to keep their coming a secret, or hide it under a bushel; the story of their escape was heralded broadcast over the country—North and South, and indeed over the civilized world. For two years or more, not the slightest fear was entertained that they were not just as safe in Boston as if they had gone to Canada. But the day the Fugitive Slave Bill passed, even the bravest abolitionist began to fear that the fugitive slave was no longer safe anywhere under the stars and stripes, North or South, and that William and Ellen Craft were liable to be captured at any moment by Georgia slave hunters. Many abolitionists counselled resistance to the death at all hazards. Instead of running to Canada, fugitives generally armed themselves and thus said, "Give me liberty or give me death."

Narrative of Philip Younger

This narrative of close observation appears in Drew's *A North-Side View of Slavery* (pages 248 to 251). Drew hoped that this book would give the cause of freedom "a new impulse." Traveling to Canada and gathering accounts at random as he went, he managed to transcribe the oral narratives of some 117 fugitive slaves.

I served in slavery fifty-five years, and am now nearly seventy-two years old. I was born in Virginia, went, at ten, to Tennessee; at twelve, to Alabama: was, all the time, body servant of a military man. My treatment was various—sometimes rough—sometimes good. Many awful scenes I have seen while moving about. I have had to put chains on men, myself, to go into a chain gang: I have seen men whipped to death—have seen them die. I have ridden hundreds of miles in Alabama, and have heard the whip going, all along from farm to farm, while they were weighing out cotton.

In Alabama, the patrols go out in companies at about dark, and ride nearly all night. If they meet a colored man without a pass, it is thirty-nine lashes; but they don't stop for the law, and if they tie a man up, he is very well off if he gets only two hundred. If there is a party assembled at the quarters, they rush in half drunk, and thrash round with their sticks, perhaps before they look at a pass—all must be whipped unless they rush out: I can't paint so bad as 't is. Sometimes a stout man will fight his way through.

As a general thing the treatment on the plantations in Alabama is very hard. Once in a while a man is kind, as kindness is out there, and then he is hated by all the other masters. They say "*his* niggers spoil *our* niggers." These servants are not allowed on the other plantations at all—if caught there, they will put as much on them as they can bear. I have as good a chance to know as any man there—I have traveled there on the plantations—I was there before the country was opened—at the war—and have seen it grow up by the colored man's labor. I have seen miles of fences around plantations, where I had been through woods with the surveyors. Escape from Alabama is almost impossible—if a man escapes, it is by the skin of his teeth.

There was a free man in Huntsville—a barber—whose wife—a free woman—was taken by a patrol, as she was walking out at dark, and put in jail, just to disgrace her—as she was in a little better standing than the patrol was. Her husband grumbled about it—a rumpus was made, and people collected. It was in front of a tavern door. The folks then called out, "Shoot the d——d nigger! shoot him!" The patrol stabbed him with a bowie-knife, and he fell in the street. He was carried in, and a doctor dressed the wound, but he was never a sound man afterwards.

I hired my time, and made some money. I bought my wife's freedom first, and sent her away. I got off by skill. I have children and grandchildren in slavery.

I had rather starve to death here, being a free man, than to have plenty in slavery. I cannot be a slave any more—nobody could hold me as a slave now, except in irons. Old as I am, I would rather face the Russian fire, or die at the point of the sword, than go into slavery.

We are placed in different circumstances here—some drag along, without doing much—some are doing well. I have a house; I have taken up fifty acres of land, and have made the payments as required; I have other property besides. Here is Henry Blue, worth twelve thousand dollars; Syddles, worth a fortune; Lucky, worth a very handsome fortune; Ramsay, a great deal of land and other property, at least twelve thousand dollars; all these were slaves at some time. And there are many others wealthy, through their own skill and industry.

Before I came here, I resided in the free States. I came here in consequence of the passage of the Fugitive Slave Bill. It was a hardship at first; but I feel better here—more like a man—I know I am—than in the States. I suffer from want of education. I manage by skill and experience and industry—but it is as if feeling my way in the dark.

Narrative of Patrick Smead

The following appears in *A North-Side View of Slavery* (pages 99 to 108).

I belonged in Savannah, Georgia. I am as white as my master was, but I was born a slave. My first master dying, I fell to one of the sons, who died when I was about fifteen. He was a sporting character. He had always promised my mother to give me my freedom at some time, as soon as I could take care of myself. I was sent to school a little while by mother, so that I could spell quite well—but I have lost it all. My master gave me no religious instruction, but I was allowed to attend a Sunday School for colored children. I was put to the cooper's trade, which I learned in five years. While my master lived I was well used. But at length he was taken sick with consumption; I attended him, and took care of him. I said nothing to him about my freedom, not feeling any great interest in the matter at that time. I have good reason to believe that he was persuaded not to set me free. At length he departed his life.

After his death, the doctor's bill of three hundred dollars had to be satisfied out of the estate. Other property being deficient, I was given up, and was for one day the property of the physician. I was then sold to a wholesale merchant for five hundred dollars. The merchant employed me about the store four years; he found me smarter than many others, and I had to work quite hard, lifting heavy bales of goods. This lifting caused me to wear a truss some time before I left. In the easiest time of the year, the summer, my working hours were from six in the morning to seven in the evening. In the fall and spring I worked from six in the morning until twelve at night, the bales of goods being opened in the night: in the winter from six to six. I had plenty of food and good common clothing. The merchant's manner of address to me was generally pleasant: I had the privilege of going to church on Sundays, if I pleased.

He never on Saturday nights allowed me any money: I liked female society as well as he did, and wanted some spending money. I was not provoked to ask for it by seeing others have money, but I felt that I ought to be allowed something for my encouragement, after performing so much hard labor. His answer was, that he gave me enough to eat. I told him that he would have to sell me, "for to work in this way I shall not." He grinned and bore it.

About a year before this I had been attentive to a young free-woman who lived with her aunt. One evening, on leaving, the aunt cautioned me to tell Billy (a boy on the place) to fasten the gate after me, as the night before he had left it open. Accordingly, on coming out, I said, "Billy, be careful to fasten the gate, for you did not fasten it the night before." There was, as I afterwards learned, a white man concealed behind a tree close by—he heard me, and fancied that what I said was meant to hit him in some way; for he meanwhile was, unbeknown to me, sustaining a peculiar relation to the very girl that I was visiting. The next day that man said he would buy me if it cost him a thousand dollars, so that he could give me a hundred lashes. My master heard of this threat—I heard of it, and believe I told my master. Some days after I met the man, told him what I had heard—that it was a mistake—that I did not know he was behind the tree, or that he had anything to do with the person I was visiting, and that I would not be in his way any further. So it blew over.

After my talk with my master about the money, he, re-membering the affair just mentioned, went to that party, and offered to sell me to him. Then the same man who had made the threat to buy me, asked me if I was willing to belong to him. I told him I would as lief belong to him as to anybody, if he would allow me a living chance. He told me that he would hire me out at my trade of coopering, and provide me with tools. He bought me—giving me a woman and two children, and a hundred dollars. I went to work as he had promised. My task was eighteen barrels a week: I could make more than twice as many, so then I began to have money. My treatment was good.

I went on in this way four years; then my colored employer was going to Liberia, with a ship load of emigrants—free people of color. He bade me goodby, and shook my hands; at this I felt an anxious wish to go with him, and from that moment I felt what liberty was. I then told him, that I hoped one day to be my own man, and if so, that I wished to go to

Liberia. He said, "I hope so, my son." He had baptized me, and was pastor of the church to which I belonged. After he left, I went on working nearly one year more, with his partner, who had bought him out.

During this time my desire for liberty grew stronger and stronger. I had spent my money as I went along. My master refused to buy me new tools after my old ones were worn out—said I dressed better than he, and must buy tools for myself. I thought this ought not to do, and I made up my mind, "it shan't do either." I had now come to a resolution, and I started for a land of liberty. I left in July, 1851, at three on a Monday morning. I reached Canada safely, and had no difficulty until two years had elapsed. Then I was employed in the summer of 1853 as a waiter in the Cataract House, on the American side of the Falls. Then a constable of Buffalo came in, one Sunday after dinner, and sent the barkeeper into the dining-room for me. I went into the hall, and met the constable—I had my jacket in my hand, and was going to put it up. He stepped up to me. "Here, Watson" (this was the name I assumed on escaping), "you waited on me, and I'll give you some change." His fingers were then in his pocket, and he dropped a quarter dollar on the floor. I told him, "I have not waited on you—you must be mistaken in the man, and I don't want another waiter's money." He approached—I suspected, and stepped back toward the dining-room door. By that time he made a grab at me, caught me by the collar of my shirt and vest—then four more constables, he had brought with him, sprung on me—they dragged me to the street door—there was a jam—I hung on by the doorway. The head constable shackled my left hand. I had on a new silk cravat twice round my neck; he hung on to this, twisting it till my tongue lolled out of my mouth, but he could not start me through the door. By this time the waiters pushed through the crowd—there were three hundred visitors there at the time—and Smith and Grave, colored waiters caught me by the hand—then the others came on, and dragged me from the officers by main force. They dragged me over chairs and every thing, down to the ferry way. I got into the cars, and the waiters were lowering me down, when the constables came and stopped them, saying, "Stop that murderer!"—they called me a *murderer*! Then I was dragged down the steps by the waiters, and flung into the ferry boat. The boatmen rowed me to within fifty feet of the Canada shore—into Canada water—when the head boatman in the other boat gave the word to row back. They did accordingly—but they could not land me at the usual place on account of the waiters. So they had to go down to Suspension Bridge; they landed me, opened a way through the crowd—shackled me, pushed me into a carriage, and away we went. The head constable then asked me "if I knew any person in Lockport." I told him "no." Then "In Buffalo?" "No." "Well, then," said he, "let's go to Buffalo—Lockport is too far." We reached Buffalo at ten o'clock at night, when I was put in jail. I told the jailer I wished he would be so good as to tell lawyer _____ to come round to the jail. Mr. _____ came, and I engaged him for my lawyer. When the constables saw that, pretending to know no one in Buffalo, I had engaged one of the best lawyers in the place, they were astonished. I told them that "as scared as they thought I was, I wanted them to know that I had my senses about me." The court was not opened until nine days; the tenth day my trial commenced. The object was, to show some evidence as if of murder, so that they could take me to _Baltimore_. On the eleventh day the claimant was defeated, and I was cleared at ten A.M. After I was cleared, and while I was yet in the court room, a telegraphic despatch came from a Judge in Savannah, saying that I was no murderer, but a fugitive slave. However, before a new warrant could be got out, I was in a carriage and on my way. I crossed over into Canada, and walked thirty miles to the Clifton House.

This broke up my summer's work at the Falls, and threw me back; and as I had to pay money to my lawyer, I have hardly got over it yet.

There is great difference in the modes of treating slaves on the plantations, according to the character of the owners—I have seen enough of slave life to know this, and I have seen slaves in Savannah used as badly as any on the plantation. I saw a man in Savannah, who had been whipped severely, and thrust into a dark hole or dungeon in a cellar. The maggots got in his flesh and he was offensive to the senses in consequence. When they turned him out, I saw the man, and saw the maggots in his flesh. I knew a Methodist, on _____ Street, who had a colored woman for cook. Something which her mistress told her to cook did not suit. The mistress complained to the minister; he shut up the cook in a stable or barn and beat her, having first tied something over her mouth.

At one time, I resided with the family in the jail-building. While there, I used to see whipping, five or six a day, or more, with a large cowskin. It is the most common thing in the world to have them whipped in the jail—that will be no news in Savannah—not over thirty-nine lashes in one day, by law. Sometimes slaves are whipped in the guard-house.

I consider that the slaves in Savannah, where I was born and raised, are poor ignorant creatures: they don't know their condition. It is ignorance that keeps them there. If they knew what I know, they could not be kept there a moment. Let a man escape, and have but a month's freedom, and he will feel the greatest animosity against slavery. I can't give slavery any name or description bad enough for it.

Narrative of Reuben Saunders

This narrative is from Drew's *A North-Side View of Slavery* (pages 274 and 275).

I was born in Greene Co., Georgia. At about twelve years old, our family was broken up by the death of my master. I was the oldest child: there were three brothers and two sisters. My master's children had grown, and were married, and settled in various parts of Georgia. We were all separated—no two went together. My mother's master was about half a mile from where the youngest child was. They did not think it would know enough to learn the way. Some of them carried her once to see her mother, and she learned the way. She used to go over to where her mother lived, and creep under the house, where she would wait till her mother came into the yard and then run to her. There were bad dogs there, but they did not trouble her. My mother's master tried to buy this child, but her owner would not sell her under six hundred dollars. He did not mean to sell. I have not seen my mother since the sale. I remained there from twelve to twenty-four years of age, and was well treated.

I was never caught there with a book in my hand, or a pen. I never saw but one slave in Georgia, who could read and write, and he was brought in from another State.

The treatment about there, seemed to depend on the number a man had. If few, they got on well, if many, they fared worse. If a man used his slaves with kindness more than the others, they disliked it.

From Georgia, I was removed to Mississippi—that being considered a money-making place. I was the only slave my master had. I went on with him. At first he engaged in rafting cypress timber, then kept a wood-yard on the Mississippi. I stayed there sixteen years. Then he brought me and my wife and children to Indiana, and set us free. He had made money fast, and he made a good use of it—for he bought my wife and three children, and my wife's brother, on purpose to set us free. My family cost him thirteen hundred dollars, and the brother, seven hundred and fifty dollars. He afterward went down the Mississippi with eight hundred dollars, and to sell some land and wind up. He was lost off the boat and drowned: some thought he was robbed and pushed overboard.

I don't think any man can of right, hold property in another. I like the condition of freedom—what I made is mine. I arrived here last April.

Narrative of John Brown

This narrative appears in *Slave Life in Georgia* (pages 256 and 257).

To prevent my running any more, Stevens fixed bells and horns on my head. This is not by any means an uncommon punishment. I have seen many slaves wearing them. A circle of iron, having a hinge behind, with a staple and padlock before, which hang under the chin, is fastened round the neck. Another circle of iron fits quite close round the crown of the head. The two are held together in this position by three rods of iron, which are fixed in each circle. These rods, or horns, stick out three feet above the head, and have a bell attached to each. The bells and horns do not weigh less than from twelve to fourteen pounds. When Stevens had fixed this ornament on my head, he turned me loose, and told me I might run off now if I liked.

I wore the bells and horns, day and night, for three months, and I do not think any description I could give of my sufferings during this time would convey anything approaching to a faint idea of them. Let alone that their weight made my head and neck ache dreadfully, especially when I stooped to my work. At night I could not lie down to rest, because the horns prevented my stretching myself, or even curling myself up; so I was obliged to sleep crouching. Of course it was impossible for me to attempt to remove them, or to get away, though I still held to my resolution to make another venture as soon as I could see my way of doing it.

I was introduced by two sturdy young men to their father, as "another of the travellers bound to the north star." The old man laid a hand upon my shoulder, and taking my other hand in his, gave me a welcome, and then conducting me into the parlour, introduced me to his wife. It was now past sunrise, and they were about going to breakfast. I was, however, taken to an upper room, where I had a good wash, in a white basin, and where clean linen and a complete suit of clothes were brought to me. After refreshing myself by this wholesome change, I was re-conducted to the parlour, and seated at the table.

It was the first time in my life I had found myself in such grand company. I was so completely abashed, and felt so out of my element, that I had no eyes, no ears, no understanding. I was quite bewildered. As to eating, it was out of the question.

"Come, friend John Brown, thee must eat," said the kind old lady, heaping my plate up with fried ham and eggs. "Thee needn't be afraid of eating."

"I'm sure thee must be hungry," added the old gentleman, handing me a great chunk of bread. "Eat away, and don't thee be afraid. We have plenty more in the house."

But it was all of no use; though an hour or even half an hour before, I felt that I could devour anything, the smoking coffee, ham, eggs, and sausages, and the nice white bread could not tempt me. For a good half hour this continued: they pressing me to eat, and I quite unable to do so. At last I began, and picked a bit now and then, receiving encouragement as my courage seemed to increase. My appetite came with my courage, and then—oh! how I did eat!

I fear my readers may think I exaggerate when I tell them that "I ate straight on for an entire hour, quite steady." I demolished all the ham and eggs and sausages they placed before me, with their due accompaniment of bread, and then a round of cold salt beef was brought up, from which I was helped abundantly. I could not but notice the looks of my new friends. The old gentleman would cough and wipe his eyes now and then, and the younger folks keep exchanging glances with one another. The old lady, fearing I should do myself an injury, made several ineffectual attempts to draw my attention off.

"Friend John Brown, we wish to talk with thee, as soon as thou can," she said; "we want to hear all about thee."

"Yes, ma'am," I answered, without leaving off: "you can go on, ma'am; I can talk and eat too."

I dare not say how long I might have gone on. I had not eaten a meal for so long, that now it seemed as though I never could satisfy my craving. At last the old lady said, decidedly:

"Friend John Brown, thee mustn't take it unkindly, but thee mustn't eat any more now. Thou canst have some more in the day-time if you like; but thou wilt make thyself ill, if thou take more now."

And so I was obliged to give in.

A chapter from the Scriptures was read after breakfast, which, including my "spell" at the table, had lasted two hours from the time we sat down.

I was then conducted into a safe retreat, where there was a comfortable bed provided for me, into which I got, and soon fell asleep. I slept until I was awakened at three in the afternoon, when I was taken down to dinner. After that we sat and chatted until suppertime, and then I went to bed again. In the middle of the night I awoke, and finding myself in a strange place, became alarmed. It was a clear, starlight night, and I could see the walls of my room, and the curtains all of a dazzling whiteness around me. I felt so singularly happy, however, notwithstanding the fear I was in at not being able to make out where I was, that I could only conclude I was in a dream, or a vision, and for some minutes I could not rid my mind of this idea. At last I became alive to the truth; that I was in a friend's house, and that I really was free and safe.

It is supposed that there are no slaves imported into the south from Africa. I am quite sure that the reverse is the case. There was a planter lived on an estate adjoining my old master Stevens. His name was Zachariah Le Mar, and he was called Squire. That man had, to my knowledge, five hundred of them, all fresh from Africa, and I know that new ones were constantly brought in. We call them "Saltbacks." I remember, too, that one day, being still at Stevens', I was down in our apple-orchard, shooting red-headed woodpeckers with a bow and arrow. John Glasgow was with me, and there came across to see him one Tony Wilson, a negro belonging to John Wilson, whose farm adjoined ours; and one Boat-swain Smith, another negro, who belonged to a Doctor Smith, living three miles from us. They were native Africans, and could speak English only very imperfectly. They met in the orchard, and had not long been in conversation, before Tony Wilson discovered that Boatswain Smith was the very man who had sold him from his country within the last two years. He got into a great rage, and fell upon Smith directly, and they both began to fight, butting at one another furiously. We had a great deal of trouble to part them, but we succeeded at last, and learned that they had both been brought direct to Savannah in Georgia, with a great many more. Boatswain Smith had been kidnapped not very long after he had been the means of sending his countrymen into slavery. This little incident may serve as a proof of the fact I am quite sure would be borne out by close inquiry, that the slave trade is still carried on between the coast of Africa and the slave states of the American Union.

Narrative of Jim Bow-Legs Alias Bill Paul

This narrative appears in Still's *Underground Railroad Records* (pages 240 to 242.).

In 1855, a traveler arrived with the above name, who, on examination, was found to possess very extraordinary characteristics. As a hero and adventurer, some passages of his history were most remarkable. His schooling had been such as could only be gathered on plantations under brutal overseers—or while fleeing—or in swamps—in prisons—or on the auction-block, etc., in which condition he was often found. Nevertheless, in these circumstances, his mind got well stored with vigorous thoughts—neither books nor friendly advisers being at his command. Yet his native intelligence as it regarded human nature, was extraordinary. His resolution and perseverance never faltered. In all respects, he was a remarkable man. He was a young man, weighing about one hundred and eighty pounds, of uncommon muscular strength. He was born in the State of Georgia, and was owned by Dr. Thomas Stephens, of Lexington. On reaching the Vigilance Committee in Philadelphia, his story was told many times over to one and another. . . .

Taking all the facts and circumstances into consideration respecting the courageous career of this successful adventurer for freedom, his case is by far more interesting than any that I have yet referred to. Indeed, for the good of the cause, and the honor of one who gained his liberty by periling his life so frequently: shot several times, making six unsuccessful attempts to escape from the far South, numberless times chased by bloodhounds, captured, imprisoned, and sold, living for months in the woods, swamps and caves, subsisting mainly on parched corn and berries . . . his narrative ought, by all means, to be published, though I doubt very much whether many could be found who could persuade themselves to believe one-tenth part of this marvellous story. . . .

His master finding him not available, on account of his absconding propensities, would gladly have offered him for sale. He was once taken to Florida, for that purpose; but generally, traders being wide awake, on inspecting him, would almost invariably pronounce him a "d—n rascal," because he would never fail to eye them sternly, as they inspected him. The obedient and submissive slave is always recognized by hanging his head and looking on the ground when looked at by a slave-holder. This lesson Jim had never learned. Hence he was not to be trusted.

His head and chest, and indeed his entire structure, as solid as a rock, indicated that he was physically no ordinary man; and not being under the influence of the spirit of "nonresistance," he had occasionally been found to be a rather formidable customer.

His father was a full-blooded Indian, brother to the noted Indian Chief, Billy Bow-Legs; his mother was quite black and of unmixed blood.

For five or six years, the greater part of Jim's time was occupied in trying to escape, and being in prison, for sale, to punish him for running away.

His mechanical genius was excellent, so were his geographical abilities. He could make shoes or do carpenter's work very handily, though he had never had the chance to learn. As to traveling by night or day, he was always road-ready and having an uncommon memory, could give exceedingly good accounts of what he saw, etc.

When he entered a swamp, and had occasion to take a nap he took care first to decide upon the posture he must take, so that if come upon unexpectedly by the hounds and slave-hunters, he might know in an instant which way to steer to defeat them. He always carried a liquid, which he had prepared to prevent hounds from scenting him, which he said had never failed. As soon as the hounds came on to the spot where he had rubbed his legs and feet with said liquid, they could follow him no further, but howled and turned immediately.

MISSISSIPPI
AND
LOUISIANA

In spite of Mississippi's strong antiabolitionist views, a number of successful escapes from the state were sufficient to arouse the suspicion in the minds of its citizens that agents of the Underground Railroad were running off slaves. Senator Jefferson Davis of Mississippi declared in the first session of the Thirty-first Congress: "Negroes do escape from Mississippi frequently, and the boats constantly passing by our long line of frontier furnish great facility to get into Ohio; and when they do escape it is with great difficulty that they are restored. We, though less than the border states, are seriously concerned in this question . . . those like myself, who live on that great highway of the West—the Mississippi River—[and] are most exposed have a present and increasing interest in this matter."

Jefferson Davis had good cause for concern about his property, for abolitionists were busy in the Deep South. Richard J. Hinton, one of John Brown's biographers, wrote that John Kagi, Brown's lieutenant, spoke of having marked out a chain of counties extending through South Carolina, Georgia, Alabama, and Mississippi. Kagi had traveled over a large portion of the region, drawing on his own knowledge and the assistance of the Canadian Negroes in Brown's band who had escaped from those states. Brown's men planned a general attack in

27

that area. The plans for the attack were set aside while plans for Harpers Ferry went forward.

The level of traditional Underground Railroad activity among runaways in Louisiana and Mississippi was very low; there are, for example, no entries for these two states or for Alabama in the index of Buckmaster's *Let My People Go.* Yet the slaves in these Deep South states did go, as the following narratives make clear.

Narrative of a Nameless Woman

This narrative appears in the *Reminiscences* of Levi Coffin (pages 254 to 256).

There lived in Mississippi, a black woman who was poor, ignorant, and a slave, but rich in the knowledge of the truth as it is in Jesus, and strong in unwavering faith. Working in the field under the driver's lash, or alone in her little hut, she never ceased praying to God, asking him to help her to escape, and assist and protect her on the long journey to the North. She had heard there was a place called Canada, far to the northward, where all were free, and learned that, in order to reach it, she must go a long way up the Mississippi River, then cross over and steer her course by the north star. Finally, her prayers seemed to be answered, and she had perfect faith that she would be preserved through all the dangers that would menace her if she ran away.

One night, when all around her were wrapped in sleep, she put a small supply of food and some clothing together, in a little bundle, and, stealing away from the negro quarters, left the plantation and plunged into the forest, which was there a labyrinth of swamps and cane-brakes. She made her way through this slowly, for several days, often hearing the bloodhounds baying on her track, or perhaps in search of other fugitives. Slaves often fled to these swamps and took refuge among the thickets, preferring the companionship of the deadly moccasin snake and the alligator, and the risk of death from starvation or exposure to the cruel treatment of their masters, and the keen cut of the overseers' lash.

This slave woman managed to evade the dogs by wading in pools and streams of water, where she knew they would lose the scent and be thrown off her trail. One time, however, she heard the deep baying of the bloodhounds coming toward her, when she was some distance from any water. There was no escape and she knew they would soon come up with her, and perhaps tear her to pieces before the pursuers could reach them. In this dire extremity, she fell on her knees and asked God to preserve her—to give her some sign of his protecting power; then, with all fear gone, she rose to her feet and calmly watched the dogs approach. As they came near, she took from her pocket a handful of crumbs—the remainder of the food she had brought—and held them out toward the hounds. They came up to her, but instead of seizing and mangling her, they gamboled about her, licked the crumbs from her hands, then ran off through the forest.

This remarkable preservation she felt was the sign she had asked of God, and, falling on her knees once more, she dedicated herself wholly to him, vowing that if she reached Canada, the rest of her life should be devoted solely and entirely to his service. She had a long journey after that, lasting for several months, and encountered many dangers, but was preserved safe through them all. She traveled at night and hid in the thickets during the day, living mostly on fruit and green corn, but venturing now and then to call at negro huts and beg for a little of the scanty food which they afforded. When she came to rivers and streams of water too deep for wading, she made rafts of logs or poles, tied together with grape-vines or hickory withes, and poled or paddled herself across as best she could. Reaching Illinois, she met with kind people who aided her on to Detroit, Michigan. Here also she found friends and was ferried across to Canada. A colored minister who witnessed her arrival says that, on landing, she fell on her knees and kissed the shore, and thanked the Lord for his wonderful mercy in preserving her through so many dangers and bringing her at last to the land of freedom. She then arose and jumped up and down for half an hour, shouting praises to God and seeming almost deliri-

ous in her great joy. We were informed that she was a
devoted Christian worker, and was earnestly endeavoring to
fulfill her vows and promises to the Lord.

Narratives of Rachel and Mary Elizabeth Parker

This narrative appears in Stowe's *Key to Uncle Tom's
Cabin* (pages 174 and 175). It concerns the kidnapping
of free black sisters who were then sold as slaves and
transported to New Orleans. Mary Elizabeth later escaped through legal action, a rare occurrence.

I [Rachel] was taken from Joseph C. Miller's about twelve
o'clock on Tuesday (Dec. 30th, 1851), by two men who came
up to the house by the *back* door. One came in and asked
Mrs. Miller where Jesse McCreary lived, and then seized me
by the arm, and pulled me out of the house. Mrs. Miller called
to her husband, who was in the *front* porch, and he ran out and
seized the man by the collar, and tried to stop him. The other,
with an oath told him to take his hands off, and if he touched me
he would kill him. He then told Miller that I belonged to Mr.
Schoolfield, in Baltimore. They then hurried me to a wagon,
where there was another large man, put me in, and drove off.

Mr. Miller ran across the field to head off the wagon, and
picked up a stake to run through the wheel, when one of the
men pulled out a sword (I think it was a sword, I never saw
one), and threatened to cut Miller's arm off. Pollock's wagon
being in the way, and he refusing to get out of the road, we
turned off to the left. After we rode away, one of the men
tore a whole in the back of the carriage, to look out to see if
they were coming after us, and they said they wished they
had given Miller and Pollock a blow.

We stopped at a tavern near the railroad, and I told the landlord (I think it was) that I was free. I also told several persons
at the car-office; and a very nice-looking man at the car-office
was talking at the door, and he said he thought that they had

better take me back again. One of the men did not come further than the tavern. I was taken to Baltimore, where we arrived about seven o'clock the same evening, and I was taken to jail.

The next morning, a man with large light-colored whiskers took me by myself, and asked me if I was not Mr. Schoolfield's slave. I told him I was not; he said that I was, and that if I did not say I was he would "cowhide me and salt me, and put me in a dungeon." I told him I was free, and that I would say nothing but the truth.

I [Mary Elizabeth] was taken from Matthew Donnelly's on Saturday night (Dec. 6th, or 13th, 1851); was caught whilst out of doors, soon after I had cleared the supper table, about seven o'clock, by two men, and put into a wagon. One of them got into the wagon with me, and rode to Elkton, Md., where I was kept until Sunday night at twelve o'clock, when I left there in the cars for Baltimore, and arrived there early on Monday morning.

At Elkton a man was brought in to see me, by one of the men, who said that I was not his father's slave. Afterwards, when on the way to Baltimore in the cars, a man told me that I must say that I was Mr. Schoolfield's slave, or he would shoot me, and pulled a "rifle" out of his pocket and showed it to me, and also threatened to whip me.

On Monday morning, Mr. Schoolfield called at the jail in Baltimore to see me; and on Tuesday morning he brought his wife and several other ladies to see me. I told them I did not know them, and then Mr. C. took me out of the room, and told me who they were, and took me back again, so that I might appear to know them. On the next Monday I was shipped to New Orleans.

It took about a month to get to New Orleans. After I had been there about a week, Mr. C. sold me to Madame C., who keeps a large flower-garden. She sends flowers to sell to the theatres, sells milk in market, etc. I went out to sell candy and flowers for her, when I lived with her. One evening, when I was coming home from the theatre, a watchman took me up, and I told him I was not a slave. He put me in the calaboose, and next morning took me before a magistrate, who sent for Madame C., who told him she bought me. He then sent for Mr. C. and told him he must account for how he got me. Mr. C. said that my mother and all the family were free, except me. The magistrate told me to go back to Madame C., and he told Madame C. that she must not let me go out at night; and he told Mr. C. that he must prove how he came by me. The magistrate afterwards called on Mrs. C., at her house, and had a long talk with her in the parlor. I do not know what he said, as they were by themselves. About a month afterwards, I was sent back to Baltimore. I lived with Madame C. about six months.

There were six slaves came in the vessel with me to Baltimore, who belonged to Mr. D., and were returned because they were sickly.

A man called to see me at the jail after I came back to Baltimore, and told me that I must say I was Mr. Schoolfield's slave, and that if I did not do it he would kill me the first time he got a chance. He said Rachel [her sister] said she came from Baltimore and was Mr. Schoolfield's slave. Afterwards some gentlemen called on me [Judge Campbell and Judge Bell, of Philadelphia, and William H. Norris, Esq., of Baltimore], and I told them I was Mr. Schoolfield's slave. They said they were my friends, and I must tell them the truth. I told them who I was, and all about it.

When I was in New Orleans, Mr. C. whipped me because I said that I was free.

Narrative of Alexander Milton Ross

Dr. Alexander Milton Ross was a Canadian abolitionist. This narrative is from his *Recollections* (pages 32 to 55).

My preparations being now completed, I engaged passage by steamer, to New Orleans, on a mission, the subject and details of which had occupied my mind exclusively for many weeks. I was accompanied to the steamer by two noble-hearted and steadfast friends of freedom [Gerrit Smith and Lewis Tappan]. Whenever a slave succeeded in making his or her escape I was to send them the information, and they in turn notified our friends north of the Ohio river to be on the lookout for "packages of hardware" (men) or "dry-goods" (females), and these Ohio friends concealed the fugitives for a time, if necessary, until they could be safely sent to Canada. . . .

From childhood I had been passionately fond of the study of Natural History, especially of Ornithology. I consequently decided to follow the pursuit of a naturalist, as a guise to my actual object.

During my stay in New Orleans I occasionally attended the slave auctions. The scenes I witnessed there will never be effaced from my memory. The cries and heart-rending agonies of the poor creatures as they were sold and separated from parents, children, husbands, or wives, will never cease to ring in my ears. Babes were torn from the arms of their mothers and sold, while parents were separated and sent to distant parts of the country. Tired and over-worked women were cruelly beaten, because they refused the outrageous demands of their wicked overseers. The horrid traffic in human beings, many of them much whiter and more intelligent than the cruel men who bought and sold them, was, without exception, the most monstrous outrage upon the rights of human beings that could possibly be imagined. . . .

My experience in New Orleans served to intensify my abhorrence and hatred of that vile and unchristian institution of slavery, and to nerve me for the work I was engaged in. On several occasions while in the Slave States I attended divine worship, and invariably remarked that whenever the subject of slavery was mentioned, it was referred to as a "wise and beneficent institution"; and one clergyman in particular declared that "the institution of slavery was devised by God for the especial benefit of the coloured race."

The route decided upon was from New Orleans to Vicksburg, and thence through the interior of Mississippi, Alabama, Georgia, South Carolina, North Carolina, and Florida. I had never before visited that section of the United States, and my field of labour was consequently surrounded by difficulties not experienced during my visit to Virginia and Tennessee, from the fact that I had not a single friend in the Cotton States.

Soon after my arrival at Vicksburg I was busily engaged in collecting ornithological specimens. I made frequent visits to the surrounding plantations seizing every favourable opportunity to converse with the more intelligent of the slaves. Many of these negroes had heard of Canada from the negroes brought from Virginia and the border Slave States; but the impression they had was, that Canada, being so far away, it would be useless to try and reach it. On these excursions I was usually accompanied by one or two smart, intelligent slaves, to whom I felt I could trust the secret of my visit. In this way I succeeded in circulating a knowledge of Canada, and the best means of reaching that country, to all the plantations for many miles around Vicksburg. . . .

I made this place my base for extensive incursions to the surrounding country, pursuing a similar course to that I adopted at Vicksburg. My ornithological collection had by this time assumed respectable and interesting proportions, and some of the planters became so much interested in my ornithological pursuits, as to offer me every facility to roam over their plantations, of which I availed myself. I had my choice of assistance from among the slaves, and selected those possessing qualities suitable for my purpose. There was not a plantation within fifteen miles of Selma that I did not visit successfully. . . .

Having completed my labours at Selma, I selected Columbus, Mississippi, for my next field of labour. I had been at work in Columbus about two weeks when a difficulty occurred which, but for the faithfulness of a negro, would have ended in my death at the hands of an infuriated mob. During one of my visits to a plantation near Columbus, I met with a negro slave of more than ordinary intelligence. His master was a man of coarse and brutal instincts, who had burned the initials of his name into the flesh of several of his slaves, to render their capture more certain, in case they ran away from this merciless wretch. I saw several of the victims of his cruelty, whose backs would forever bear the marks of his branding iron and lash. He was a veritable "Legree." On one of my excursions over his plantation I was accompanied by the slave mentioned. During our rambles he gave me a history of his life and sufferings, and expressed an earnest desire to gain his freedom. I felt that he could be relied upon, and imparted to him the secret object of my visit to the South. He listened with absorbing earnestness whilst I explained to him the difficulties and dangers he would have to encounter on so long and perilous a journey. He, however, declared his determination to make the attempt, saying, that death itself was preferable to his present existence. On the following day

(Saturday) I again visited the plantation, and selected this slave for my companion. He informed me he had decided to start for Canada, as soon as he could communicate with a brother who was a slave on a plantation a few miles distant. He wished to take this brother with him, if possible. I gave him instructions for his guidance after he should cross the Ohio river; the names of friends at Evansville (Ind.), and Cleveland (Ohio), to whom he could apply for assistance. I also furnished him with a pistol, knife, and pocket compass, and directed him to travel by night until he reached friends north of the Ohio river.

On the following Monday evening, while seated at the supper table of the hotel at which I was stopping, I heard loud and excited talking in the adjoining room. In a few minutes the landlord came up to me with an excited look, and said, "Col. _____ wishes to speak with you. You had better go out and meet him." I immediately rose, and went into the room from which the loud talking emanated. As I entered, the Colonel, in a loud and brutal tone, said, "That's him, arrest him." Upon which a man stepped up and said, "You are my prisoner." I demanded the reason why I was arrested. Whereupon the doughty Colonel strode toward me with his fist clenched, and charged me with being a d——d abolitionist. He said he would have my heart's blood; that I had enticed away his nigger "Joe"; for the nigger had not been seen since he went out with me on the previous Saturday. The room was filled with an excited crowd of men, who glared upon me with fierce and fiendish looks. . . .

In the meantime the constable had produced a pair of iron handcuffs, and fastened them around my wrists. . . . I quietly asked if they would allow me to say a few words, at the same time making a Masonic sign of distress, in hope that there might be a Mason in the crowd with sufficient courage to sustain my request. I had no sooner made "the sign of distress," than a voice near me said, "Yes, let's hear what he has to say. He ought to be allowed to speak." I was encouraged, and very quietly said: "Gentlemen, I am a total stranger here, without friends. I am your prisoner in irons. The Colonel has charged me with violating your laws! Will you act the part of cowards by allowing this man to incite you to commit a murder? or will you, like brave men, grant the only request I have to make, that is, a fair trial before your magistrates?"

Several persons at once spoke up in my favour, among whom was the landlord and his brave little wife.

I was then, much to the chagrin of the Colonel, led to the lock-up, and confined to a filthy room. . . .

A crowd of people had gathered to see an abolitionist have the mockery of a trial. Col. "Legree" was asked by the Justice to state his case, which he did in true slave-driving style, as if determined to force the case against me. In fact, my case seemed hopeless. I saw no way of escape from my desperate situation. . . .

At length the Colonel finished his statement, which, reduced to simple facts, was, that I had called at his residence on Saturday last, and requested permission to roam over his plantation to shoot birds; that he had given me permission, and allowed his servant "Joe" to accompany me; that "Joe" had not returned, nor could he be found; that he was sure I had aided him to escape; and demanded of the Justice that I should be punished as a "negro thief" deserved. His remarks were loudly applauded by the slave-hounds that surrounded him. The Justice turned to me, and, in a coarse, stern voice, said, "Have you anything to say?" At this moment a voice outside the room shouted, "Here's Joe! here's Joe!" and a rush was made toward the door.

"Joe" was ushered into the court room, and fell on his knees before the Colonel, asking his forgiveness for leaving the plantation without permission. He said he wanted to see his brother "powerful bad," and had gone to the plantation on which his brother was living, about eight miles distant, on Saturday night, expecting to return by Sunday evening; but, having sprained his ankle, he could not move until Monday evening, when he started for home, travelling nearly all night. As soon as he reached the Colonel's he was told of my arrest, and early that morning had come into Columbus to save me. The Justice ordered the constable to release me at once, and expressed his regret that I had been subjected to so much annoyance.

The Colonel was completely chopfallen at the turn affairs had taken, while I was surrounded by several Masonic friends, who expressed their gratification at my release. I addressed the Colonel, saying, that as he had put me to much inconvenience and trouble, I claimed a favour of him. He asked what it was. I begged him not to punish "Joe" for what he had done, and to allow me to present the brave fellow with a gift, as a mark of gratitude for his fidelity to me. . . . I then handed "Joe" twenty dollars in gold, for which he looked a thousand thanks. I was thus enabled to evince my gratitude for what he had done for me, and at the same time present him with the means to aid him in escaping from bondage.

Two years after this occurrence, while dining at the American Hotel, in Boston, I observed a coloured waiter eyeing me very closely; at length he recognized me, and asked if I remembered him. It was "Joe," my saviour, the former slave of Col. "Legree." . . . "Joe" subsequently gave me the following particulars of his escape from slavery:

On Sunday evening following my arrest and acquittal his brother joined him in a piece of woods, near the Col.'s plantation, where he had secreted sufficient food to last them several days.

At midnight they started together, moving as rapidly as they could through the fields and woods, keeping the north star in front of them. Whenever it was possible they walked in the creeks and marshy grounds, to throw the slave-hunters off their tracks. Thus, night after night, they kept on their weary way, hungry and sorefooted. On the morning of the seventeenth day of their freedom, they reached the Ohio river, nearly opposite a large town. All day they lay secreted in the bushes, at night they crossed the river in a small boat, and travelled rapidly, taking a north-easterly course. After enduring many hardships, they reached Cleveland, Ohio, and went to the house of a friend whose name I had given "Joe." They were there kindly received, and supplied with clothing and other comforts. Resting a week, they were sent on to Canada, where "Joe's" brother still lives. . . .

TEXAS
AND
MISSOURI

The settlers in prestatehood Texas, drawn from all parts of the Union but with most from the slaveholding South, formed a compact society that sturdily resisted any agreement with antislavery forces. Tension mounted as more and more slaveholders migrated from every part of the South. There was a strong movement from the beginning for annexation to the United States. In 1848, in spite of abolitionists' pleas against incorporating another slave state into the Union, Texas became a state.

Frederick Law Olmsted, who became famous later in life as an architect and designer of Central Park in New York City, was commissioned by *The New York Times* to write his impressions of the South. He toured the region, focusing primarily on the subject of slavery. The following account from his book *A Journey in the Back Country* (pages 171 to 173) relates his visit to a cotton plantation near New Orleans and his conversation with a planter regarding runaway slaves in Mexico:

PLANTER: I suppose there's a heap of Americans flocking in and settling up that country along the line, ain't there, sir?

OLMSTED: No, sir, very few. I saw none, in fact, only a few Irishmen and Frenchmen who called themselves

Americans. Those were the only foreigners I saw, except for negroes.

PLANTER: Niggers! Where they from?

OLMSTED: They were runaways from Texas.

PLANTER: But their masters go there and get them again, don't they?

OLMSTED: No sir, they can't.

PLANTER: Why not?

OLMSTED: The Mexicans are friendly to niggers, and protect them.

PLANTER: But why not go to the government?

OLMSTED: The government considers them free, and will not let them be taken back.

PLANTER: But that's stealing, that is; the same as stealing, sir. Why don't our government make them deliver them up? What good is the government to us if it don't preserve the rights of property, sir? Niggers are property, ain't they? And if a man steals my property, ain't the government bound to get it for me? Niggers are property, the same as horses and cattle, and nobody's any more rights to help a nigger that run away than he has to steal a horse.

He spoke angrily, and was excited. Perhaps he was indirectly addressing me, as a northern man, on the general subject of fugitive slaves. I said that it was necessary to have special treaty stipulations about such matters. The Mexicans lost their peons—bounded servants; they ran away to our side, but the United States government never took any measures to restore them, nor did the Mexicans ask it. "But," he answered, in a tone of indignation, "those aren't niggers, are they? They are white people, just as white as the Mexicans themselves, and just as much right to be free."

On December 19, 1859, John Brown camped at Bain's Fort, Kansas, and was introduced to a fugitive slave named Jim Daniels. A slave of one James Lawrence of Missouri, he had heard of Brown and, securing a pass from his master to travel about and sell brooms, had used the opportunity to make his way to Brown's camp for help. Never one to refuse the request of a fugitive slave seeking freedom, the well-known abolitionist divided his forces into two divisions and made his famous raid on Missouri. Brown provides us with his account of the raid in a letter to the New York *Tribune* of January 1859, published in Sanborn's edition of his letters (page 481):

On Sunday, December 19, a Negro man called Jim came over to the Osage settlement from Missouri, and stated that he, together with his wife, two children, and other men was to be sold within a day or two, and begged for help to get away. On Monday (the following) night, two small companies were made up to go to Missouri and forcibly liberate the five slaves, together with other slaves. One of these companies I assigned to direct. We proceeded to the place, surrounded the buildings, liberated the slaves, and took certain property supposed to belong to the estate. We, however, learned before leaving that a portion of the articles we had taken belonged to a man living on the plantation as a tenant, and was supposed to have no interest in the estate. We promptly returned to him all we had taken. We then went to another plantation, where we found five more slaves, took some property and two white men. We moved all slowly away into the territory for some distance, and then sent the white men back, telling them to follow us as soon as they chose to do so. The other company freed one female slave, took some property and, as I am informed, killed one white man (the master), who fought against liberation. Now for a comparison. Eleven persons are forcibly restored to their natural and inalienable rights, with but one man killed, and "all hell is stirred from beneath."

Siebert provides us with additional information when he writes in his classic study that the company responsible for shooting the slaveowner, David Cruse, was in the charge of John Kagi and Charles Stephens, also known as Whipple. Siebert continues (page 167):

> Thus Brown was led to undertake one of his boldest adventures, one of the boldest indeed in the history of the Underground Railroad. With a mere handful of men, he proposed to escort his band of freed men on a journey of twenty-five hundred miles to Canada, in the dead of winter and surrounded by dangers [resulting from] the publicity of his foray and the announcement of a reward of three-thousand dollars for his arrest by Governor Stewart of Missouri.

President James Buchanan, a proslavery sympathizer who was distinctively silent when antislavery emigrants were murdered, offered an additional two hundred and fifty dollars to the reward posted by the governor. The rewards seem to have ignited Old Brown's abolitionist blood as he directed his guerrilla band northward. According to the historian, Henrietta Buckmaster in *Let My People Go* (page 259):

> There was no time for rest or hesitation. The reward stirred the greed of men. The Brown party paused long enough to add a new baby to their crew, and pushed on, across the prairie, covered in December snow, across the wild bleak hills where little foxes ran and the wind came down like piercing blades of steel. They beat off a posse, fighting the Battle of the Spurs with the objects which they had at hand. They took prisoners. They heard the dull quick thudding of Kagi and his forty men riding hard as horses could carry them to catch up with the old man and drive off fresh pursuers. They crossed the ice of the Missouri River, and pushed toward their friends at the Underground Railroad station in Springdale, Iowa, where they distributed themselves among the Quakers.

However, their rest was short. Rumors were afloat that the deputy United States marshal was closing in on Springdale. It became necessary for Brown to gather his men and the runaway slaves. Abolitionist friends secured a freight car on a siding at West Liberty. Here they climbed aboard during the night. The coal train gained speed as the cold hills of Iowa led into frozen Illinois and, at length, Chicago, where they were affectionately greeted by the cunning Underground Railroad agent and famous detective, Alan Pinkerton. Pinkerton forwarded Brown and his charges toward Detroit. From that city, Brown ferried them across the Detroit River to Windsor, Canada. The dramatic escape from Missouri to Queen Victoria's Canada had consumed three weeks and created great excitement throughout the nation, especially in Missouri. According to Brown's biographer James Redpath, writing in 1860 (page 220):

> When the news of the invasion of Missouri spread, a wild panic went with it, which in a few days resulted in clearing Bates and Vernon counties of their slaves. Large numbers were sold south; many ran into the Territory and escaped; others were removed farther inland. When John Brown made his invasion there were five hundred slaves in that district, where there are not fifty now.

Over a decade before John Brown's notorious kidnapping of fugitive slaves from Missouri, there were other pioneers in the antislavery cause. George Thompson described in his narrative written in 1847 how he served time in a prison at Jefferson City, Missouri, for attempting to aid fugitive slaves. Thompson crossed the Mississippi River from Quincy, Illinois, with James Burr, another student of the Congregationalist Mission Institute of Reverend Moses Hunter, and Alanson Work, one of Hunter's employees, intending to rescue certain slaves. However, the young and daring abolitionists were betrayed by a black decoy who caused their arrest. The trio were captured and taken to jail at Palmyra. In September they were sentenced to twelve years in prison for the crime of "Grand Larceny (Abolition)."

William Wells Brown and his attractive, fair-skinned

mother, Elizabeth, attempted to escape to Canada in the spring of 1833, but they were recaptured in central Illinois and returned to bondage, later to be sold to a third master, Enoch Price, a riverboat captain. Brown was taken to Cincinnati, where one day he walked off the boat and never returned. On the fifth or sixth day of his escape, he was caught in a freezing rain. While traveling at night, according to Brown (see *Life of William W. Brown,* page 98), he became so "chilled and benumbed" that he had to seek shelter in a barn to keep from freezing. "Nothing but the providence of God," he recalled, "and that old barn, saved me from freezing to death." Brown further stated that because his feet had been frostbitten from time to time, he walked with difficulty. He continued his nerve-wracking journey. One cold morning he concealed himself "behind some logs and brush" near a narrow road and waited for a Good Samaritan:

> The first person that passed was a man in a buggy-wagon. He looked too genteel for me to hail him. Very soon, another passed by on horseback, and I attempted speaking to him but fear made my voice fail me. As he passed, I left my hiding-place and was approaching the road, when I observed an old man walking towards me, leading a white horse. He had on a broad-rimmed hat and a very long coat, and was evidently walking for exercise. As soon as I saw him and observed his dress, I thought to myself, "You are the man I have been looking for!" Nor was I mistaken. He was the very man!

The Good Samaritan extended his hand and offered to help Brown in his quest for freedom. Brown didn't forget the good deed of the one helper whom he found during his flight. To Wells Brown, from whom he received a surname, he later dedicated his fugitive slave's narrative.

Brown, shortly after his escape, hired himself at the age of twenty-one to a lake captain. He worked at various jobs in Cleveland and in Buffalo, and during his spare time, he studied spelling books, grammars, and history books. Distinguishing himself as a public speaker, he was called by William Lloyd Garrison in 1847 to serve as a lecturer and Underground Railroad agent with the Massachusetts Anti-Slavery Society, possibly to replace Frederick Douglass, who left to publish his paper, the *North Star*. Although Brown could not rival Douglass as an orator, he lectured almost without interruption in America and Europe. His daughter Josephine wrote that Brown delivered more than a thousand addresses while he was in Great Britain from July 1849 to September 1854.

A prolific author, Brown became America's first black man of letters. To him belongs the multiple distinction of being the first black novelist, dramatist, historian, and travel writer. His novel *Clotel, or The President's Daughter* was published in London in 1853, and in the United States in 1864, and was widely read. Brown was also a self-taught doctor and practiced medicine after the Civil War.

Hannibal, Missouri, the home of storyteller Mark Twain, was in the heart of "Little Dixie." The town and the region around it were known havens for slave-hunters from Kentucky, Tennessee, and elsewhere. A court trial during this period involved three abolitionists who had attempted to help five escaped slaves but were betrayed by one of the fugitives and caught. Mark Twain's father served on the jury that sent them to jail for twelve years. Twain, early in his career, showed compassion for the helpers and wrote about the case in his story "A Scrap of Curious History."

Bethany, Joplin, Potosi, and Kansas City have been confirmed by written records as stations on Missouri's Underground Railroad.

KANSAS AND NEBRASKA TERRITORIES

B. F. Stringfellow, a proslavery leader from Missouri, declared in Washington in 1855 that "two thousand slaves, actually lodged in Kansas, will make a slave state. Once fairly there, nobody will disturb them." No one except John Brown, who gladly accepted the challenge. He arrived in Kansas in 1855, in response to appeals for arms from his sons, five of whom preceded him to the territory and settled at Osawatomie. He found them living in uncomfortable circumstances—"No houses to shelter one of them; no hay or corn-fodder of any account secured; shivering over their fires, all exposed to the dreadfully cutting winds, morning and evening on stormy days."

It was not to make a home for himself in Kansas, nor to aid his sons in their wilderness struggle, that John Brown came to Kansas. Rather, it was his conviction that there was an opportunity to make Kansas instead of Canada a terminal on the Underground Railroad. It was with this intention that John Brown left his North Elba, New York, home and transported a wagonload of weapons to lead his Charge of the Abolition Brigade.

The abolitionist town of Lawrence had been gutted and burned by some eight hundred heavily armed proslavers, including Missouri forces, who had been designated a posse by Sheriff Samuel Jones. Charles Sumner, in a terse denunciation, declared this to be "a crime without example in the history of the west."

In *Let My People Go* (page 241), Underground Railroad historian Henrietta Buckmaster vividly describes what followed:

> John Brown swooped down on Pottawatomie and avenged Lawrence—and Sumner. It was a bloody and ruthless revenge, a midnight raid in which five pro-slavery settlers were dragged from their beds and cut to death with an old army cutlass. War was on with a vengeance. Guerrilla bands of Missourians stalked the territory by day and night, throwing their pickets across the borders of Iowa and Nebraska, shooting, turning back the emigrants from the east, finally blockading the Missouri River and sending down its currents, tied to logs, those who attempted to pass into Kansas.

Believing that he was divinely inspired, Brown later denied that he, personally, participated in the bloody massacre in Pottawatomie. Brown stated a few years later to James Redpath, his first biographer (see Redpath, page 119), "I do not say this to exculpate myself; for although I took no hand in it, I would have advised it had I known the circumstances. I endorse it as it was. Again, time and the honest verdict of posterity," said Brown in his Virginia cell, "will approve of every act of mine."

John Brown recalled the grim specter of Kansas. "Once," he said, "I saw three mutilated bodies, two were dead and one still lived, but riddled with twenty bullet holes and buck-shot holes; the two murdered men had been lying eighteen hours on the ground, a prey to the flies. One of these young men was my own son." "The war" was becoming a common phrase in Kansas, both sides profoundly stirred by it.

Nebraska was involved like Kansas in the fierce struggle concerning slavery in the territories after the passage of the Kansas-Nebraska Bill in 1854, which established those territories. The fighting occurred generally in Kansas, however, where the Underground Railroad movement was widespread. In Nebraska, the Underground Railroad movement was centered in Nebraska City, Camp Creek, and Little Nemaha.

Narrative of John Brown

John Brown wrote the following in a letter to his wife and children in June 1856 (from Sanborn's *Letters of John Brown*, pages 240 to 241).

Every one,

It is now about five weeks since I have seen a line from North Elba, or had any chance of writing you. During that period we here have passed through an almost constant series of very trying events. We were called to go to the relief of Lawrence on May 22 and every man (eight in all) except Orson, turned out; he staying with the women and children and to take care of the cattle. John was captain of a company to which Jason belonged; the other six were a little company by ourselves. On our way to Lawrence, we learned that it had been already destroyed and we encamped with John's company overnight. Next day, our little company left, and during the day we stopped and searched three men.

Lawrence was destroyed in this way: Their leading men had (as I think) decided, in a very cowardly manner, not to resist any process having any government official to serve it, notwithstanding the process might be wholly a bogus affair. The consequence was that a man called a United States Marshal came on with a horde of ruffians which he called his posse and, after arresting few persons, turned the ruffians loose on the defenseless people. They robbed the inhabitants of their money and other property and even women of their ornaments, and burned considerable of the town. On the second day and evening after we left John's men [John Brown,

Jr.], we encountered quite a number of pro-slavery men and took quite a number of prisoners. Our prisoners, we let go; but we kept some four or five horses.

Narrative of William Wells Brown

Brown was born in Kentucky and grew up in Missouri, believing that his mulatto mother's father was Daniel Boone. Brown's white father was "connected with some of the first families of Kentucky." This passage is from his *Narrative*, published in Boston in 1847 (pages 13 to 30).

I was born in Lexington, Ky. The man who stole me as soon as I was born, recorded the births of all the infants which he claimed to be born his property, in a book which he kept for that purpose. My mother's name was Elizabeth. She had seven children, viz.: Solomon, Leander, Benjamin, Joseph, Millford, Elizabeth, and myself. No two of us were children of the same father. My father's name, as I learned from my mother, was George Higgins. He was a white man, a relative of my master, and connected with some of the first families in Kentucky.

My master owned about forty slaves, twenty-five of whom were field hands. He removed from Kentucky to Missouri when I was quite young, and settled thirty or forty miles above St. Charles, on the Missouri, where, in addition to his practice as a physician, he carried on milling, merchandizing, and farming. He had a large farm, the principal productions of which were tobacco and hemp. The slave cabins were situated on the back part of the farm, with the house of the overseer, whose name was Grove Cook, in their midst. He had the entire charge of the farm, and having no family was allowed a woman to keep house for him, whose business it was to deal out the provisions for the hands.

Soon afterwards, my master removed to the city of St. Louis, and purchased a farm four miles from there, which he placed under the charge of an overseer by the name of Friend

Haskell. He was a regular Yankee from New England. The Yankees are noted for making the most cruel overseers.

My mother was hired out in the city, and I was also hired out there to Major Freeland, who kept a public house. He was formerly from Virginia, and was a horse-racer, cock-fighter, gambler, and withal an inveterate drunkard. There were ten or twelve servants in the house, and when he was present, it was cut and slash—knock down and drag out. In his fits of anger, he would take up a chair, and throw it at a servant; and in his more rational moments, when he wished to chastise one, he would tie them up in the smokehouse, and whip them; after which, he would cause a fire to be made of tobacco stems, and smoke them. This he called *"Virginia play."*

I complained to my master of the treatment which I received from Major Freeland; but it made no difference. He cared nothing about it, so long as he received the money for my labor. After living with Major Freeland five or six months, I ran away, and went into the woods back of the city; and when night came on, I made my way to my master's farm, but was afraid to be seen, knowing that if Mr. Haskell, the overseer, should discover me, I should be again carried back to Major Freeland; so I kept in the woods. One day, while in the woods, I heard the barking and howling of dogs, and in a short time they came so near that I knew them to be the bloodhounds of Major Benjamin O'Fallon. He kept five or six, to hunt runaways slaves with.

As soon as I was convinced that it was them. I knew there was no chance of escape. I took refuge in the top of a tree and the hounds were soon at its base, and there remained until the hunters came up in a half or three quarters of an hour afterwards. There were two men with the dogs, who, as soon as they came up, ordered me to descend. I came down, was tied, and taken to St. Louis jail. Major Freeland soon made his appearance, and took me out, and ordered me to follow him, which I did. After we returned home I was tied up in the smokehouse, and was very severely whipped. After the major had flogged me to his satisfaction, he sent out his son Robert, a young man eighteen or twenty years of age, to see that I was well smoked. He made a fire of tobacco stems, which soon set me to coughing and sneezing. This, Robert told me, was the way his father used to do to his slaves in

Virginia. After giving me what they conceived to be a decent smoking, I was untied and again set to work.

Robert Freeland was a "chip off the old block." Though quite young, it was not unfrequently that he came home in a state of intoxication. He is now, I believe, a popular commander of a steamboat on the Mississippi river. Major Freeland soon after failed in business, and I was put on board the steamboat Missouri, which plied between St. Louis and Galena. The commander of the boat was William B. Culver. I remained on her during the sailing season, which was the most pleasant time for me that I had ever experienced. At the close of navigation I was hired to Mr. John Colburn, keeper of the Missouri Hotel. He was from one of the free states; but a more inveterate hater of the negro I do not believe ever walked God's green earth. This hotel was at that time one of the largest in the city, and there were employed in it twenty or thirty servants, mostly slaves. . . .

While living at the Missouri hotel, a circumstance occurred which caused me great unhappiness. My master sold my mother, and all her children, except myself. They were sold to different persons in the city of St. Louis.

After a miserable stay with Colburn at the Missouri Hotel, Brown was replaced in 1830 and was then employed in the printing office of an abolitionist, the Reverend Elijah P. Lovejoy, publisher and editor of the St. Louis Times. (Lovejoy was later murdered at Alton, Illinois, because of his abolitionist activities.)

Mr. Lovejoy was a very good man, and decidedly the best master that I had ever had. I am chiefly indebted to him, and to my employment in the printing office, for what little learning I obtained while in slavery. . . .

While living with Mr. Lovejoy, I was often sent on errands to the office of the "Missouri Republican," published by Mr. Edward Charles. Once, while returning to the office with type, I was attacked by several large boys, sons of slaveholders, who pelted me with snow-balls. Having the heavy form of type in my hands, I could not make my escape by running; so I laid down the type and gave them battle. They gathered round me, pelting me with stones and sticks, until they over-powered me, and would have captured me, if I had not restored to my heels. Upon my retreat they took possession of the type; and what to do to regain it I could not devise. Knowing Mr. Lovejoy to be a very humane man, I went to the office and laid the case before him. He told me to remain in the office. He took one of the apprentices with him and went after the type, and soon returned with it; but on his return informed me that Samuel McKinney had told him he would whip me, because I had hurt his boy. Soon after, McKinney was seen making his way to the office by one of the printers, who informed me of the fact, and I made my escape through the back door.

McKinney, not being able to find me on his arrival, left the office in a great rage, swearing that he would whip me to death. A few days after, as I was walking along Main Street, he seized me by the collar, and struck me over the head five or six times with a large cane, which caused the blood to gush from my nose and ears in such a manner that my clothes were completely saturated with blood. After beating me to his satisfaction he let me go, and I returned to the office so weak from the loss of blood that Mr. Lovejoy sent me home to my master. It was five weeks before I was able to walk again. During this time it was necessary to have some one to supply my place at the office, and I lost the situation.

After my recovery, I was hired to Capt. Otis Reynolds, as a waiter on board the steamboat Enterprise, owned by Messrs. John and Edward Walsh, commission merchants at St. Louis. This boat was then running on the upper Mississippi. My employment on board was to wait on gentlemen, and the captain being a good man, the situation was a pleasant one to me—but in passing from place to place, and seeing new faces every day, and knowing that they could go where they pleased, I soon became unhappy, and several times thought of leaving the boat at some landing-place, and trying to make my escape to Canada, which I had heard much about as a place where the slave might live, be free, and be protected.

SOUTH
CAROLINA

A large portion of the slaves of South Carolina lived in the tidewater area and when planning escape often looked toward the coast and its sailing vessels with captains who might pilot them to the North or to the West Indies and freedom closer to home.

Most slaves on the plantations knew nothing of the Underground Railroad or of northern abolitionists, unless they were told by city slaves or sympathetic northern white travelers. However, they did know of the many instances of planned rebellions against the state, including the one commanded by the Charleston carpenter Denmark Vesey, who had bought his own freedom. The revolt had been planned to occur in 1822 and is considered one of the most extensive slave revolts ever recorded in America, with as many as nine thousand slaves recruited for the rebellion. Vesey was betrayed by a house slave, and was later put to death with three dozen others of the more than ten dozen arrested. Twenty-two were hanged together on the same gallows.

Dr. Alexander M. Ross traveled through South Carolina for the express purpose of spreading information about Canada and the routes by which the country could be reached. His *Recollections and Experiences of an Abolitionist* tells of some of the dangers (pages 50 and 51):

A few days after my arrival, one of the Charleston papers contained a dispatch from Augusta which stated that several first-class Negro men had disappeared from that place within a week; and that a very general impression prevailed there that abolitionists were at work inciting Negroes to escape from their masters. I left Charleston that evening and went to Raleigh, North Carolina. While at breakfast the next morning, two men seated near me entered into conversation relative to the escape of slaves from Augusta. One of them remarked that an Englishman, who had been stopping in Augusta for several weeks, was suspected of doing the mischief, and that it was supposed he had gone with the fugitives, as he had not been seen since the slaves were missed; but if he should be caught, no mercy would be shown him, as it was time to make an example of the Negro thieves that infested the South. I lost no time, obviously, and left by the first train to Washington.

The task of tracing the origin of fugitive slave escapes in South Carolina would be most difficult without historian Peter Wood's scholarly introduction to slave life in the colony, *Black Majority,* from which the following is taken (page 163):

Whether slaves departed singly or together, by sea or land, armed or unarmed, toward north or south, their chances of successful escape became increasingly slight. This did not preclude desperate slaves from undertaking such escapes, as the Stono Uprising will make clear, but it meant that Negroes who actually took flight from South Carolina in various directions were only a minority of the entire runaway population.

Many more slaves seem to have succeeded in going "underground" intermittently or for good, without leaving the colony. It is hard to estimate how many people simply disappeared temporarily and endured a set punishment on return.

The practice of free Negroes concealing fugitives persisted, in spite of cruel punishments, for the *Charleston Courier* of August 13, 1827, reports the following story:

> A trial of much interest took place on Saturday last, at the city hall before a court composed of John Michel, Esq., Justice of the Quorum and two Freeholders. The parties put upon their trial were Hannah Elliot, a free black woman, together with her daughter Judy, and her sons Simon and Sam. They were severally indicted under the act of 1740 for harbouring, concealing, and entertaining two female children, aged six and nine years, the property of a lady of this city, the extraordinary concealment and discovery of which was mentioned a short time since.

Not all whites openly identified themselves with the slaveholding gentry, and antislavery sentiment was occasionally expressed within prominent families. Sarah and Angelina, daughters of Judge John F. Grimke, a distinguished jurist, planter, and slaveholder, left Charleston because of their opposition to slavery. They moved to Philadelphia, where Angelina joined the Society of Friends and became active in the abolition movement. In 1837, at a time when few American women dared to speak in public, they toured New England lecturing in over sixty towns on behalf of the antislavery cause. Angelina married Theodore Weld, one of the nation's leading abolitionists. Throughout the South postmasters and other officials destroyed copies of Angelina's famous pamphlet, *Appeal to the Christian Women in the South,* and the citizens of Charleston banned her from the city of her birth because of her efforts to end slavery.

Her fellow Carolinians, intent upon keeping slavery, had the great advantages of public opinion and of pulpit, of the use of law, and of the use of dogs to track runaways. The fear of bloodhounds was justified. A Columbia, South Carolina, newspaper reported that: "Mr. J. L. Bryan of Moore County, sold at auction, on the 20th instant a pack of ten bloodhounds trained for hunting runaway negroes, for the sum of $1540. The highest price paid for any one dog was $301." One English traveler confirmed that slave-hunters took particular pride in their dogs:

> When I was traveling through the southern portion of the United States, I remained for a few days at Columbia, South Carolina, the seat of the State legislature. One evening, I was much surprised to see a great number of men on horseback, accompanied by dogs. Upon inquiring who they were, I was informed that they were negro-hunters, whose horrible business consisted in tracking and catching runaway slaves. They came into the yard attached to the boarding-house at which I was stopping. When they had kennelled their dogs, and were about to feed them, I felt a curiosity to go out and see them. The dogs were of a species between the bloodhound and fox hound, and were ferocious, gaunt, and savage-looking animals. Their monsters fed them exclusively on Indian cornbread. This kind of food, they told me, made the dogs eager and lively for their business. It is the practice, when these wretches come to a town, for any white person, who has lost slaves, to go to the "nigger-catchers," as they term them, and as nearly as they can to put them on the track; of course giving a sufficient remuneration for their trouble. Even in this slaveholding community, such is the odium and contempt with which these creatures are regarded, that none but the very scum of society can be found to pursue so inhuman an occupation.

According to Alexander Ross (pages 50–51), "bloodhounds are larger and more compact than ordinary hounds, with hair straight and sleek as that of the finest race horse, colored between yellow and brown, short-eared, rather long-nosed, and built for scenting, quick action, and speed," and his description is of further value since he was also a naturalist.

Narrative of John Jackson

This escape narrative was printed in the Rochester, New York, *Union and Advertiser* on August 9, 1893.

I was born and bred on the plantation of old Mars Robert English, one hundred miles from Charleston. My younger days were happy ones. I played with the massa's children until I became seven or eight years old, then I had to go into the field with the other black folks and work hard all day from earliest dawn till late at night. We ate twice a day, that is, when we got up in the morning we were driven out into the fields and were called into breakfast at noon by the blast of an old tin horn.

All we got to eat then was three corn cake dumplins and one plate of soup. No meat unless there happened to be a rotten piece in the smoke house. This would be given to us to make our soup. Why the dogs got better eating than we poor colored folks. We would go out into the fields again and work very hard until dark, when we were driven in by the crack of the overseer's lash and frequently that crack meant blood from some unfortunate creature's back, who, becoming weary had shown signs of faltering.

In the evening those of us who felt inclined would play on something we had made from corn stalks and skin, but not very often. Our overseer was a mean fellow, that he was, sir. I was whipped before my father's face many and many a time. My poor father couldn't help himself, though. After [the overseer] had whipped me to his heart's content—it didn't seem as if he had a heart—he would send me back bleeding and sore to work on until noon, when he blowed the horn.

I would have to tell him about half past seven o'clock every morning, to go and get his breakfast while we worked on in the boiling sun, without food since the night before. I growed up and married when I was very young and I loved my little girl wife. Life was not a burden then. I never minded the whippings I got.

I was happy and it made old Mars Robert angry. He frequently would come out and whip me himself and say "you will have to give up that wife of yours or I will thrash you till you can't stand." I always declared I wouldn't and then he would whip me, oh! how he would whip me. My flesh even now has a quivering feeling when I think of those horrible times. Old Mars Robert went crazy soon afterward and then he could not whip me any more.

One day the overseer said to me, "I'm going to marry that girl of yours to Enoch." He was another slave. I said to him that no one should take her while I was around and then he whipped me till I fainted. That night I determined to run away to the free north and see if I could not get some one to help me steal my girl wife out of slavery. It was a dark, rainy night. Everybody had gone to sleep and even the bloodhounds had crept into their master's house for shelter.

I kissed my wife and babe goodbye. I can see her now, my poor wife, with the tears glistening in her eyes. The dying fire cast its fitful glow upon the wall and I was going from my dear ones never to see them more, for they married my dear wife to another slave and she and my baby boy died soon after and got out of slavery, thank the good Lord.

I made way to Charleston and got into the hold of a northern bound sailing vessel. I remained for seven days and nights in my hiding place. Hunger and thirst at last compelled me to bore a hole through the planking of the ship with the gimlet I had. I stuck out a straw and attracted the attention of the captain, who ordered the sailors to release me. After a long while I was taken out of my close confinement and was taken to the captain, who asked me if I knew him or his vessel. I said I did not. He said all right and took me down to the cabin and gave me something to eat.

The vessel was bound for Boston. I asked the captain if he could help me get my wife and child. He told me to get some minister to write, as I could not write myself. I did and then learned she had been married to another slave and a short time afterward died.

I made my way to Toronto from Boston and from there to England. While in England I belonged to the Rev. Mr. Spurgeon's church and was the only black man in the congregation.

I came back to this country after the war. I'm getting old and feeble and I only want to live till I get the money for the Home, and then I will go down to Old Carliny and there is where I want to die, down in my old cabin home.

Narrative of Daniel Fisher

This narrative appeared in the *New Era Press* of Deep River, Connecticut, on November 23, 1900, and was reprinted in Strother's *The Underground Railroad in Connecticut,* 1962 (pages 48 to 51).

I was born in Westmoreland County, Virginia, about the year of 1808. I had five brothers and two sisters and was known as Daniel Fisher. Our master's name was Henry Cox. When I was about twenty years of age my master was obliged, on account of heavy losses, to sell me, and I was sent to Richmond to be sold on the block to the highest bidder. The sale took place and the price paid for me was five hundred and fifty dollars. I was taken by my new master to South Carolina. This was in the month of March. I remained there until October when, in company with another slave, we stole a horse and started to make our escape. In order not to tire the animal, we traveled from ten o'clock at night until daybreak the next morning when we ran the horse into the woods and left him, for we knew what would happen to us if two slaves were seen having a horse in their possession. We kept on our way on foot, hiding by day and walking by night. We were without knowledge of the country, and with nothing to guide us other than the north star, which was oftentimes obscured by clouds, we would unwittingly retrace our steps and find ourselves back at the starting point. Finally, after days of tedious walking and privations, fearing to ask for food and getting but little from the slaves we met, we reached Petersburg. From Petersburg we easily found our way to Richmond and then, after wandering in the woods for three days and nights, we came to my old home at Westmoreland Court House.

One of the greatest obstacles we had to contend with was the crossing of rivers, as slaves were not allowed to cross bridges without a pass from their masters. For that reason, when we came to the Rappahannock we had to wait our chance and steal a fisherman's boat in order to cross. Upon my arrival at my old plantation, I called upon my young master and begged him to buy me back. He said he would gladly do it, but he was poorer than when he sold me. He advised me to stow myself away on some vessel going north, and as the north meant freedom I decided to act upon his advice. While awaiting the opportunity to do so, we (the same slave who had accompanied me from South Carolina being with me) secured shovels and dug us three dens in different localities in the neighboring woods. In these dens we lived during the day, and foraged for food in the night time, staying there about three months. At the end of that time we managed to stow ourselves away on a vessel loaded with wood bound for Washington. We were four days without food and suffered much. When we reached Washington the captain of the vessel put on a coat of a certain color, and started out for the public market, telling us to follow and keep him in sight.

At the market he fed us and told us in what direction to go, starting us on our journey, giving us two loaves of bread each for food. We took the railroad track and started for Baltimore. We had gone scarcely a mile before we met an Irishman, who decided that we were runaways, and was determined to give us to the authorities. However, by telling him a smooth story that we were sent for by our masters to come to a certain house just ahead, he let us by. Thinking our bundles of bread were endangering our safety by raising suspicion, we threw them away. After we went several days without food, traveling day and night, we reached the Delaware [Susquehanna?] River. We walked along the bank of the river for some five miles in search of a bridge. We finally came to one, but on attempting to cross were stopped, as we had no passes. It was a toll bridge, and there was a woman in charge of it, who upon our payment of a penny for each and the promise to come back immediately, allowed us to go by. By this time we were hungry, but had no food. At the other end of the bridge we were stopped again, as the gates were opened only for teams. However, by exercising our ingenuity and pretending to look around, we finally managed to slip by in the shadow of a team, and then—glorious thought!—we were at last on the free soil of Pennsylvania.

We again took to the woods, knowing that we were liable to be apprehended at any time. We made a fire, which attracted attention, and we were soon run out of our hiding place. We sought another place and built another fire, and again we were chased away. We made no more fires. In the course of our further wanderings we were chased by men and hounds, but managed to escape capture, and finally arrived in Philadelphia, being three days on the road. In Philadelphia we found friends who gave us the choice of liquor or food. I took the food, my companion the liquor.

As kidnappers were plenty, it was thought best for our safety that we separate, and we parted. The only weapon for defense which I had was a razor, one which I had carried all through my wanderings. In company with some Philadelphia colored people, I was taken to New York, and it was there I first met members of the Abolition party. At New York I was put on board a steamboat for New Haven. Arrived in that city, a colored man took me to the Tontine Hotel, where a woman gave me a part of a suit of clothes. I was fed and made comfortable, and then directed to Deep River, with instructions that upon arriving there I was to inquire for George Read or Judge Warner. I walked all the way from New Haven to Deep River, begging food by the way from the women of the farm houses, as I was afraid to apply to the men, not knowing but what they would detail me and give me up. I traveled the Old Stage Road from New Haven to Deep River and in going through Killingworth I stopped at the tavern kept by Landlord Redfield but was driven away. Upon reaching the "Plains" this side of Winthrop, I could not read the signs on the post at the forks of the road, and asked the way of Mrs. Griffing. She drove me away, but called out, "Take that road," and pointed to it. Further on I met Harrison Smith, who had a load of wood which he said was for Deacon Read, the man I was looking for.

I reached Deep River at last, weary and frightened. I called at Deacon Read's, told him my circumstances and gave him my name as Daniel Fisher. All this was in secret. The good deacon immediately told me that I must nevermore be known as Daniel Fisher, but must take the name of "William Winters," the name which I have borne to this day. He furthermore told me that I must thereafter wear a wig at all times and in all places. After that I worked at different times for Ambrose Webb and Judge Warner in Chester, and for Deacon Stevens in Deep River, getting along very nicely, though always afraid of being taken by day or night and carried again to the South.

NORTH
CAROLINA

Underground activities evidently developed early in North Carolina, for in 1741 the colony passed an act providing that, "any person harbouring a runaway shall be prosecuted and compelled to pay the sum of twenty-five pounds or serve the owner of the slave, should he be convicted and suffer accordingly."

As late as 1860, all suspected of being fugitive slaves were questioned or lodged in jail and held until their owners came to get them, and there is unmistakable evidence that the runaways were a continuous source of trouble to their owners. Newspapers throughout the state contained advertisements for runaways, offering rewards for their apprehension, and the American Anti-Slavery Society reported that two thousand escaped from North Carolina in the last year before the Civil War.

In North Carolina, Underground methods are known to have been employed by white persons as early as 1819. According to Siebert (*The Underground Railroad,* page 117), "Vestal Coffin organized the Underground Railroad near the present Guilford College in 1819. Addison Coffin, his son, entered its service as a conductor in early youth and still survives in hale old age. Vestal's cousin, Levi Coffin became an antislavery apostle in early youth and continued unflinching to the end. His early years were spent in North Carolina, whence he helped many slaves to reach the West." Levi Coffin removed to Indi-

61

ana in 1826. Of his own and his cousin's activities in behalf of slaves while still a resident of North Carolina, Coffin wrote:

> Runaway slaves used frequently to conceal themselves in the woods and thickets of New Garden, waiting opportunities to make their escape to the North, and I generally learned their places of concealment and rendered them all the service in my power. These outlying slaves knew where I lived, and, when reduced to extremity of want or danger, often came to my room, in the silence and darkness of the night, to obtain food or assistance. In my efforts to aid these fugitives I had a zealous coworker in my friend and cousin Vestal Coffin, who was then, and continued to the time of his death—a few years later—a staunch friend to the slave.

There were stations in Jamestown, now High Point, and Goldsboro, where Quaker communities made it a part of their religious duties to render aid to fugitive slaves. Mount Jefferson, overlooking Jefferson and West Jefferson in Ashe County, was until recently known as Nigger Mountain, because northern sympathizers befriended escaping slaves by hiding them on its slopes, also supplying them with food and loaning them horses.

Several North Carolina fugitives wrote narratives of their lives or became subjects of biographies. Lunsford Lane of Raleigh purchased his freedom after spending thirty-two years in bondage and serving as a "waiter and messenger" for two of the state governors. He was described as a modest, intelligent man of prepossessing appearance by Garrison's *Liberator.* He removed his family to Boston and soon after became an agent and speaker for the antislavery cause. In 1842, his book, *The Narrative of Lunsford Lane, formerly of Raleigh, North Carolina,* was published and in 1863 his life story was retold in a full-length biography.

Narratives also came from such fugitives as Moses Roper, born in Caswell County, who published his *Narrative of the Adventures and Escape from American Slavery* in 1838. After surviving sadistic maltreatment and being sold from master to master, Roper coaxed a semi-literate white boy of Savannah, Georgia, into preparing free papers that described him as an Indian. The papers enabled Roper to obtain employment on a vessel bound for New York City.

Nearly twenty years later a slave who was born on the John Hawes plantation in Hanover County published his *Experiences of Thomas H. Jones Who Was a Slave for Forty-Three Years.* After buying his family's freedom and sending them to New York City, Jones stowed away on a vessel for the same city. He was betrayed before landing, but managed to elude his captors by jumping from the vessel. Soon he arrived in Brooklyn, met his family, and moved to Connecticut. Jones finally settled in Worcester, Massachusetts.

Narrative of Harry Grimes

This narrative appears in Still's *Underground Railroad Records* (pages 422 to 425).

As Harry, from having suffered most, was the hero of this party, and withal was an intelligent man, he was first called upon to make his statement as to how times had been with him in the prison house, from his youth up. He was about forty-six years of age, according to his reckoning, full six feet high, and in muscular appearance was very rugged, and in his countenance were evident marks of firmness. He said that he was born a slave in North Carolina, and had been sold three times. He was first sold when a child three years of age, the second time when he was thirteen years old, and the third and last time he was sold to Jesse Moore, from whom he fled. Prior to his coming into the hands of Moore he had not experienced any very hard usage, at least nothing more severe than fell to the common lot of slave-boys, therefore the period of his early youth was deemed of too little interest to record in detail. In fact time only could be afforded for noticing very briefly some of the more remarkable events of his bondage. The examining Committee [a committee to interrogate slaves to see if they were spies] confined their interrogations to his last taskmaster.

"How did Moore come by you?" was one of the inquiries. "He bought me," said Harry, "of a man by the name of Taylor, nine or ten years ago; he was as bad as he could be, couldn't be any worse to be alive. He was about fifty years of age, when I left him, a right red-looking man, big bellied old fellow, weighs about two hundred and forty pounds. He drinks hard, he is just like a rattlesnake, just as cross and crabbed when he speaks, seems like he could go through you.

"I have been treated bad. One day we were grubbing and master said we didn't do work enough. 'How come there was no more work done that day?' said master to me. I told him I did work. In a more stormy manner he 'peated the question. I then spoke up and said: 'Massa, I don't know what to say.' At once massa plunged his knife into my neck causing me to stagger. Massa was drunk. He then drove me down to the black folks' houses [cabins of the slaves]. He then got his gun, called the overseer, and told him to get some ropes. While he was gone I said, 'Massa, now you are going to tie me up and cut me all to pieces for nothing. I would just as leave you would take your gun and shoot me down as to tie me up and cut me all to pieces for nothing.' In a great rage he said 'go.' I jumped, and he put up his gun and snapped both barrels at me. He then set his dogs on me, but as I had been in the habit of making much of them, feeding them, etc., they would not follow me, and I kept on straight to the woods. My master and the overseer cotched the horses and tried to run me down, but as the dogs would not follow me they couldn't make nothing of it. It was the last of August a year ago. The devil was into him, and he flogged and beat four of the slaves, one man and three of the women, and said if he could only get hold of me he wouldn't strike me, 'nary-a-lick,' but would tie me to a tree and empty both barrels into me.

"In the woods I lived on nothing, you may say, and something too. I had bread, and roasting ears, and 'taters. I stayed in the hollow of a big poplar tree for seven months; the other part of the time I stayed in a cave. I suffered mighty bad with the cold and for something to eat. Once I got me some charcoal and made me a nice fire in my tree to warm me, and it liked to killed me, so I had to take the fire out. One time a snake come to the tree, poked its head in the hollow and was coming in, and I took my axe and chopped him in two. It was a poplar leaf moccasin, the poisonest kind of a snake we have. While in the woods all my thoughts was how to get away to a free country.''

Subsequently, in going back over his past history, he referred to the fact, that on an occasion long before the cave and tree existence, already noticed, when suffering under this brutal master, he sought protection in the woods and abode twenty-seven months in a cave, before he surrendered himself, or was captured. His offence, in this instance, was simply because he desired to see his wife, and ''stole'' away from his master's plantation and went a distance of five miles, to where she lived, to see her. For this grave crime his master threatened to give him a hundred lashes, and to shoot him; in order to avoid this punishment, he escaped to the woods, etc. The lapse of a dozen years and recent struggles for an existence, made him think lightly of his former troubles and he would, doubtless, have failed to recall his earlier conflicts but for the desire manifested by the Committee to get all the information out of him they could.

He was next asked, ''Had you a wife and family?'' ''Yes, sir,'' he answered, ''I had a wife and eight children, belonged to the widow Slade.'' Harry gave the names of his wife and children as follows: Wife, Susan, and children, Oliver, Sabey, Washington, Daniel, Jonas, Harriet, Moses and Rosetta, the last named he had never seen. ''Between my mistress and my master there was not much difference.''

Narrative of Passmore Williamson

This narrative appears in Still's *Underground Railroad Records* (pages 86 to 91). The legality of slaves becoming free when brought by their masters into a free state was finally decided by the Supreme Court in the famous Dred Scott case. The speaker in this case is Still himself.

The Vigilance Committee referred to is that of the Philadelphia Vigilance Association, which questioned all those
who came to it for assistance in order to protect itself
against spies.

Among other duties devolving on the Vigilance Committee
when hearing of slaves brought into the State by their owners,
was immediately to inform such persons that as they were not
fugitives, but were brought into the State by their masters,
they were entitled to their freedom without another moment's
service, and that they could have the assistance of the Committee and the advice of counsel without charge, by simply
availing themselves of these proffered favors.

Many slave-holders fully understood the law in this particular, and were also equally posted with regard to the vigilance
of abolitionists. Consequently they avoided bringing slaves
beyond Mason and Dixon's Line in traveling North. But some
slave-holders were not thus mindful of the laws, or were too
arrogant to take heed, as may be seen in the case of Colonel
John H. Wheeler, of North Carolina, the United States Minister to Nicaragua. In passing through Philadelphia from Washington, one very warm July day in 1855, accompanied by
three of his slaves, his high official equilibrium, as well as his
assumed rights under the Constitution, received a terrible
shock at the hands of the Committee.

In order to bring fully before the reader the beginning of
this interesting and exciting case, it seems only necessary to
publish the subjoined letter, written by one of the actors in
this drama, and addressed to the New York Tribune, and an
additional paragraph which may be requisite to throw light on
a special point, which Judge Kane decided was concealed in
the "obstinate" breast of Passmore Williamson, as said Williamson persistently refused before the said Judge's court, to
own that he had a knowledge of the mystery in question.
After which, a brief glance at some of the more important
points of the case must suffice.

The following note was placed in my hands by a colored
boy whom I had never seen before, to my recollection:

Mr. Still—Sir: Will you come down to Bloodgood's
Hotel as soon as possible—as there are three fugitive

slaves here and they want liberty. Their master is here
with them, on his way to New York.

The note was without date, and the signature so indistinctly
written as not to be understood by me, having evidently been
penned in a moment of haste.

Without delay I ran with the note to Mr. P. Williamson's
office, Seventh and Arch, found him at his desk, and gave it
to him, and after reading it, he remarked that he could not go
down, as he had to go to Harrisburg that night on business—
but he advised me to go, and to get the names of the slaveholder and the slaves, in order to telegraph to New York to
have them arrested there, as no time remained to procure a
writ of habeas corpus here.

I could not have been two minutes in Mr. W.'s office
before starting in haste for the wharf. To my surprise, however, when I reached the wharf, there I found Mr. W., his
mind having undergone a sudden change; he was soon on the
spot.

I saw three or four colored persons in the hall at Bloodgood's,
none of whom I recognized except the boy who brought me
the note. Before having time for making inquiry some one
said they had gone on board the boat. "Get their description," said Mr. W. I instantly inquired of one of the colored
persons for the desired description, and was told that she was
"a tall, dark woman, with two little boys."

Mr. W. and myself ran on board of the boat, looked among
the passengers on the first deck, but saw them not. "They are
up on the second deck," an unknown voice uttered. In a
second we were in their presence. We approached the anxious-
looking slave-mother with her two boys on her left-hand; close
on her right sat an ill-favored white man having a cane in his
hand which I took to be a sword-cane. (As to its being a
sword-cane, however, I might have been mistaken.)

The first words to the mother were: "Are you traveling?"
"Yes," was the prompt answer. "With whom?" She nodded
her head toward the ill-favored man, signifying with him.
Fidgeting on his seat, he said something, exactly what I do
not now recollect. In reply I remarked: "Do they belong to
you, Sir?" "Yes, they are in my charge," was his answer.
Turning from him to the mother and her sons, in substance,
and word for word, as near as I can remember, the following

remarks were earnestly though calmly addressed by the individuals who rejoiced to meet them on free soil, and who felt
unmistakably assured that they were justified by the laws of
Pennsylvania as well as the Law of God, in informing them
of their rights:

"You are entitled to your freedom according to the laws of
Pennsylvania, having been brought into the State by your
owner. If you prefer freedom to slavery, as we suppose
everybody does, you have the chance to accept it now. Act
calmly—don't be frightened by your master—you are as much
entitled to your freedom as we are, or as he is—be determined and you need have no fears but that you will be
protected by the law. Judges have time and again decided
cases in this city and State similar to yours in favor of
freedom! Of course, if you want to remain a slave with your
master, we cannot force you to leave; we only want to make
you sensible of your rights. *Remember, if you lose this chance
you may never get such another,"* etc.

This advice to the woman was made in the hearing of a
number of persons present, white and colored; and one el-
derly white gentleman of genteel address, who seemed to take
much interest in what was going on, remarked that they
would have the same chance for their freedom in New Jersey
and New York as they then had—seeming to sympathize
with the woman, etc.

During the few moments in which the above remarks were
made, the slaveholder frequently interrupted—said she understood all about the laws making her free, and her right to
leave if she wanted to; but contended that she did not want to
leave—that she was on a visit to New York to see her
friends—afterwards *wished to return to her three children
whom she left in Virginia, from whom it would be HARD to
separate her.* Furthermore, he diligently tried to constrain her
to say that she did not want to be interfered with—that she
wanted to go with him—that she was on a visit to New
York—had children in the South, etc.; but the woman's
desire to be free was altogether too strong to allow her to
make a single acknowledgement favorable to his wishes in the
matter. On the contrary, she repeatedly said, distinctly and
firmly, *"I am not free, but I want my freedom—ALWAYS
wanted to be free!! but he holds me."*

While the slaveholder claimed that she belonged to him, he

said *that she was free!* Again he said that he was *"going to give her her freedom,"* etc. When his eyes would be off of hers, such eagerness as her looks expressed, indicative of her entreaty that we would not forsake her and her little ones in their weakness, it had never been my lot to witness before, under any circumstances.

The last bell tolled! The last moment for further delay passed! The arm of the woman being slightly touched, accompanied with the word, "Come!" she instantly arose, "Go along—go along!" said some, who sympathized, to the boys, at the same time taking hold of their arms. By this time the parties were fairly moving toward the stairway leading to the deck below. Instantly on their starting, the slaveholder rushed at the woman and her children, to prevent their leaving; and, if I am not mistaken, he simultaneously took hold of the woman and Mr. Williamson, which resistance on his part caused Mr. W. to take hold of him and set him aside quickly.

The passengers were looking on all around, but none interfered in behalf of the slaveholder except one man, whom I took to be another slaveholder. He said harshly, "Let them alone; they are his *property!*" The youngest boy, about seven years of age—too young to know what these things meant—cried "Massa John! Massa John!" The elder boy, eleven years of age, took the matter more dispassionately, and the mother *quite calmly.* The mother and her sympathizers all moved down the stairs together in the presence of quite a number of spectators on the first deck and on the wharf, all of whom, as far as I was able to discern, seemed to look upon the whole affair with the greatest indifference. The woman and children were assisted, but not forced to leave. Nor were there any violence or threatenings as I saw or heard. The only words that I heard from any one of an objectionable character, were "Knock him down; knock him down!", but who uttered or who was meant I knew not, nor have I since been informed. However, if it was uttered by a colored man, I regret it, as there was not the slightest cause for such language, especially as the sympathies of the spectators and citizens seemed to justify the course pursued.

While passing off of the wharf and down Delaware Avenue to Dock St., and up Dock to Front, where a carriage was procured, the slaveholder and one police officer were of the

party, if no more. The youngest boy on being put in the
carriage was told that he was "a fool for crying so after
'Massa John,' who would sell him if he ever caught him."
Not another whine was heard on the subject.

The carriage drove down town slowly, the horses being
fatigued and the weather intensely hot; the inmates were put
out on Tenth Street—not at any house—after which they soon
found hospitable friends and quietude. The excitement of the
moment having passed by, the mother *seemed very cheerful,
and rejoiced greatly that herself and boys had been, as she
thought, "so providentially delivered from the house of bondage!"* For the first time in her life she could look upon herself
and children and feel free!

Having felt the iron in her heart for the best half of her
days—having been sold with her children on the auction
block—having had one of her children sold far away from
her without hope of her seeing him again—she very naturally
and wisely concluded to go to Canada, fearing if she remained in this city—as some assured her she could do with
entire safety—that she might again find herself in the clutches
of the tyrant from whom she had fled.

A few items of what she related concerning the character of
her master may be interesting to the reader— Within the last
two years he had sold all his slaves—between thirty and forty
in number—having purchased the present ones in that space
of time. She said that before leaving Washington, coming on
the cars, and at his father-in-law's in the city, a number of
persons had told him that in bringing his slaves into Pennsylvania they would be free. When told at his father-in-law's, as
she overheard it, that he "could not have done a worse
thing," &c., he replied that "Jane would not leave him."

As much, however, as he affected to have such implicit
confidence in Jane, he scarcely allowed her to be out of his
presence a moment while in this city. To use Jane's language,
he was "on her heels every minute," fearing that some one
might get to her ears the sweet music of freedom. By the
way, Jane had it deep in her heart before leaving the South,
and was bent on succeeding in New York, if disappointed in
Philadelphia.

At Bloodgood's, after having been belated and left by the
two o'clock train, while waiting for the five o'clock line, his
appetite tempted her "master" to take a hasty dinner. So after

placing Jane where he thought she would be pretty secure from "evil communications" from the colored waiters, and after giving her a double counselling, he made his way to the table; remained but a little while, however, before leaving to look after Jane; finding her composed, looking over a bannister near where he left her, he returned to the table again and finished his meal.

But, alas, for the slave-holder! Jane had her "top eye open," and in that brief space had appealed to the sympathies of a person whom she ventured to trust, saying, "I and my children are slaves, and we want liberty!" I am not certain, but suppose that person, in the goodness of his heart, was the cause of the note being sent to the Anti-Slavery office, and hence the result.

As to her going on to New York to see her friends, and wishing to return to her three children in the South, and his going to free her, &c., Jane declared repeatedly and very positively, that there was not a particle of truth in what her master said on these points. The truth is she had not the slightest hope of freedom through any act of his. She had only left one boy in the South, who had been sold far away, where she scarcely ever heard from him, indeed never expected to see him any more.

In appearance Jane is tall and well formed, with a high and large forehead, of genteel manners, chestnut color, and seems to possess, naturally, uncommon good sense, though of course she has never been allowed to read.

Thus I have given as truthful report as I am capable of doing, of Jane and the circumstances connected with her deliverance.

TENNESSEE AND KENTUCKY

"If Ohio is ever abolitionized," Unitarian minister Samuel May, Jr., wrote in an undated note now in the Boston Public Library, "it will be by the fugitive slaves from Kentucky; their flight through the State is the best lecture—the pattering of their feet, that's the talk." The fugitives crossed from Virginia or Kentucky into Ohio, which had a boundary of nearly four hundred miles along these two slave states, or they came from Kentucky into Indiana and moved north across Lake Erie or by way of Detroit into Canada.

The Underground Railroad had its villains, who used unsavory methods to secure money from trusting fugitives. In 1854, a former Kentucky slave, Henry Bibb, published in his Canadian newspaper, *Voice of the Fugitive,* a warning against such procedures: "If any professed friend refuses to aid you or your friends in making their escape from Slavery, unless they are paid an extravagant price for it, they are not to be trusted; no matter whether they are white or black." Bibb went on to say it had been reported that a "certain free coloured person" made a practice of extorting from fifty to three hundred dollars for about three or four days' use of his time in helping fugitives on their escapes. Then "the poor fugitives would be betrayed and dragged back into a living death." In addition to his newspaper, Bibb wrote an outstanding narrative of his experiences and later achievements. John Greenleaf Whittier called him an example of what intelligent blacks in America could accomplish. Among other achievements, Bibb organized the Refugee Home Colony, which purchased thirteen hundred acres of land in Canada for the settlement of fugitive slaves.

The Ohio–Kentucky Underground Railroad probably served more fugitives than any others in the North. Agent William M. Cockrum, who for many years served as a conductor in the Midwest, said that at a point midway between Rockport, Indiana, and Owensboro, Kentucky, "many slaves crossed over the Ohio River and went on the Lakes to Canada." Berea College was started by the Reverend John G. Fee, son of a Kentucky slaveholder, who hid slaves in his interracial school.

Most of the fugitives from Tennessee went either by river or overland through Kentucky, spurred on by the success of others and the activity of abolitionists. The more intense abolitionism grew, however, the more sectional the movement became. The South became more and more attached to slavery and would not tolerate any attack on it. Not only was the old-time abolitionist in danger there after 1840, but anyone who even suggested an antislavery bias was in danger. Proslavery citizens drove Cassius M. Clay out of Lexington, Kentucky, after he expressed antislavery sentiments in *The True American.* Dr. Reuben Crandall of New York was arrested and imprisoned after loaning copies of the *Emancipator* to some of his white friends.

Narrative of Jarmain Wesley Loguen

The Tennessee Underground Railroad had among its passengers Jarmain W. Loguen. After reaching Canada, Loguen later settled in Syracuse, New York, where he became a minister and trustworthy station keeper on the

Underground, working with Gerrit Smith and Samuel Ward. The following exchange of letters between Loguen and his former owner was published in Loguen's book, *The Rev. J. W. Loguen, as a Slave and as a Freeman* (pages 451 to 455).

Maury Co., State of Tennessee
February 20th, 1860

To Jarm:

. . . I write you these lines to let you know the situation we are in—partly in consequence of your running away and stealing Old Rock, our fine mare. . . . I am cripple, but I am still able to get about. The rest of the family are all well. . . . Though we got the mare back, she was never worth much after you took her, and, as I now stand in need of some funds, I have determined to sell you. If you will send me one thousand dollars and pay for the old mare I will give up all claim I have to you. . . .

In consequence of your running away, we had to sell Abe and Ann and twelve acres of land; and I want you to send me the money that I may be able to redeem the land that you was the cause of our selling, and on receipt of the above named sum of money, I will send you your bill of sale. If you do not comply with my request, I will sell you to some one else. . . .

I understand that you are a preacher. . . . I would like to know if you read your Bible? If so, can you tell what will become of the thief if he does not repent? and, if the blind lead the blind, what will the consequence be? . . . You know that we reared you as we reared our own children; that you was never abused, and that shortly before you ran away, when your master asked you if you would like to be sold, you said you would not leave him to go with any body.

—Sarah Logue

Syracuse, N.Y., March 28th, 1860

Mrs. Sarah Logue:

. . . You sold my brother and sister, Abe and Ann, and twelve acres of land, you say, because I run away. Now you have the unutterable meanness to ask me to return and be your miserable chattel, or in lieu thereof send you one thousand dollars to enable you to redeem the *land,* but not to redeem my poor brother and sister! If I were to send you money it would be to get my brother and sister, and not that you should get land. You say you are *cripple,* and doubtless you say it to stir my pity, for you know I was susceptible in that direction. I do pity you. . . . Wretched woman! Be it known to you that I value my freedom, to say nothing of my mother, brothers, and sisters, more than your whole body; more indeed, than my own life; more than all the lives of all the slaveholders and tyrants under heaven. . . .

You say, "You know we raised you as we did our own children?" Woman, did you raise your *own children* for the market? Did you raise them for the whipping post? Did you raise them to be drove off in a coffle in chains? Where are my poor bleeding brothers and sisters? Can you tell? Who was it that sent them off into sugar and cotton fields, to be kicked, and cuffed, and whipped, and to groan and die; and where no kin can hear their groans, or attend and sympathize at their dying bed, or follow in their funeral?

. . . You say I am a thief, because I took the old mare along with me. Have you got to learn that I had a better right to the old mare, as you call her, than *Manasseth Logue* had to me? Is it a greater sin for me to steal his horse, than it was for him to rob my mother's cradle and steal me? If he and you infer that I forfeit all my rights to you, shall not I infer that you forfeit all your rights to me? Have you got to learn that human rights are mutual and reciprocal, and if you take my liberty and life, you forfeit me your own liberty and life? Before God and High Heaven, is there a law for one man which is not law for every other man?

If you or any other speculator on my body and rights, wish to know how I regard my rights, they need but come here and lay their hands on me to enslave me. Do you think to terrify me by presenting the alternative to give my money to you, or give my body to Slavery? . . . I stand among a free people, who, I thank God, sympathize with my rights, and the rights of mankind; and if your emissaries and venders come here, to re-inslave me, and escape the unshrinking vigor of my own right arm, I trust my strong and brave friends, in this City and State, will be my rescuers and avengers.

Yours,

—J. W. Loguen

Narrative of Lewis Hayden

This narrative appears in Stowe's *Key to Uncle Tom's Cabin* (pages 154 and 155).

I belonged to the Reverend Adam Runkin, a Presbyterian minister in Lexington, Kentucky. My mother was of mixed blood—white and Indian. She married my father when he was working in a bagging factory near by. After a while my father's owner moved off and took my father with him, which broke up the marriage. She was a very handsome woman. My master kept a large dairy, and she was the milk-woman. Lexington was a small town in those days, and the dairy was in the town. Back of the college was the Masonic Lodge. A man who belonged to the lodge saw my mother when she was about her work. He made proposals of a base nature to her. When she would have nothing to say to him, he told her that she need not be so independent, for if money could buy her he would have her. My mother told old mistress, and begged that master might not sell her. But he did sell her. My mother had a high spirit, being part Indian. She would not consent to live with this man, as he wished; and he sent her to prison, and had her flogged, and punished her in various ways, so that at last she began to have crazy turns. When I read in *Uncle Tom's Cabin* about Cassy, it put me in mind of my mother, and I wanted to tell Mrs. S——— about her. She tried to kill herself several times, once with a knife and once by hanging. She had long, straight black hair, but after this it all turned white, like an old person's. When she had her raving turns she always talked about her children. The jailer told the owner that if he would let her go to her children, perhaps she would get quiet. They let her out one time, and she came to the place where we were. I might have been seven or eight years old—don't know my age exactly. I was not at home when she came. I came in and found her in one of the cabins near the kitchen. She sprung and caught my arms, and seemed going to break them, and then said, "I'll fix *you* so they'll never get you!" I screamed, for I thought she was going to kill me; they came in and took me away. They tied her, and carried her off. Sometimes, when she was in her right mind, she used to tell me what things they had done to her. At last her owner sold her, for a small sum, to a man named Lackey. While with him she had another husband and several children. After a while this husband either died or was sold, I do not remember which. The man then sold her to another person named Bryant. My own father's owner now came and lived in the neighborhood of this man, and brought my mother [father?] with him. He had had another wife and family of children where he had been living. He and my mother came together again, and finished their days together. My mother almost recovered her mind in her last days.

I never saw anything in Kentucky which made me suppose that ministers or professors of religion considered it any more wrong to separate the families of slaves by sale than to separate any domestic animals.

There may be ministers and professors of religion who think it is wrong, but I never met with them. My master was a minister, and yet he sold my mother, as I have related.

When he was going to leave Kentucky for Pennsylvania, he sold all my brothers and sisters at auction. I stood by and saw them sold. When I was just going up on to the block, he swapped me off for a pair of carriage-horses. I looked at those horses with strange feelings. I had indulged hopes that master would take me into Pennsylvania with him, and I should get free. How I looked at those horses, and walked round them, and thought for *them* I was sold!

It was commonly reported that my master had said in the pulpit that there was no more harm in separating a family of slaves than a litter of pigs. I did not hear him say it, and so cannot say whether this is true or not.

It may seem strange, but it is a fact—I had more sympathy and kind advice in my efforts to get my freedom, from gamblers and such sort of men, than Christians. Some of the gamblers were very kind to me.

I never knew a slave-trader that did not seem to think, in his heart, that the trade was a bad one. I knew a great many of them, such as Neal, McAnn, Cobb, Stone, Pulliam, and Davis, &c. They were like Haley—they meant to repent when they got through.

Intelligent colored people in my circle of acquaintance, as a general thing, *felt no security whatever for their family ties.*

Some, it is true, who belonged to rich families, felt some security; but those of us who looked deeper, and knew how many were not rich that seemed so, and saw how fast money slipped away, were always miserable. The trader was all around, the slave-pens at hand, and we did not know what time any of us might be in it. Then there were the rice-swamps, and the sugar and cotton plantations; we had had them held before us as terrors, by our masters and mistresses, all our lives. We knew about them all; and when a friend was carried off, why, it was the same as death, for we could not write or hear and never expected to see them again.

I have one child who is buried in Kentucky, and that grave is pleasant to think of. I've got another that is sold nobody knows where, and that I never can bear to think of.

Narrative of Eliza Harris

This narrative is from Coffin's *Reminiscences* (pages 147 to 151).

Eliza Harris, of *Uncle Tom's Cabin* notoriety, the slave woman who crossed the Ohio River, near Ripley, on the drifting ice with her child in her arms, was sheltered under our roof and fed at our table for several days. This was while we lived at Newport, Indiana, which is six miles west of the State line of Ohio. To elude the pursuers who were following closely on her track, she was sent across to our line of the Underground Railroad.

The story of this slave woman, so graphically told by Harriet Beecher Stowe in *Uncle Tom's Cabin*, will, no doubt, be remembered by every reader of that deeply interesting book. The cruelties of slavery depicted in that remarkable work are not overdrawn. The stories are founded on facts that really occurred, real names being wisely withheld, and fictitious names and imaginary conversations often inserted. From the fact that Eliza Harris was sheltered at our house several days, it was generally believed among those acquainted with the circumstances that I and my wife were the veritable

Simeon and Rachel Halliday, the Quaker couple alluded to in *Uncle Tom's Cabin*. I will give a short sketch of the fugitive's story, as she related it.

She said she was a slave from Kentucky, the property of a man who lived a few miles back from Ohio River, below Ripley, Ohio. Her master and mistress were kind to her, and she had a comfortable home, but her master got into some peculiar difficulty, and she found that she and her only child were to be separated. She had buried two children, and was doubly attached to the one she had left, a bright, promising child, over two year old. When she found that it was to be taken from her, she was filled with grief and dismay, and resolved to make her escape that night if possible. She watched her opportunity, and when darkness had settled down and all the family had retired to sleep, she started with her child in her arms and walked straight toward the Ohio River. She knew that it was frozen over, at that season of the year, and hoped to cross without difficulty on the ice, but when she reached its banks at daylight, she found that the ice had broken up and was slowly drifting in large cakes. She ventured to go to a house nearby, where she was kindly received and permitted to remain through the day. She hoped to find some way to cross the river the next night, but there seemed little prospect of any one being able to cross in safety, for during the day the ice became more broken and dangerous to cross. In the evening she discovered pursuers nearing the house, and with desperate courage she determined to cross the river, or perish in the attempt. Clasping her child in her arms she darted out of the back door and ran toward the river, followed by her pursuers, who had just dismounted from their horses when they caught sight of her. No fear or thought of personal danger entered Eliza's mind, for she felt that she had rather be drowned than to be captured and separated from her child. Clasping her babe to her bosom with her left arm, she sprang on to the first cake of ice, then from that to another and another. Some times the cake she was on would sink beneath her weight, then she would slide her child on to the next cake, pull herself on with her hands, and so continue her hazardous journey. She became wet to the waist with ice water and her hands were benumbed with cold, but as she made her way from one cake of ice to another, she felt that surely the Lord was preserving and upholding her, and that nothing could harm her.

When she reached the Ohio side, near Ripley, she was completely exhausted and almost breathless. A man, who had been standing on the bank watching her progress with amazement and expecting every moment to see her go down, assisted her up the bank. After she had recovered her strength a little he directed her to a house on the hill, in the outskirts of town. She made her way to the place, and was kindly received and cared for. It was not considered safe for her to remain there during the night, so, after resting a while and being provided with food and dry clothing, she was conducted to a station on the Underground Railroad, a few miles farther from the river. The next night she was forwarded on from station to station to our house in Newport, where she arrived safely and remained several days.

Other fugitives arrived in the meantime, and Eliza and her child were sent with them, by the Greenville branch of the Underground Railroad, to Sandusky, Ohio. They reached that place in safety, and crossed the Lake to Canada, locating finally at Chatham, Canada West.

In the summer of 1854 I was on a visit to Canada, accompanied by my wife and daughter, and Laura S. Haviland, of Michigan. At the close of a meeting which we attended, at one of the colored churches, a woman came up to my wife, seized her hand, and exclaimed: "How are you, Aunt Katie? God bless you!" etc. My wife did not recognize her, but she soon called herself to our remembrance by referring to the time she was at our house in the days of her distress, when my wife gave her the name of Eliza Harris, and by relating other particulars. We visited her at her house while at Chatham, and found her comfortable and contented.

Many other fugitives came and spoke to us, whom we did not recognize or remember until they related some incident that recalled them to mind. Such circumstances occurred in nearly every neighborhood we visited in Canada. Hundreds who had been sheltered under our roof and fed at our table, when fleeing from the land of whips and chains, introduced themselves to us and referred to the time, often fifteen or twenty years before, when we had aided them.

On the first day of August, 1854, we went, with a large company from Windsor, to attend a celebration of the West

India emancipation. The meeting was held in a dense settlement of fugitives, about eight miles south of Windsor. Several public speakers from Detroit were in our party. A platform had been erected in a grove near the schoolhouse, where Laura S. Haviland had established a school for fugitives. The day was fine, and there was a large crowd of colored people, who had come from various settlements to hear the speaking. Here we met quite a number of those whom we had helped on their way to freedom, and the gratitude they expressed was quite affecting. One old white-headed man came to my wife, and said he wanted to get hold of her hand. She reached her hand to him, and while he held it, he said, "Don't you 'member me, Misses?"

She looked at him closely, and said, "No, I believe I do not remember thee."

Then the old negro said, "La me! Misses, don't you 'member when dey was close after me to take me an' you hid me in de feather bed and saved me? Why, bress your heart! if it hadn't been for you I should nebber been here. It's more dan twenty years ago, and my head is white, but I hasn't forgot dat time."

MARYLAND

As southern ways and sympathies persisted among slaveowners below the Mason-Dixon line, those slaves who sought freedom fled from Maryland into eastern and western Pennsylvania. By the 1830s, slave self-protection and refugee societies had been formed by free blacks in Pennsylvania in the towns of Columbia, in Lancaster County, and York and Gettysburg. These received escaping slaves and worked against the agents of slaveholders. Though many of the fugitives had other northern destinations as their goal, many were content to establish homes in southeastern and southwestern Pennsylvania.

When runaway slaves were denied the opportunity to escape across the Mason-Dixon line, they sometimes gravitated toward Baltimore. Professor Richard C. Wade recorded in his book *Slave in the Cities* that a jailer's account for 1837 revealed that in Baltimore 149 blacks had been arrested as runaways and 148 more for not having papers. Some of the latter were subsequently declared fugitives. Two decades later, despite a precipitous drop in the number of slaves there, 62 were charged with escaping and 421 with being "without proper security." The number living illegally in the city must have been several times the number who were discovered.

No account of the network of the Underground Railroad in Maryland could be complete without some notice of the Eastern Shore. The Eastern Shore comprises the peninsula lying between Chesapeake Bay and the Atlantic Ocean, whose land area includes the whole of Delaware, with nine counties of Maryland and two of Virginia. Abolitionists and fugitive slaves found it desirable to use this large river- and bay-drained area as part of their secret escape system.

The flow of fugitive slaves from this area steadily increased. In his biography of Harriet Tubman (page 27), Earl Conrad wrote that servitude in the Eastern Shore region must have been very oppressive, for it produced so many of the foremost Negro revolutionaries, including Harriet Tubman, Samuel R. Ward, James W. C. Pennington, Hezekiah Grice, and Henry Highland Garnet.

It is evident from the works of William Still and other Underground Railroad historians that more fugitive slaves escaped into the North from Maryland than from any other slave state. Still was told that they had escaped from the following towns and counties: Hagerstown, Frederick, Westminster, Laurel, Bel Air, Towson, Havre de Grace, Elkton, Easton, Cambridge, and Hereford.

Many slaves found refuge in vessels sailing from the ports of Annapolis and Baltimore, while others were transported in small boats on the Chesapeake Bay into the Susquehanna River and delivered to waiting conductors in Pennsylvania. Slaves fleeing from western Maryland evidently used the Appalachian route, reputed to have been one of the most important passages to the North, extending as far south as Alabama and Georgia.

The insecurity of life for the Underground Railroad sympathizers operating below the Mason-Dixon line is illustrated by the following episode. On June 29, 1850, the *Baltimore Sun*'s headline read: "Lynch Law in Maryland—A Man and Woman Tarred and Feathered." The newspaper stated: "The slave owners of Kent County, Maryland, have within a year or two, suffered heavy losses by running off of slaves, not less than sixty having escaped in 1848, and a large number since. These mysterious escapes created no little excitement." Two white persons, James I. Bowers and his wife, of Kent County, "well known to entertain strong antislavery sentiments," were charged with assisting the slaves to escape. When they were acquitted by the court because of insufficient evidence, a mob of slaveholders seized the couple in their home, tarred and feathered them, and drove them out of the community.

One Baltimore rabbi, David Einhorn, became so immersed in the fight against slavery that he was driven out of the state immediately after the Civil War began. Einhorn arrived in Philadelphia about 1862 where he preached regularly against slavery.

In Baltimore, the home of black conductor William Watkins and his family was an important station on the Railroad. Watkins won fame as a teacher and abolitionist. His niece, Frances Ellen Watkins Harper, who was born in 1825 and orphaned at an early age, had by the late 1850s gained considerable fame as an antislavery poet, novelist, and speaker. She became associated with Frederick Douglass and assisted Douglass with his antislavery paper, the *North Star*. William Still called her the "leading colored poet" of his day. She committed herself totally and passionately to the Underground Railroad movement.

The most powerful abolitionist orator and political statesman during this era was Frederick Douglass. Born in February 1817 in Tuckahoe, Talbot County, Maryland, Douglass was the son of a slave, Harriet Bailey, and an unidentified white man. Once when Douglass was asked exactly when and where he was born, he declared, "I cannot answer; don't know my age. Slaves have no family records."

As a small boy, he was intelligent and ambitious. A rebellious and spirited child, he bore the marks of many beatings and whippings. He witnessed his aunt strung up by the hands for hours and beaten at intervals because she had been "impudent." He also saw a girl cousin turned out and starved because her burned hands would not let her work. Douglass taught himself to read and write and at the age of twenty-one he stole away to freedom.

On March 27, 1893, many years after his flight, the illustrious Douglass wrote to historian Wilbur H. Siebert: "My connection with the Underground Railroad began long before I left the South, and was continued as long as slavery continued, whether I lived in New Bedford, Lynn [both in Massachusetts], or Rochester, N.Y. In the latter place, I had *as many as eleven* fugitives under my roof at one time." In his autobiography Douglass declared about this work: "My agency was all the more exciting and interesting because not altogether free from danger. I could take not a step in it without exposing myself to fine and imprisonment . . . but in face of this fact, I can say, I never did more congenial, attractive, fascinating, and satisfactory work."

Originally named Araminta, Harriet Tubman was renamed after her mother. She was born a slave, in a family of eleven children, on the Brodas plantation in Bucktown, Dorchester County, Maryland, about 1820. Dark complexioned, medium in height, with a full broad face, topped by a colorful head bandana, Tubman developed almost extraordinary physical endurance and muscular strength, as well as mental fortitude. She was described by William Still in his book *The Underground Railroad* (page 296) as "a woman of no pretentions, a most ordinary specimen of humanity."

Tubman appears to have been a unique compound of practical shrewdness and visionary enthusiasm. She believed in dreams and omens warning and instructing her in her illegal enterprises. At times she would break forth into wild and strange rhapsodies. A deeply religious woman with an indomitable sense of purpose, she gave all the credit to God during her dangerous journeys. During her youth she had been haunted by a vision: she saw a line, dividing slavery from freedom; on the northern slope stood people stretching their hands across the boundary to welcome her and calling her "Moses."

Tubman's flight to freedom occurred during the summer of 1849. She had been warned by a slave from another plantation that she and her brothers were to be sold. She would later recall her thoughts at that moment: "There's two things I got a right to and these are Death and Liberty. One or the other I mean to have. No one will take me back alive; I shall fight for my liberty, and when the time has come for me to go, the Lord will let them kill me."

Cautiously she set off to follow the North Star. From time to time she was aided on her journey by members of the Underground Railroad. Early one morning she crossed over into free territory in Pennsylvania. She later said, "I looked at my hands to see if I was the same person. There was such a glory over everything. The sun came up like gold through the trees, and I felt like I was in Heaven" (see Conrad, page 297). Shortly after her arrival in Philadelphia she met William Still and found employment as a domestic worker in a hotel in that city.

Again and again she risked the wrath of slave-hunters, making nineteen perilous excursions in all to bring others to freedom. Included among her freedom train passengers were her parents, whom she conducted all the way to Canada.

Tubman always carried a pistol to ward off pursuers and opium to quiet crying babies. Whenever her passengers became frightened and threatened to leave, she would slowly raise the pistol and declare, "Dead niggers tell no tales. You go or die." Later she proudly proclaimed, "I never run my train off the track and I never lost a passenger."

Although the great Underground Railroad navigator did not keep a journal, she did describe her routes of escape from the Eastern Shore to her friend Sarah Bradford and others. They varied. Sometimes she headed toward mountains, always acting by faith and intuition. Usually she followed the lone trail that led from Cambridge over the big Choptank River bridge to the Delaware towns of Camden, Dover, Smyrna, and Odessa, to Wilmington, where her close friend Thomas Garrett was always waiting with food and funds. From his friendly home she led the way through southern Chester County, Pennsylvania, into Philadelphia before continuing her dangerous journey into upstate New York and finally across the suspended bridge at Niagara Falls into Canada.

Pauline Hopkins, noted black author around the turn of the century, eulogized Tubman as follows: "Harriet Tubman, though one of the earth's lowliest ones, displayed an amount of heroism in her character rarely possessed by those of any station in life. Her name deserves to be handed down to posterity side by side with those of Grace Darling, Joan of Arc, and Florence Nightingale; no one of them has shown more courage and power of endurance in facing danger and death to relieve human suffering than this woman in her successful and heroic endeavors to reach and save all whom she might of her oppressed people." (See Cunard, page 13.)

Narrative of Margaret Ward and Infant Son, Samuel Ringgold Ward

Eber Pettit's *Sketches in the History of the Underground Railroad,* 1870, includes this narrative (pages 80 to 85). The infant in the narrative published in 1855 his own *Autobiography of a Fugitive Negro,* which was of great importance to the abolitionists.

On the eastern shore of the Chesapeake, in the state of Maryland, there lived, about forty years ago, a remarkable woman by the name of Margaret. She was born on a slave ship on its way from Africa to Baltimore, just before the importation of slaves was prohibited. She, with her mother, fell into the hands of a family who gave them religious instruction, and Margaret, while young, exhibited traits of character that were regarded as remarkable for one of her race. Of a proud, indomitable spirit, yet having acute moral sense, a disposition naturally amiable, of cheerful temperament, and crushed with a sense of her degraded condition, she was unusually capable in all kinds of housework, and especially active and competent as nurse when any of the family were sick.

At sixteen years of age she went to live with her young mistress, who was married to a planter in that fertile country known as the "Eastern Shore." At eighteen Margaret was a large woman, tall and well formed, her complexion black as jet, her countenance always pleasant, though she seldom laughed. She talked but little, even to those of her own race. At twenty years of age she became the wife of a worthy young man to whom she had given her best affections. Not long after, her young master became very angry with her for what he called stubbornness and resistance to his will, and threatened to chastise her by whipping—a degradation that she had always felt that she could not submit to, and yet to obey her master in the thing he demanded would be still worse. She therefore told him that she would not be whipped, she would rather die, and gave him warning that any attempt to execute his threat would surely result in the death of one of them. He knew her too well to risk the experiment, and decided to punish her in another way. He sold her husband, and she saw him bound in chains and driven off with a large drove of men and women for the New Orleans market. He then put her in the hands of a brutal overseer, with directions to work her to the extent of her ability on a tobacco plantation, which command was enforced up to the day of the birth of her child. At the end of one week she was driven again to the field and compelled to perform a full task, having at no time any abatement of her work on account of her situation, with the exception of one week. It was the custom on the plantation to establish nurseries, presided over by old, broken down slaves, where mothers might leave their infants during the work hours, but this privilege was denied to Margaret. She was obliged to leave her child under the shade of a bush in the field, returning to it but twice during the long day. On returning to the child one evening she found it apparently senseless, exhausted with crying, and a large serpent lying across it. Although she felt that it would be better for both herself and child if it were dead, yet a mother's heart impelled her to make an effort to save it, and by caressing him and careful handling she resuscitated it.

As soon as she heard its feeble, wailing cry, she made a vow to deliver her boy from the cruel power of slavery or die in the attempt, and falling prostrate, she prayed for strength to perform her vow, and for grace and patience to sustain her in her suffering, toil, and hunger; then pressing her child to her bosom, she fled with all the speed of which she was capable toward the North Star. Having gone a mile or two, she heard something pursuing her; on looking round she saw Watch, the old house dog. Watch was a large mastiff, somewhat old, and with him Margaret had ever been a favorite, and since she had been driven to the field, Watch often visited her at her cabin in the evening. She feared it would not be safe to allow

Watch to go with her, but she could not induce him to go
back, so she resumed her flight, accompanied by her faithful
escort. At break of day she hid herself on the border of a
plantation and soon fell asleep.

Toward evening she was aroused by the noise made by the
slaves returning to their quarters, and seeing an old woman
lingering behind all the others, she called her, told her troubles and asked for food. The old woman returned about
midnight with a pretty good supply of food, which Margaret
divided with Watch, and then started on, taking the north star
for her guide. The second day after she left, the Overseer
employed a hunter with his dogs to find her. He started with
an old slut and three whelps, thinking, no doubt, that as the
game was only a woman and her infant child, it would be a
good time to train his pups.

Margaret had been missed at roll call the morning after her
flight, but the Overseer supposed she was hiding near the
place for a day or two, and that hunger would soon drive her
up; therefore, when the hunter started, he led the old dog,
expecting to find her in an hour or two, but not overtaking her
the first day, on the next morning, he let his hounds loose,
intending to follow on horseback, guided by their voices.
About noon, the old dog struck the track at the place where
Margaret had made her little camp the day before, and she
bounded off with fresh vigor, leaving the man and the younger dogs beyond sight and hearing. The young dogs soon lost
the track where Margaret forded the streams, and the old dog
was miles away, leaving the hunter without a guide to direct
him.

Margaret had been lying in the woods on the bank of a
river, intending to start again as soon as it was dark, when
she was startled by the whining and nervous motions of old
Watch, and listening, she heard the hoarse ringing bay of a
blood-hound. Although she had expected that she would be
hunted with dogs, and recalled over and over again the shock-
ing accounts related by Overseers to the slaves, of fugitives
overtaken and torn in pieces by the savage Spanish bloodhounds, she had not, until now, realized the horrors of her
situation. She expected to have to witness the destruction of
her child by the savage brute, and then be torn in pieces
herself. She did not, however, lose her presence of mind. The
river or inlet near her camp was too wide and too deep to be

forded at that place, but she fastened her child to her shoulders and waded in as far as she could, taking a club to defend herself. Meanwhile, old Watch lay with his nose between his feet, facing the coming foe. The hound, rendered more fierce by the freshness of the track, came rushing headlong with nose to the ground, scenting her prey, and seemed not to see old Watch, until, leaping to pass over him, she found her wind-pipe suddenly collapsed in the massive jaws of the old mastiff. The struggle was not very noisy, for Watch would not even growl, and the hound could not, but it was terribly energetic. The hound made rapid and persuasive gestures with her paws and tail, but it was of no use, the jaws of old Watch relaxed not until all signs of life in his enemy had ceased. Margaret came back from the river, and would have embraced her faithful friend, but fearing that a stronger pack was following, she hastily threw the dead hound into the river and pursued her journey.

Within a few hours after her providential escape by the aid of her faithful friend, old Watch, from the fangs of the slave hunter's hound, she fell into the hands of friends, who kept her secreted until she could be sent into a free State; while there, she learned about the pursuit by the hunter, and that he never knew what became of his best hound. After the chase was abandoned, she, through a regular line, similar to our U.G.R.R., was sent to Philadelphia and then to New York, where she became a celebrated nurse, and always befriended the poor of all colors and all nationalities. She rented a good house which was a home for herself and boy, and also for old Watch while he lived. When her boy, whom she called Samuel, was old enough to go to school, she found a place for him in Westchester Co., where he obtained the rudiments of an education, and afterwards in the family of a gentleman in Central New York [Gerrit Smith] he enjoyed the advantages of a thorough education, and became a devoted minister of the gospel in the Congregational Church. I often met him during the early history of the U.G.R.R., of which he was an efficient agent. Samuel was one of the most eloquent men I have ever heard speak. He was a fine looking man, though he was so black it was sometimes said that it grew dark when he entered a room; but it grew light when he began to speak.

Narrative of Samuel Green, Jr.

Still's *Underground Railroad Records* includes this narrative (pages 246 to 250). It makes clear the grave danger in which fugitives place family members left behind.

Samuel Green Alias Wesley Kinnard, August 28th, 1854.

The passenger answering to the above name left Indian Creek, Chester County, Maryland, where he had been held to service or labor, by Dr. James Muse. One week had elapsed from the time he set out until his arrival in Philadelphia. Although he had never enjoyed school privileges of any kind, yet he was not devoid of intelligence. He had profited by his daily experiences as a slave, and withal, had managed to learn to read and write a little, despite law and usage to the contrary. Sam was about twenty-five years of age and by trade, a blacksmith. Before running away, his general character for sobriety, industry, and religion, had evidently been considered good, but in coveting his freedom and running away to obtain it, he had sunk far below the utmost limit of forgiveness or mercy in the estimation of the slave-holders of Indian Creek.

During his intercourse with the Vigilance Committee, while rejoicing over his triumphant flight, he gave, with no appearance of excitement, but calmly, and in a common-sense-like manner, a brief description of his master, which was entered on the record book substantially as follows: "Dr. James Muse is thought by the servants to be the worst man in Maryland, inflicting whipping and all manner of cruelties upon the servants."

While Sam gave reasons for this sweeping charge, which left no room for doubt, on the part of the Committee, of his sincerity and good judgment, it was not deemed necessary to make a note of more of the doctor's character than seemed actually needed, in order to show why Sam had taken passage on the Underground Rail Road. For several years, Sam was hired out by the doctor at blacksmithing; in this situation, daily wearing the yoke of unrequited labor, through the kindness of Harriet Tubman (sometimes called "Moses"), the light of the Underground Rail Road and Canada suddenly illuminated his mind. It was new to him, but he was quite too intelligent and liberty-loving, not to heed the valuable information which this sister of humanity imparted. Thenceforth he was in love with Canada, and likewise a decided admirer of the U. R. Road. Harriet was herself, a shrewd and fearless agent, and well understood the entire route from that part of the country to Canada. The spring previous, she had paid a visit to the very neighborhood in which Sam lived, expressly to lead her own brothers out of "Egypt." She succeeded. To Sam this was cheering and glorious news, and he made up his mind, that before a great while, Indian Creek should have one less slave and that Canada should have one more citizen. Faithfully did he watch an opportunity to carry out his resolution. In due time a good Providence opened the way, and to Sam's satisfaction he reached Philadelphia, having encountered no peculiar difficulties. The Committee, perceiving that he was smart, active, and promising, encouraged his undertaking, and having given him friendly advice aided him in the usual manner. Letters of introduction were given him, and he was duly forwarded on his way. He had left his father, mother, and one sister behind. Samuel and Catharine were the names of his parents. Thus far, his escape would seem not to affect his parents, nor was it apparent that there was any other cause why the owner should revenge himself upon them.

The father was an old local preacher in the Methodist Church—much esteemed as an inoffensive, industrious man; earning his bread by the sweat of his brow, and contriving to move along in the narrow road allotted colored people bond or free, without exciting a spirit of ill will in the pro-slavery power of his community. But the rancor awakened in the breast of slave-holders in consequence of the high-handed step the son had taken, brought the father under suspicion and hate. Under the circumstances, the eye of Slavery could do nothing more than watch for an occasion to pounce upon him. It was not long before the desired opportunity presented itself. Moved by parental affection, the old man concluded to pay a visit to his boy, to see how he was faring in a distant land, and among strangers. This resolution he quietly carried into effect. He found his son in Canada, doing well; industrious; a man of sobriety, and following his father's footsteps religiously. That the old man's heart was delighted with what his eyes saw and his ears heard in Canada, none can doubt. But in the simplicity of his imagination, he never dreamed that this visit was to be made the means of his destruction. During the best portion of his days he had faithfully worn the badge of Slavery, had afterwards purchased his freedom, and thus become a free man. He innocently conceived the idea that he was doing no harm in availing himself not only of his God-given rights, but of the rights that he had also purchased by the hard toil of his own hands. But the enemy was lurking in ambush for him—thirsting for his blood. To his utter consternation, not long after his return from his visit to his son "a party of gentlemen from the New Market district, went at night to Green's house and made search, whereupon was found a copy of *Uncle Tom's Cabin*, etc." This was enough, the hour had come, wherein to wreak vengeance upon poor Green. The course pursued and the result, may be seen in the following statement taken from the Cambridge (Md.), "Democrat," of April 29th, 1857, and communicated by the writer to the "Provincial Freeman."

SAM GREEN

The case of the State against Sam Green (free negro) indicted for having in his possession, papers, pamphlets, and pictorial representations, having a tendency to create discontent, etc., among the people of color in the State, was tried before the court on Friday last.

This case was of the utmost importance, and has created in the public mind a great deal of interest—it being the first case of the kind ever having occurred in our county.

It appeared, in evidence, that this Green has a son in Canada to whom Green made a visit last summer. Since his return to this county, suspicion has fastened upon him, as giving aid and assisting slaves who have since absconded and reached Canada, and several weeks ago, a party of gentlemen from New Market district, went at night, to Green's house and made search, whereupon was found a volume of *Uncle Tom's Cabin*, a map of Canada, several schedules of routes to the North, and a letter from his son in Canada, detailing the pleasant trip he had, the number of friends he met with on the way, with plenty to eat, drink, etc., and concludes with a request to his father, that he shall tell other slaves, naming them, to come on, which slaves, it is well known, did leave shortly afterwards, and have reached Canada. The case was argued with great ability, the counsel on both sides displaying a great deal of ingenuity, learning, and eloquence. The first indictment was for having in possession the letter, map, and route schedules.

Notwithstanding the mass of evidence given, to show the prisoner's guilt, in unlawfully having in his possession these documents, and that nine-tenths of the community in which he lived, believed that he had a hand in the running away of slaves, it was the opinion of the court, that the law under which he was indicted, was not applicable to the case, and that he must, accordingly, render a verdict of not guilty.

He was immediately arraigned upon another indictment, for having in possession *Uncle Tom's Cabin,* and tried; in this case the court has not yet rendered a verdict, but holds it under *curia* till after the Somerset county court. It is to be hoped, the court will find the evidence in this case sufficient to bring it within the scope of the law under which the prisoner is indicted (that of 1842, chap. 272), and that the prisoner may meet his due reward—be what it may.

That there is something required to be done by our Legislators, for the protection of slave property, is evident from the variety of constructions put upon the statute in this case, and we trust, that at the next meeting of the Legislature there will be such amendments, as to make the law on this subject, perfectly clear and comprehensible to the understanding of everyone.

In the language of the assistant counsel for the State, "Slavery must be protected or it may be abolished."

From the same sheet, of May 20th, the terrible doom of Samuel Green is announced in the following words:

In the case of the State against Sam Green, (free negro) who was tried at the April term of the Circuit

Court of this county, for having in his possession abolition pamphlets, among which was *Uncle Tom's Cabin,*
[and] has been found guilty by the court, and sentenced
to the penitentiary for the term of ten years—until the
14th of May, 1867.

The son, a refugee in Canada, hearing the distressing news
of his father's sad fate at the hands of the relentless ''gentlemen,'' often wrote to know if there was any prospect of his
deliverance.

In this dark hour the friends of the Slave could do but little
more than sympathize with this heart-stricken son and grey-
haired father. The aged follower of the Rejected and Cruci-
fied had like Him to bear the ''reproach of many,'' and make
his bed with the wicked in the Penitentiary. Doubtless there were
a few friends in his neighborhood who sympathized with him,
but they were powerless to aid the old man. But thanks to a
kind Providence, the great deliverance brought about during the
Rebellion by which so many captives were freed, also unlocked
Samuel Green's prison-doors and he was allowed to go free.

After his liberation from the Penitentiary, we had from his
own lips narrations of his years of suffering—of the bitter
cup, that he was compelled to drink, and of his being sustained by the almighty Arm—but no notes were taken at that
time, consequently we have nothing more to add concerning
him, save a faithful likeness.

Narrative of Frederick Douglass

The material in italic type below appears in Frederick
Holland's 1891 biography of Douglass (pages 33 to 35).
The material in roman type is from the autobiography of
1855 (beginning at page 32).

On Monday, the third day of September, 1838, in accordance
with my resolution, I bade farewell to the city of Baltimore,
and to that slavery which had been my abhorrence from
childhood. . . .

Before, however, proceeding with this narration, it is, perhaps, proper that I should frankly state, in advance, my intention to withhold a part of the facts connected with my escape from slavery. There are reasons for this suppression, which I trust the readers will deem altogether valid. It may be easily conceived, that a full and complete statement of all the facts pertaining to the flight of a bondman, might implicate and embarrass some who may have, wittingly or unwittingly, assisted him; and no one can wish me to involve any man or woman who has befriended me, even in the liability of embarrassment or trouble. . . .

I have never approved of the very public manner, in which some of our western friends have conducted what *they* call the *"Under-ground Railroad,"* but which, I think, by their open declarations, has been made, most emphatically, the *"Upper*-ground Railroad." Its stations are far better known to the slaveholders than to the slaves. I honor those good men and women for their noble daring, in willingly subjecting themselves to persecution, by openly avowing their participation in the escape of slaves; nevertheless, the good resulting from such avowals, is of a very questionable character. It may kindle an enthusiasm, very pleasant to inhale; but that is of no practical benefit to themselves, nor to the slaves escaping. Nothing is more evident, than that such disclosures are a positive evil to the slaves remaining, and seeking to escape. In publishing such accounts, the anti-slavery man addresses the slaveholder, *not the slave;* he stimulates the former to greater watchfulness, and adds to his facilities for capturing his slave. We owe something to the slaves, south of Mason and Dixon's line, as well as to those north of it; and, in discharging the duty of aiding the latter, on their way to freedom, we should be careful to do nothing which would be likely to hinder the former, in making their escape from slavery. . . .

My condition in the year (1838) of my escape, was, comparatively, a free and easy one, so far, at least, as the wants of the physical man were concerned; but the reader will bear in mind, that my troubles from the beginning, have been less physical than mental, and he will thus be prepared to find, after what is narrated in the previous chapters, that slave life was adding nothing to its charms for me, as I grew older, and became better acquainted with it. The practice, from week to week, of openly robbing me of all my earnings, kept the nature and character of slavery constantly before me. I could be robbed by *indirection,* but this was *too* open and barefaced to be endured. I could see no reason why I should, at the end of each week, pour the reward of my honest toil into the purse of any man. The thought itself vexed me, and the manner in which Master Hugh received my wages, vexed me more than the original wrong. Carefully counting the money and rolling it out, dollar by dollar, he would look me in the face, as if he would search my heart as well as my pocket, and reproachfully ask me, *"Is that all?"*—implying that I had, perhaps, kept back part of my wages; or, if not so, the demand was made, possibly, to make me feel, that, after all, I was an "unprofitable servant." Draining me of the last cent of my hard earnings, he would, however, occasionally—when I brought home an extra large sum—dole out to me a sixpence or a shilling, with a view, perhaps, of kindling up my gratitude; but this practice had the opposite effect—it was an admission *of my right to the whole sum.* The fact, that he gave me any part of my wages, was proof that he suspected that I had a right to *the whole of them.* I always felt uncomfortable, after having received anything in this way, for I feared that the giving me a few cents, might, possibly, ease his conscience, and make him feel himself a pretty honorable robber, after all!

Held to a strict account, and kept under a close watch—the old suspicion of my running away not having been entirely removed—escape from slavery, even in Baltimore, was very difficult. The railroad from Baltimore to Philadelphia was under regulations so stringent, that even *free* colored travelers were almost excluded. They must have *free* papers; they must be measured and carefully examined, before they were allowed to enter the cars; they only went in the day time, even when so examined. The steamboats were under regulations equally stringent. All the great turnpikes, leading northward, were beset with kidnappers, a class of men who watched the newspapers for advertisements for runaway slaves, making their living by the accursed reward of slave hunting.

My discontent grew upon me, and I was on the lookout for means of escape. With money, I could easily have managed the matter, and, therefore, I hit upon the plan of soliciting the privilege of hiring my time. It is quite common, in Baltimore, to allow slaves this privilege, and it is the practice, also, in New Orleans. A slave who is considered trustworthy, can, by paying his master a definite sum regularly, at the end of each week, dispose of his time as he likes. It so happened that I was not in very good odor, and I was far from being a trustworthy slave. . . .

My object, therefore, in working steadily, was to remove suspicion, and in this I succeeded admirably. He probably thought I was never better satisfied with my condition, than at the very time I was planning my escape. The second week passed, and again I carried him my full week's wages—*nine dollars;* and so well pleased was he, that he gave me *twenty-five cents!* and "bade me make good use of it!" I told him I would, for one of the uses to which I meant to put it, was to pay my fare on the underground railroad.

The laws of Maryland required every free negro to carry papers describing him accurately and to pay liberally for this protection. Slaves often escaped by borrowing papers from a friend, to whom the precious documents would be returned by mail. Whenever a colored man came with free papers to the railroad station to buy a ticket, he was always examined carefully enough to insure the detection of a runaway, unless the resemblance was very close. Our hero was not acquainted with any free negro who looked much like him; but he found out that passengers who paid on the cars were not scrutinized so minutely as those who bought tickets, and also that sailors were treated with peculiar indulgence by the conductors. The dominant party was doing all it could to encourage the shipping interest, and rapidly reducing the tariff. The cry of "Free Trade and Sailors' Rights" meant in this instance "Free Labor and the Rights of the Slave."

Among his friends was a sailor who was of much darker hue than he was himself, but who owned a protection, setting forth his occupation, and bearing the sacred figure of the American eagle. This was borrowed; sailor's clothes were purchased, and, on Monday morning, the fugitive jumped on the train just as it started. His baggage had been put aboard by a friendly hackman. He was greatly troubled, for, as he wrote to his master, ten years later, I was making a leap in the dark. The probabilities, so far as I could by reason determine them, were stoutly against the undertaking. The preliminaries and precautions I had adopted previously, all

worked badly. I was like one going to war without weapons—
ten chances of defeat to one of victory. One in whom I had
confided, and one who had promised me assistance, appalled
by fear at the trial hour, deserted me. However, gloomy as
was the prospect, thanks be to the Most High, who is ever the
God of the oppressed, at the moment which was to determine
my whole earthly career, His grace was sufficient; my mind
was made up.

*His anxiety increased in consequence of the harshness with
which the conductor questioned other passengers in the negro
car. The sailor, however, was addressed kindly and told,
after a mere glance at the protection, that it was all right.
Thus far he was safe; but there were several people on the
train who would have known him at once in any other clothes.
A German blacksmith looked at him intently, and apparently
recognized him, but said nothing. On the ferry boat, by which
they crossed the Susquehanna, he found an old acquaintance
employed, and was asked some dangerous questions. On they
went, however, until they stopped to let the train from Philadelphia pass. At a window sat a man under whom the runaway had been at work but a few days before. He might
easily have recognized him, and would certainly have him
arrested; but fortunately he was looking another way. The
passengers went on from Wilmington by steamer to Philadelphia, where one of them took the train for New York and
arrived early on Tuesday. In less than twenty-four hours the
slave had made himself a free man. It was but a few months
since he had become twenty-one.*

The flight was a bold and perilous one; but here I am, in
the great city of New York, safe and sound, without loss of
blood or bone. In less than a week after leaving Baltimore, I
was walking amid the hurrying throng, and gazing upon the
dazzling wonders of Broadway. The dreams of my childhood
and the purposes of my manhood were now fulfilled. A free
state around me, and a free earth under my feet! What a
moment was this to me! A whole year was pressed into a
single day. A new world burst upon my agitated vision. I
have often been asked, by kind friends to whom I have told
my story, how I felt when first I found myself beyond the
limits of slavery; and I must say here, as I have often said to
them, there is scarcely anything about which I could not give
a more satisfactory answer. It was a moment of joyous excite-

ment, which no words can describe. In a letter to a friend, written soon after reaching New York, I said I felt as one might be supposed to feel, on escaping from a den of hungry lions. But, in a moment like that, sensations are too intense and too rapid for words. Anguish and grief, like darkness and rain, may be described, but joy and gladness, like the rainbow of promise, defy alike the pen and pencil. . . .

Free and joyous, however, as I was, joy was not the only sensation I experienced. It was like the quick blaze, beautiful at the first, but which subsiding, leaves the building charred and desolate. I was soon taught that I was still in an enemy's land. A sense of loneliness and insecurity oppressed me sadly. I had been but a few hours in New York, before I was met in the streets by a fugitive slave, well known to me, and the information I got from him respecting New York, did nothing to lessen apprehension of danger. The fugitive in question was "Allender's Jake," in Baltimore; but, said he, I am "William Dixon," in New York! I knew Jake well, and knew when Tolly Allender and Mr. Price, (for the latter employed Master Hugh as his foreman, in his shipyard on Fell's Point) made an attempt to recapture Jake, and failed. Jake told me all about his circumstances, and how narrowly he escaped being taken back to slavery; that the city was now full of southerners, returning from the springs, that the black people in New York were not to be trusted; that there were hired men on the lookout for fugitives from slavery, and who, for a few dollars, would betray me into the hands of the slave-catchers; that I must trust no man with my secret; that I must not think of going either on the wharves to work, or to a boarding-house to board; and, worse still, this same Jake told me it was not in his power to help me. He seemed, even while cautioning me, to be fearing lest, after all, I might be a party to a second attempt to recapture him. Under the inspiration of this thought, I must suppose it was, he gave signs of a wish to get rid of me, and soon left me—his whitewash brush in hand—as he said, for his work. He was soon lost to sight among the throng, and I was alone again, an easy prey to the kidnappers, if any should happen to be on my track.

New York, seventeen years ago, was less a place of safety for a runaway slave than now, and all know how unsafe it now is, under the new fugitive slave bill. I was much troubled. I had very little money—enough to buy me a few loaves of bread, but not enough to pay board, outside a lumber yard. I saw the wisdom of keeping away from the shipyards, for if Master Hugh pursued me, he would naturally expect to find me looking for work among the calkers. For a time, every door seemed closed against me. A sense of my loneliness and helplessness crept over me, and covered me with something bordering on despair. In the midst of thousands of my fellowmen, and yet a perfect stranger! In the midst of human brothers, and yet more fearful of them than of hungry wolves! I was without home, without friends, without work, without money, and without any definite knowledge of which way to go, or where to look for succor. . . .

I found my man in the person of one who said his name was Stewart. He was a sailor, warm-hearted and generous, and he listened to my story with a brother's interest. I told him I was running for my freedom—knew not where to go—money almost gone—was hungry—thought it unsafe to go to the shipyards for work, and needed a friend. Stewart promptly put me in the way of getting out of trouble. He took me to his house, and went in search of the late David Ruggles, who was then the secretary of the New York Vigilance Committee, and a very active man in all anti-slavery works. Once in the hands of Mr. Ruggles, I was comparatively safe. I was hidden with Mr. Ruggles several days. In the meantime, my intended wife, Anna, came on from Baltimore—to whom I had written, informing her of my safe arrival at New York—and, in the presence of Mrs. Mitchell and Mr. Ruggles, we were married, by Rev. James W. C. Pennington.

Mr. Ruggles was the first officer on the under-ground railroad with whom I met after reaching the north, and, indeed, first of whom I ever heard anything. Learning that I was a calker by trade, he promptly decided that New Bedford was the proper place to send me. "Many ships," said he, "are there fitted out for the whaling business, and you may there find work at your trade, and make a good living." Thus, in one fortnight after my flight from Maryland, I was safe in New Bedford, regularly entered upon the exercise of the rights, responsibilities, and duties of a freeman.

Narrative of Harriet Tubman

The material here is from interviews appearing in the *Commonwealth* of July 17, 1863, and in the first volume of the *Freeman's Record* of March 1865 (pages 34 to 38).

One of the teachers lately commissioned by the New-England Freedmen's Aid Society is probably the most remarkable woman of this age. That is to say, she has performed more wonderful deeds by the native power of her own spirit against adverse circumstances than any other. She is well known to many by the various names which her eventful life has given her; Harriet Garrison, Gen. Tubman, &c.; but among the slaves she is universally known by her well earned title of Moses,—Moses the deliverer. She is a rare instance, in the midst of high civilization and intellectual culture, of a being of great native powers, working powerfully, and to beneficient ends, entirely untaught by schools or books.

Her maiden name was Araminta Ross. She is the grand-daughter of a native African, and has not a drop of white blood in her veins. She was born in 1820 or 1821, on the Eastern Shore of Maryland. Her parents were slaves, but married and faithful to each other, and the family affection is very strong. She claims that she was legally freed by a will of her first master, but his wishes were not carried into effect.

She seldom lived with her owner, but was usually "hired out" to different persons. She once "hired her time," and employed it in rudest farming labors, ploughing, carting, driving the oxen, &c., to so good advantage that she was able in one year to buy a pair of steers worth forty dollars.

When quite young she lived with a very pious mistress; but the slaveholder's religion did not prevent her from whipping the young girl for every slight or fancied fault. Araminta found that this was usually a morning exercise; so she prepared for it by putting on all the thick clothes she could procure to protect her skin. She made sufficient outcry, however, to convince her mistress that her blows had full effect; and in the afternoon she would take off her wrappings, and dress as well as she could. When invited into family prayers, she preferred to stay on the landing, and pray for herself; "and I prayed to God," she says "to make me strong and able to fight and that's what I've allers prayed for ever since." It is in vain to try to persuade her that her prayer was a wrong one. She always maintains it to be sincere and right, and it has certainly been fully answered.

In her youth she received a severe blow on her head from a heavy weight thrown by her master at another slave, but which accidentally hit her. The blow produced a disease of the brain which was severe for a long time, and still makes her very lethargic. She cannot remain quiet fifteen minutes without appearing to fall asleep. It is not refreshing slumber; but a heavy, weary condition which exhausts her. She therefore loves great physical activity, and direct heat of the sun, which keeps her blood actively circulating. She was married about 1844 to a free colored man named John Tubman, but never had any children. Owing to changes in her owner's family, it was determined to sell her and some other slaves; but her health was so much injured, that a purchaser was not easily found. At length she became convinced that she would soon be carried away, and she decided to escape. Her brothers did not agree with her plans; and she walked off alone, following the guidance of the brooks, which she had observed to run North. The evening before she left, she wished very much to bid her companions farewell, but was afraid of being betrayed, if any one knew of her intentions; so she passed through the street singing, "Good bye, I'm going to leave you, Good bye, I'll meet you in the kingdom," and similar snatches of Methodist songs. As she passed on singing, she saw her master, Dr. Thompson, standing at his gate, and her native humor breaking out, she sung yet louder, bowing down to him, "Good bye, I'm going for to leave you." He stopped and looked after her as she passed on; and he afterwards said, that, as her voice came floating back in the evening air it seemed as if "A wave of trouble never rolled across her peaceful breast."

Wise judges are we of each other!—She was only quitting home, husband, father, mother, friends, to go out alone, friendless and penniless into the world.

She remained two years in Philadelphia working hard and carefully hoarding her money. Then she hired a room, furnished it as well as she could, bought a nice suit of men's clothes, and went back to Maryland for her husband. But the faithless man had taken to himself another wife. Harriet did not dare venture into her presence, but sent word to her husband where she was. He declined joining her. At first her grief and anger were excessive. She said, "she did not care what massa did to her, she thought she would go right in and make all the trouble she could, she was determined to see her old man once more;" but finally she thought "how foolish it was just for temper to make mischief;" and that, "if he could do without her, she could without him," and so "he dropped out of her heart," and she determined to give her life to brave deeds. Thus all personal aims died out of her heart; and with her simple brave motto, "I can't die but once," she began the work which has made her Moses,—the deliverer of her people. Seven or eight times she has returned to the neighborhood of her former home, always at the risk of death in the most terrible forms, and each time has brought away a company of fugitive slaves, and led them safely to the free States, or to Canada. Every time she went, the dangers increased. In 1857 she brought away her old parents, and, as they were too feeble to walk, she was obliged to hire a wagon, which added greatly to the perils of the journey. In 1860 she went for the last time, and among her troop was an infant whom they were obliged to keep stupefied with laudanum to prevent its outcries. This was at the period of great excitement, and Moses was not safe even in New York State; but her anxious friends insisted upon her taking refuge in Canada. So various and interesting are the incidents of the journeys, that we know not how to select from them. She has shown in them all the characteristics of a great leader: courage, foresight, prudence, self-control, ingenuity, subtle perception, command over others' minds. Her nature is at once profoundly practical and highly imaginative. She is economical as Dr. Franklin, and as firm in the conviction of supernatural help as Mahomet. A clergyman once said, that her stories convinced you of their truth by their simplicity as do the gospel narratives. She never went to the South to bring away fugitives without being provided with money; money for the most part earned by drudgery in the kitchen, until within the last few years, when friends have aided her. She had to leave her sister's two orphan children in slavery the last time, for the want of thirty dollars. Thirty pieces of silver; an embroidered handkerchief or a silk dress to one, or the price of freedom to two orphan children to another! She would never allow more to join her than she could properly care for, though she often gave others directions by which they succeeded in escaping. She always came in the winter when the nights are long and dark, and people who have homes stay in them. She was never seen on the plantation herself; but appointed a rendezvous for her company eight or ten miles distant, so that if they were discovered at the first start she was not compromised. She started on Saturday night; the slaves at that time being allowed to go away from home to visit their friends—so that they would not be missed until Monday morning. Even then they were supposed to have loitered on the way, and it would often be late on Monday afternoon before the flight would be certainly known. If by any further delay the advertisement was not sent out before Tuesday morning, she felt secure of keeping ahead of it; but if it were, it required all her ingenuity to escape. She resorted to various devices, she had confidential friends all along the road. She would hire a man to follow the one who put up the notices, and take them down as soon as his back was turned. She crossed creeks on railroad bridges by night, she hid her company in the woods while she herself not being advertised went into the towns in search of information. If met on the road, her face was always to the south, and she was always a very respectable looking darkey, not at all a poor fugitive. She would get into the cars near her pursuers and manage to hear their plans.

The expedition was governed by the strictest rules. If any man gave out, he must be shot. "Would you really do that?" she was asked. "Yes," she replied, "if he was weak enough to give out, he'd be weak enough to betray us all, and all who had helped us; and do you think I'd let so many die just for one coward man." "Did you ever have to shoot any one?" she was asked. "One time," she said, "a man gave out the second night; his feet were sore and swollen, he couldn't go any further; he'd rather go back and die, if he must." They tried all arguments in vain, bathed his feet, tried to strengthen him, but it was of no use, he would go back. Then she said, "I told the boys to get their guns ready, and shoot him. They'd have done it in a minute; but when he heard that, he jumped right up and went on as well as any body." She can tell the time by the stars, and find her way by natural signs as well as any hunter; and yet she scarcely knows of the existence of England or any other foreign country.

When going on these journeys she often lay alone in the forests all night. Her whole soul was filled with awe of the mysterious Unseen Presence, which thrilled her with such depths of emotion, that all other care and fear vanished. Then she seemed to speak with her Maker "as a man talketh with his friend;" her child-like petitions had direct answers, and beautiful visions lifted her up above all doubt and anxiety into serene trust and faith. No man can be a hero without this faith in some form; the sense that he walks not in his own strength, but leaning on an almighty arm. Call it fate, destiny, what you will, Moses of old, Moses of to-day, believed it to be Almighty God.

She loves to describe her visions, which are very real to her; but she must tell them word for word as they lie in her untutored mind, with endless repetitions and details; she cannot shorten or condense them, whatever be your haste. She has great dramatic power; the scene rises before you as she saw it, and her voice and language change with her different actors. Often these visions came to her in the midst of her work. She once said, "We'd been carting manure all day, and t'other girl and I were gwine home on the sides of the cart, and another boy was driving, when suddenly I heard such music as filled all the air;" and, she saw a vision which she described in language which sounded like the old prophets in its grand flow; interrupted now and then by what t'other girl said, by Massa's coming and calling her to wake up, and her protests that she wasn't asleep.

One of her most characteristic prayers was when on board a steamboat with a party of fugitives. The clerk of the boat declined to give her tickets, and told her to wait. She thought he suspected her, and was at a loss how to save herself and her charge, if he did; so she went alone into the bow of the boat, and she says, "I drew in my breath and I sent it out to the Lord, but that was all I could say; and then again the third time, and just then I felt a touch on my shoulder, and looked round, and the clerk said, 'Here's your tickets.' "

Her efforts were not confined to the escape of slaves. She conducted them to Canada, watched over their welfare, collected clothing, organized them into societies, and was always occupied with plans for their benefit. She first came to Boston in the spring of 1859, to ask aid of the friends of her race to build a house for her aged father and mother. She brought recommendations from Gerrit Smith, and at once won many friends who aided her to accomplish her purpose. Her parents are now settled in Auburn, and all that Harriet seems to desire in reward for her labors is the privilege of making their old age comfortable. She has a very affectionate nature, and forms the strongest personal attachments. She has great simplicity of character; she states her wants very freely, and believes you are ready to help her; but if you have nothing to give, or have given to another, she is content. She is not sensitive to indignities to her color in her own person; but knows and claims her rights. She will eat at your table if she sees you really desire it; but she goes as willingly to the kitchen. She is very abstemious in her diet, fruit being the only luxury she cares for. Her personal appearance is very peculiar. She is thoroughly negro, and very plain. She has needed disguise so often, that she seems to have command over her face, and can banish all expression from her features, and look so stupid that nobody would suspect her of knowing enough to be dangerous; but her eye flashes with intelligence and power when she is roused.

VIRGINIA

For more than ten years John Brown had cherished a plan for the liberation of the slaves. This he had revealed to Frederick Douglass as early as 1847. In his *Life and Times* Douglass wrote (page 280):

"The true object to be sought," said Brown, "is first of all to destroy the money value of slave property; and that can only be done by rendering such property insecure. My plan then is to take at first about twenty-five picked men, and begin on a small scale; supply them arms and ammunition; post them in squads of five on a line of twenty-five miles, the most persuasive and judicious of whom shall go down to the fields from time to time, as opportunity offers, and induce the slaves to join them, seeking and selecting the most restless and daring." . . . With care and enterprise he thought he could soon gather a force of one hundred hardy men. . . . When they were properly drilled . . . they would run off the slaves in larger numbers, retain the brave and strong ones in the mountains, and send the weak and timid to the North by the Underground Railroad: his operations would be confined to one locality. . . . "If," said Brown, "we could drive slavery out of the county . . . it would weaken the system throughout the state." The enemy's country would afford subsistence, the fastnesses of the Alleghanies abundant protection, and a series of stations through Pennsylvania to the Canadian border a means of egress for timid slaves.

Early in 1858, Captain Brown, as he was sometimes called, asserted that "what we need is action—action!" He plotted actively to collect a band of devoted followers, seize and fortify a position in the mountains of Virginia, and from it make raids into the nearby farming communities to liberate slaves.

"Men, get on your arms; we will proceed to the Ferry." With these bold words, John Brown, Commander-in-Chief of the Provisional Army, set in motion his troop of liberators on a peaceful Sunday, October 16, 1859, and began his march on the road to Harpers Ferry. Brown was fifty-nine years old, triumphantly wearing a long, white, messianic beard. With his band of twenty-one men of both races, he began his famous raid on the federal arsenal, and was successful in getting inside after a battle during which no attackers were killed.

On the afternoon of October 18, 1859, a detachment of Marines commanded by Colonel Robert E. Lee, assisted by Lieutenant J. E. B. Stuart, surrounded the arsenal and captured the notorious Underground Railroad commander with four of his men. Seven of Brown's men escaped and ten were killed, two of the slain his own sons.

Brown was imprisoned in the county jail at Charlestown (now Charleston), where he waited trial, while cries of "Lynch the nigger-thief" were heard throughout the town and throughout the South.

John Brown's trial was the subject of national and international conversation. He made his last speech on November 2, 1859, during his trial:

I have, may it please the Court, a few words to say.

In the first place, I deny everything but what I have all along admitted—the design on my part to free the slaves. I intended certainly to have made a clean thing of that matter, as I did last winter when I went into Missouri and there took slaves without the snapping of a gun on either side, moved them through the country, and finally left them in Canada. I designed to have done the same thing again, on a larger scale.

Of his comrades-in-arms, Brown said:

> There is not one of them but joined me of his own accord, and the greater part of them at their own expense. A number of them I never saw, and never had a word of conversation with, till the day they came to me; and that was for the purpose I have stated.
> Now I have done.

On the morning of his execution, on his way out of jail, he handed his last written words to a guard. They were:

> I John Brown, now am quite certain that the crimes of this guilty land will never be washed away except with blood. I had, as I now think, vainly flattered myself that, without much bloodshed, it might be done.

Brown walked to the gallows on that bright and clear Friday morning of December 2, 1859, surrounded by fifteen hundred federal troops and hundreds of other curious witnesses. There had been numerous plans to rescue him by his northern followers, but he discouraged any attempt at rescue.

Speaking soon after, in northern Kansas, Abraham Lincoln, referring to Brown's hanging, declared him a man of surpassing courage and rare selflessness for whom punishment for murderous treason was nonetheless just. Soon afterward the Republicans nominated Lincoln for president.

Barrie Stavis, one of John Brown's biographers, wrote that Brown's attack on Harpers Ferry was not an ill-conceived maneuver but a commando tactic of such brilliance that it enabled him and his handful of men to capture all of their military objectives without firing a shot. Had they then fled to the nearby mountains, as earlier planned, the raid would have been a stunning victory.

John Brown became a martyr, and his death made him a lasting symbol. In 1862, while visiting Washington, D.C., Julia Ward Howe heard a company of black Union soldiers singing "John Brown's body lies a-mouldering in the grave, his soul goes marching on" and, overcome by emotion, decided to write other words based upon the tune of their song. Her new words became "The Battle Hymn of the Republic."

In the network of Underground Railroad routes, Virginia was the site of several junctions. The fugitives who traveled over these routes crossed the Ohio River in the vicinity of Parkersburg and Point Pleasant, in what is now West Virginia, and proceeded north twenty or thirty miles with the help of abolitionists before reaching Morgan County, Ohio.

Wheeling was also an important stop on the Underground before the new free state was established, and hundreds of fugitive slaves were brought here to cross into freedom on the other side of the Ohio River.

The vast Dismal Swamp on the Virginia-North Carolina border was a popular retreat for a large colony of refugees. Although the swamp abounded with deadly snakes, red-bugs, yellow flies, mosquitoes, and ticks, for nearly two thousand fugitives over the years, this was home. By hunting, fishing, and stealing, most of these exiles managed to avoid recapture and stay alive. A runaway slave belonging to Augustus Holly of Bertie County, North Carolina, when finally recaptured in the swamp, was found to be wearing "a coat that was impervious to shot, it being thickly wadded with turkey feathers."

If it took great courage for fugitives to live in the wilds of the Dismal Swamp, one can imagine the bravery of the slaves who escaped as stowaways or fled on horse or foot at night. The Virginia roads were especially dangerous: heavily patrolled by slaveholders and bounty-hunters. Passengers on the Underground Railroad came from such places as Richmond, Petersburg, Norfolk, and Roanoke. Robert Brown, alias Thomas Jones, swam the Potomac River on horseback on Christmas night to escape the dread of slavery. His wife and children had been sold only five days earlier because she had resisted the sexual advances of her master. Although Brown arrived safely in Harrisburg, he was still in grief over his loss.

Narrative of Captain Fountain

This narrative of a white ship captain is from Still's *Underground Railroad Records* (pages 165 to 168).

Captain F. was certainly no ordinary man. Although he had been living a sea-faring life for many years, and the marks of this calling were plainly enough visible in his manners and speech, he was, nevertheless, unlike the great mass of this class of men, not addicted to intemperance and profanity. On the contrary, he was a man of thought, and possessed, in a large measure, those humane traits of character which lead men to sympathize with suffering humanity wherever met with.

It must be admitted, however, that the first impressions gathered from a hasty survey of his rough appearance, his large head, large mouth, large eyes, and heavy eye-brows, with a natural gift at keeping concealed the inner-workings of his mind and feelings, were not calculated to inspire the belief, that he was fitted to be entrusted with the lives of unprotected females, and helpless children; that he could take pleasure in risking his own life to rescue them from the hell of Slavery; that he could deliberately enter the enemy's domain, and with the faith of a martyr, face the dread slave-holder, with his Bowie-knives and revolvers—slave hunters, and blood hounds, lynchings and penitentiaries, for humanity's sake. But his deeds proved him to be a true friend of the slave; whilst his skill, bravery, and success stamped him as one of the most daring and heroic Captains ever connected with the Underground Rail Road cause.

At the time he was doing most for humanity in rescuing bondsmen from Slavery, slave-laws were actually being the most rigidly executed. To show mercy, in any sense, to men or women, who might be caught assisting a poor slave to flee from the prison-house, was a matter not to be thought of in Virginia.

This was perfectly well understood by Captain F.; indeed he did not hesitate to say, that his hazardous operations might any day result in the "sacrifice" of his life. But on this point he seemed to give himself no more concern than he would have done to know which way the wind would blow the next day. He had his own convictions about dying and the future, and he declared, that he had "no fear of death," however it might come. Still, he was not disposed to be reckless or needlessly to imperil his life or the lives of those he undertook to aid. Nor was he averse to receiving compensation for his services. In Richmond, Norfolk, Petersburg, and other places where he traded, many slaves were fully awake to their condition. The great slave sales were the agencies that served to awaken a large number. Then the various mechanical trades were necessarily given to the slaves, for the master had no taste for "greasy, northern mechanics." Then, again, the stores had to be supplied with porters, draymen, etc., from the slave population. In the hearts of many of the more intelligent amongst the slaves, the men, as mechanics, etc., the women, as dressmakers, chambermaids, etc., notwithstanding all the opposition and hard laws, the spirit of Freedom was steadily burning. Many of the slaves were half brothers, and sisters, cousins, nephews, and nieces of their owners, and of course "blood would tell."

It was only necessary for the fact to be made known to a single reliable and intelligent slave, that a man with a boat running North had the love of Freedom for all mankind in his bosom to make that man an object of the greatest interest. If an angel had appeared amongst them doubtless his presence would not have inspired greater anxiety and hope than did the presence of Captain F. The class most anxious to obtain freedom could generally manage to acquire some means which they would willingly offer to captains or conductors in the South for such assistance as was indispensable to their escape. Many of the slaves learned if they could manage to cross Mason and Dixon's line, even though they might be utterly destitute and penniless, that they would then receive aid and protection from the Vigilance Committee. Here it may be well to state that, whilst the Committee gladly received and aided all who might come or be brought to them, they never employed agents or captains to go into the South with a view of enticing or running off slaves. So when captains operated, they did so with the full understanding that they alone were responsible for any failures attending their movements.

The way is now clear to present Captain F. with his
schooner lying at the wharf in Norfolk, loading with wheat,
and at the same time with twenty-one fugitives secreted therein.
While the boat was thus lying at her mooring, the rumor was
flying all over town that a number of slaves had escaped,
which created a general excitement a degree less, perhaps,
than if the citizens had been visited by an earthquake.

The mayor of the city with a posse of officers with axes
and long spears repaired to Captain F.'s boat. The fearless
commander received his Honor very coolly, and as gracefully
as the circumstances would admit. The mayor gave him to
understand who he was, and by what authority he appeared
on the boat, and what he meant to do. "Very well," replied
Captain F., "here I am and this is my boat, go ahead and
search." His Honor with his deputies looked quickly around,
and then an order went forth from the mayor to "spear the
wheat thoroughly." The deputies obeyed the command with
alacrity. But the spears brought neither blood nor groans, and
the sagacious mayor obviously concluded that he was "barking up the wrong tree." But the mayor was not there for
nothing. "Take the axes and go to work," was the next
order; and the axe was used with terrible effect by one of the
deputies. The deck and other parts of the boat were chopped
and split; no greater judgment being exercised when using the
axe than when spearing the wheat; Captain F. all the while
wearing an air of utter indifference or rather of entire compo-
sure. Indeed every step they took proved conclusively that
they were wholly ignorant with regard to boat searching. At
this point, with remarkable shrewdness, Captain F. saw wherein
he could still further confuse them by a bold strategical move.
As though about out of patience with the mayor's blunder, the
captain instantly reminded his Honor that he had "stood still
long enough" while his boat was being "damaged, chopped
up," &c. "Now if you want to search," continued he, "give
me the axe, and then point out the spot you want opened and
I will open it for you very quick." While uttering these words
he presented, as he was capable of doing, an indignant and
defiant countenance, and intimated that it mattered not where
or when a man died provided he was in the right, and as
though he wished to give particularly strong emphasis to what
he was saying, he raised the axe, and brought it down edge
foremost on the deck with startling effect, at the same time

causing the splinters to fly from the boards. The mayor and his posse seemed, if not dreadfully frightened, completely confounded, and by the time Captain F. had again brought down his axe with increased power, demanding where they would have him open, they looked as though it was time for them to retire, and in a few minutes after they actually gave up the search and left the boat without finding a soul. Daniel in the lions' den was not safer than were the twenty-one passengers secreted on Captain F.'s boat. The law had been carried out with a vengeance, but did not avail with this skilled captain. The "five dollars" were paid for being searched, the amount which was lawfully required of every captain sailing from Virginia. And the captain steered direct for the City of Brotherly Love. The wind of heaven favoring the good cause, he arrived safely in due time, and delivered his precious freight in the vicinity of Philadelphia within the reach of the Vigilance Committee.

Narrative of Charles Peyton Lucas

This narrative appears in Drew's *A North-Side View of Slavery* (pages 107 to 109).

In one week's time I started for the North with two companions; but it was cock-crowing before we reached the Potomac; so we went on a hill, and hid until the next (Sunday) night. Then we came down, and tied our provisions into bundles on our backs, and started for the Potomac river—whether to wade it, swim it, or get drowned, we knew not. We waded and swam, changing our ground as the water deepened. At last we reached the opposite bank in Maryland: we merely stopped to pour the water out of our boots, and then traveled on all wet, until morning: then we hid in the bushes. We traveled by night and concealed ourselves by day, for ten days and nights, suffering greatly from hunger and from rain, without shelter. One day in September, we sat on a mountain, exposed to a hot, broiling sun, and without food or drink. We could hear people at their work about us, but we did not dare ask for aid. For three days, we had neither food nor drink, excepting green corn. We sucked the juice for drink, and the corn itself was our only food. The effect of this was to weaken us very much.

One night we came to a farmer's spring-house—I broke the lock and got a good pan of milk, but before I could find anything else, the dogs began to bark, so that we had to hurry off. We quaffed the milk with a good relish and it did us a deal of service. We drank at times muddy water from horse tracks: on one occasion, we were run very severely by dogs and men, but we got away from them. One morning between two and four o'clock, we came to a white man tending a lime-kiln—he was asleep. We knew nothing of the way; so we concluded to awaken him, and ask the way, and if he tried to stop us, or have us caught, that we would kill him and throw him into the kiln. We awoke him and told him that our harvesting was done—we were hunting for work, as we had two days of work in. He did not believe it—said we were runaways. I took out my pistol, cocked and capped it, and the others produced, one a bayonet, and the other a bowie knife. The man approached us, saying still we were runaways. Had he offered to touch us we would have killed him, but he proved to be the best friend we had ever had. He told us our way, and regretted that he had no food. Said he, "If you travel on, by day-light you will cross Mason and Dixon's line, and get among the Dutch. Keep away from the big road, walk near it, but not in it—walk in the daytime, but keep in the woods." We followed his directions, and at ten o'clock next morning, we reached a Dutchman's house. The man was out—but the woman and girls set the table. We ate all they had in the house—I ate till I was ashamed. The good woman told us to avoid Shippensburg, as six had been carried back from there just before. She told us, if anybody questioned us, to say that we were going to Horse Shoe Bottom camp meeting on the Susquehanna. We did accordingly, and soon struck the track of the underground railroad, which we followed into the northern free States.

At ———, I went to work on a building. One day a druggist came to me, and said that an advertisement describing me was in the tavern—"tawny colored man, tall, spare, and of pleasing countenance when spoken to, and he works at blacksmithing. No scars recollected, except one on his neck.

Any person who will return him to me, or lodge him in jail, so that I can get him, shall have a reward of five hundred dollars.'' My friends advised me to remove further. I worked in Geneva, N.Y., until the passage of the fugitive slave law, when my friends advised me to go to Canada. . . . I feel that I am out of the lion's paw, and I feel that *there is no curse on God's earth, equal to slavery.*

Narrative of Henry Box Brown

This daring escape, from Still's *Underground Railroad Records* (pages 81 to 83), was the object of great public excitement during the 1840's. Sheet music was even written to celebrate the exploit. Samuel A. Smith, the white Richmond carpenter who crated Brown, was convicted and imprisoned for eight years when caught in two similar attempts to deliver boxed slaves. Brown himself went to Boston, where he became an active worker on the Underground Railroad.

Brown was a man of invention as well as a hero. In point of interest, however, his case is no more remarkable than many others. Indeed, neither before nor after escaping did he suffer one-half what many others have experienced.

He was decidedly an unhappy piece of property in the city of Richmond, Va. In the condition of a slave he felt that it would be impossible for him to remain. Full well did he know, however, that it was no holiday task to escape the vigilance of Virginia slave-hunters, or the wrath of an enraged master for committing the unpardonable sin of attempting to escape to a land of liberty. So Brown counted well the cost before venturing upon his hazardous undertaking. Ordinary modes of travel he concluded might prove disastrous to his hopes; he, therefore, hit upon a new invention altogether, which was to have himself boxed up and forwarded to Philadelphia direct by express. The size of the box and how it was to be made to fit him most comfortably, was of his own ordering. Two feet eight inches deep, two feet wide, and three feet long were the exact dimensions of the box, lined with baize. His resources in regard to food and water consisted of the following: One bladder of water and a few small biscuits. His mechanical implement to meet the death-struggle for fresh air, all told, was one large gimlet. Satisfied that it would be far better to peril his life for freedom in this way than to remain under the galling yoke of Slavery, he entered his box, which was safely nailed up and hooped with five hickory hoops, and then was addressed by his next friend, James A. Smith, a shoe dealer, to Wm. H. Johnson, Arch Street, Philadelphia, marked, "This side up with care." In this condition he was sent to Adams' Express office in a dray, and thence by overland express to Philadelphia. It was twenty-six hours from the time he left Richmond until his arrival in the city of Brotherly Love. The notice, "This side up, etc.," did not avail with the different expressmen, who hesitated not to handle the box in the usual rough manner common to this class of men. For a while they actually had the box upside down, and had him on his head for miles. A few days before he was expected, certain intimation was conveyed to a member of the Vigilance Committee that a box might be expected by the three o'clock morning train from the South, which might contain a man. One of the most serious walks he ever took—and they had not been a few—to meet and accompany passengers, he took at half past two o'clock that morning to the depot. Not once, but for more than a score of times, he fancied the slave would be dead. He anxiously looked while the freight was being unloaded from the cars, to see if he could recognize a box that might contain a man; one alone had that appearance, and he confessed it really seemed as if there was the scent of death about it. But on inquiry, he soon learned that it was not the one he was looking after, and he was free to say he experienced a marked sense of relief. That same afternoon, however, he received from Richmond a telegram, which read thus, "Your case of goods is shipped and will arrive tomorrow morning."

At this exciting juncture of affairs, Mr. McKim, who had been engineering this important undertaking, deemed it expedient to change the programme slightly in one particular at least to insure greater safety. Instead of having a member of the Committee go again to the depot for the box, which might excite suspicion, it was decided that it would be safest to have the express bring it direct to the Anti-Slavery Office.

But all apprehension of danger did not now disappear, for there was no room to suppose that Adams' Express office had any sympathy with the Abolitionist or the fugitive, consequently for Mr. McKim to appear personally at the express office to give directions with reference to the coming of a box from Richmond which would be directed to Arch Street, and yet not intended for that street, but for the Anti-Slavery office at 107 North Fifth Street, it needed of course no great discernment to foresee that a step of this kind was wholly impracticable and that a more indirect and covert method would have to be adopted. In this dreadful crisis Mr. McKim, with his usual good judgment and remarkably quick, strategical mind, especially in matters pertaining to the U.G.R.R., hit upon the following plan, namely, to go to his friend, E. M. Davis, who was then extensively engaged in mercantile business, and relate the circumstances. Having daily intercourse with said Adams' Express office, and being well acquainted with the firm and some of the drivers, Mr. Davis could, as Mr. McKim thought, talk about "boxes, freight, etc.," from any part of the country without risk. Mr. Davis heard Mr. McKim's plan and instantly approved of it, and was heartily at his service. "Dan, an Irishman, one of Adams' Express drivers, is just the fellow to go to the depot after the box," said Davis. "He drinks a little too much whiskey sometimes, but he will do anything I ask him to do, promptly and obligingly. I'll trust Dan, for I believe he is the very man." The difficulty which Mr. McKim had been so anxious to overcome was thus pretty well settled. It was agreed that Dan should go after the box next morning before daylight and bring it to the Anti-Slavery office direct, and to make it all the more agreeable for Dan to get up out of his warm bed and go on this errand before day, it was decided that he should have a five dollar gold piece for himself. Thus these preliminaries having been satisfactorily arranged, it only remained for Mr. Davis to see Dan and give him instructions accordingly, etc. Next morning, according to arrangement, the box was at the Anti-Slavery office in due time. The witnesses present to behold the resurrection were J. M. McKim, Professor C. D. Cleveland, Lewis Thompson, and the writer.

Mr. McKim was deeply interested; but having been long

identified with the Anti-Slavery cause as one of its oldest and ablest advocates in the darkest days of slavery and mobs, and always found by the side of the fugitive to counsel and succor, he was on this occasion perfectly composed.

Professor Cleveland, however, was greatly moved. His zeal and earnestness in the cause of freedom, especially in rendering aid to passengers, knew no limit. Ordinarily he could not too often visit these travelers, shake them too warmly by hand, or impart to them too freely of his substance to aid them on their journey. But now his emotion was overpowering.

Mr. Thompson, of the firm of Merrihew & Thompson— about the only printers in the city who for many years dared to print such incendiary documents as anti-slavery papers and pamphlets—one of the truest friends of the slave, was composed and prepared to witness the scene.

All was quiet. The door had been safely locked. The proceedings commenced. Mr. McKim rapped quietly on the lid of the box and called out, "All right!" Instantly came the answer from within, "All right, sir!"

The witnesses will never forget that moment. Saw and hatchet quickly had the five hickory hoops cut and the lid off, and the marvellous resurrection of Brown ensued. Rising up in the box, he reached out his hand, saying, "How do you do, gentlemen?" The little assemblage hardly knew what to think or do at the moment. He was about as wet as if he had come up out of the Delaware. Very soon he remarked that, before leaving Richmond he had selected for his arrival hymn (if he lived) the Psalm beginning with these words: *"I waited patiently for the Lord, and He heard my prayer."* And most touchingly did he sing the psalm, much to his own relief, as well as to the delight of his small audience.

Narrative of John Fairfield

This account is taken from Levi Coffin's *Reminiscences* (beginning at page 428).

It is seldom that one hears of a person who has been brought up in the midst of slavery, surrounded by its influences from his earliest recollection, being a hater of the "peculiar institution," but there are several such cases on record. Among them is that of John Fairfield, who has already figured in these pages in connection with a party of twenty-eight fugitives, whom he conducted to Cincinnati from their homes in Kentucky.

His early home was in Virginia, east of the mountains, where he imbibed anti-slavery sentiments—from what source it is unknown, certainly not from his relatives, who were all slaveholders. When quite a young man, he decided to make a visit to the State of Ohio, and seek his fortunes in a free State. Thinking that it would be a good opportunity to put his anti-slavery principles into practice, he planned to take with him one of his uncle's slaves, a bright, intelligent young man, about his own age, to whom he was much attached. John and this young colored man had played together when boys, and had been brought up together. They had often discussed plans by which Bill, the slave, could make his escape to Canada, but no attempt had been made to carry them out, until young Fairfield determined to visit Ohio. The arrangement was then made for Bill to take one of his master's horses, and make his escape the night before Fairfield started, and wait for him at a rendezvous appointed. This plan was carried out, and Bill traveled as Fairfield's servant until they reached Ohio. Not feeling safe in that State, he went on to Canada, accompanied by Fairfield, who spent several weeks there looking at the country. Bill, in the meanwhile, found a good situation, and when Fairfield left him he was rejoicing in his newly achieved liberty and prosperity.

When Fairfield told me the story, some years afterward, I asked him if he did not feel guilty of encouraging horse-stealing, as well as negro-stealing. I knew that death was the penalty for each of these crimes, according to the laws of Virginia and North Carolina.

The reply was: "No! I knew that Bill had earned several horses for his master, and he took only one. Bill had been a faithful fellow, and worked hard for many years, and that horse was all the pay he got. As to negro-stealing, I would steal all the slaves in Virginia if I could."

After spending several months in Ohio, John Fairfield returned to Virginia, but did not remain long. His uncle suspected him of having helped his ablebodied and valuable servant to escape, and having obtained evidence from some source—probably from Ohio—he set about procuring a writ and having his nephew arrested.

Fairfield learned of his uncle's intention, and concluded to leave that part of the country. Actuated by a feeling of spite, or some other motive, he resolved to take other slaves, as he had taken Bill, and succeeded in getting away with several, some of whom belonged to his uncle. They traveled during the night and hid themselves during the day. Sometimes when they were safely secreted for the day, Fairfield went forward a few miles and purchased provisions, under the pretense of buying for movers in camp; then returned and supplied the party of fugitives. They finally arrived safely in Canada, and Fairfield, liking the country, concluded to make his home there. Bill was now married and comfortably settled.

Fairfield's success in conducting the slaves from Virginia to Canada was soon known to many of the fugitives settled in that country, and having confidence in him, they importuned him to bring away from slavery the husbands, wives, children, or other relatives which they had left behind them in various parts of the South. Some of them had accumulated small sums of money, and offered to pay him if he would undertake the mission.

Fairfield was a young man without family, and was fond of adventure and excitement. He wanted employment, and agreed to take the money offered by the fugitives and engage in the undertaking. He obtained the names of masters and slaves, and an exact knowledge of the different localities to be visited, together with other information that might be of use to him; then acted as his shrewd judgment dictated, under different circumstances. He would go South, into the neighborhood where the slaves were whom he intended to conduct away, and, under an assumed name and a false pretense of business, engage boarding, perhaps at the house of the master whose stock of valuable property he intended to decrease. He would proclaim himself to be a Virginian, and profess to be strongly pro-slavery in his sentiments, thus lulling the suspicions of slave holders while he established a secret understanding with the slaves—gaining their confidence and making arrangements for their escape. Then he would suddenly disappear from the neighborhood, and several slaves would be missing at the same time.

Fairfield succeeded well in his daring adventures, and in many instances brought members of families together in Canada, who had been separated for several years. Husbands and wives were again united, and there were joyful meetings between parents and children. The fugitives settled in Canada had unbounded confidence in Fairfield, and were constantly begging him to bring away their friends and relatives from slavery. He continued this unique business for more than twelve years, and during that time aided, it is said, several thousand slaves to escape from bondage and reach Canada. He was a wicked man, daring and reckless in his actions, yet faithful to the trust reposed in him, and benevolent to the poor. He seemed to have no fear for his personal safety—was always ready to risk his life and liberty in order to rescue the slaves from bondage.

He was an inveterate hater of slavery, and this feeling supplied a motive for the actions of his whole life. He believed that every slave was justly entitled to freedom, and that if any person came between him and liberty, the slave had a perfect right to shoot him down. He always went heavily armed himself, and did not scruple to use his weapons whenever he thought the occasion required their use. He resorted to many stratagems to effect his object in the South, and brought away numbers of slaves from nearly every slave State in the Union. He often stopped at Cincinnati, on his way South, and generally made his home among the colored people. He frequently called to see me, and told me of his daring exploits and plans of operation, to all of which I objected. I could have no sympathy with his mode of action, and at various times urged him to cease his operations in the South and return to his home in Canada and remain there. I would have nothing to do with aiding him to carry out his plans, for I could not indorse the principles he acted upon. . . .

Fairfield was always ready to take money for his services from the slaves if they had it to offer, but if they did not he helped them all the same. Sometimes the slaves in the South had accumulated a little money, which they gave gladly to any one who would conduct them out of the house of bondage; and sometimes the fugitives in the North gave their little hoard to Fairfield, and begged him to rescue their relatives from slavery. Though always willing to take money for his services, he was equally ready to spend it in the same cause, and, if necessary, would part with his last dollar to effect his object. . . .

Fairfield was several times betrayed and arrested, in the South, and put in prison, but being a Free Mason, high in the Order, he managed to get out of prison without being tried. He broke jail once or twice and escaped. He often had to endure privation and hardship, but was ready to undergo any suffering, for the sake of effecting his object. He sometimes divided his clothing with a destitute fugitive, and was willing to make any sacrifice of personal comfort. We often heard of his arrival in Canada with large companies of fugitives, whom he had conducted thither by some line of the Underground Railroad. . . .

Free colored people in the Northern States who had relatives in slavery heard of Fairfield's successful efforts, and applied to him to bring their friends out of bondage, sometimes offering him several hundred dollars. . . .

Narrative of John Hall and Mary Weaver

This narrative is taken from Still's *Underground Railroad Records* (pages 250 to 253).

April 27, 1855. John Hall arrived safely from Richmond, Va., per schooner (Captain B). One hundred dollars were paid for his passage. In Richmond he was owned by James Dunlap, a merchant. John had been sold several times, in consequence of which, he had possessed very good opportunities of experiencing the effect of change of owners. Then too, the personal examination made before sale, and the gratification afforded his master when he [John], brought a good price—left no very pleasing impressions on his mind.

By one of his owners, named Burke, John alleged that he had been "cruelly used." When quite young, both he and his sister, together with their mother, were sold by Burke. From that time he had seen neither mother nor sister. They were sold separately. For three or four years the desire to seek liberty had been fondly cherished, and nothing but the want of a favorable opportunity had deterred him from carrying out his designs. He considered himself much "imposed upon" by his master, particularly as he was allowed "no choice about living" as he "desired." This was indeed ill-treatment as John viewed the matter. John may have wanted too much. He was about thirty-five years of age, light complexion, tall, rather handsome-looking, intelligent, and of good manners. But notwithstanding these prepossessing features, John's owner valued him at only one thousand dollars. If he had been a few shades darker and only half as intelligent as he was, he would have been worth at least five hundred dollars more. The idea of having had a white father, in many instances, depreciated the pecuniary value of male slaves, if not of the other sex. John emphatically was one of this injured class; he evidently had blood in his veins which decidedly warred against submitting to the yoke. In addition to the influence which such rebellious blood exerted over him, together with a considerable amount of intelligence, he was also under the influence and advice of a daughter of old Ireland. She was heart and soul with John in all his plans which looked Canada-ward. This it was that "sent him away."

It is very certain, that this Irish girl was not annoyed by the kinks in John's hair. Nor was she overly fastidious about the small percentage of colored blood visible in John's complexion. It was, however, a strange occurrence and very hard to understand. Not a stone was left unturned until John was safely on the Underground Railroad. Doubtless she helped to earn the money which was paid for his passage. And when he was safe off, it is not too much to say, that John was not a whit more delighted than was his intended Irish lassie, Mary Weaver. John had no sooner reached Canada than Mary's heart was there, too. Circumstances, however, required that she should remain in Richmond a number of months for the purpose of winding up some of her affairs. As soon as the way opened for her, she followed him. It was quite manifest, that she had not let a single opportunity slide, but seized the first chance and arrived partly by means of the Underground Rail Road and partly by the regular train. Many difficulties were surmounted before and after leaving Richmond, by which they earned their merited success. From Canada, where they anticipated entering upon the matrimonial career with mutual satisfaction, it seemed to afford them great pleasure to write back frequently, expressing their heartfelt gratitude for assistance.

Narrative of Eber Pettit

This narrative is in Pettit's *Sketches,* 1870 (pages 17 to 23).

Something over twenty years ago, I stopped a few days at the City Hotel in Wheeling, Va. The hotel was located on the southern border of the city, adjoining a small plantation in the rear of the garden. The landlord was a pleasant, social gentleman, well informed on all topics of interest, and preferred hiring his help rather than to be the owner of a human being. Having learned this, I was less guarded in talking about their institutions than I should otherwise have been. Among the guests at the hotel was a family of Quakers on their way from Eastern Virginia to Indiana. One of the young men told me that he had never been outside of the State of Virginia; had long been disgusted with the wickedness and cruelty of slavery which he could not avoid seeing and hearing every day. The horrors of the everyday life on the plantations as described by him exceeded everything related in *Uncle Tom's Cabin,* and he had sold out, and the family were going to settle in a free State.

I was sitting on the piazza talking with this man, when a coffle of slaves came in front of the house and were hustled along by the driver; the men were fine looking fellows, though they were bare-footed, and most of them bare-headed; they were chained by the right wrist to the long bar of iron. The women were not fettered, some of them carried infants in their arms, and some children rode on the wagon with the corn on which they all were fed. They soon started toward a steamboat lying at the levee, and were shipped for the New Orleans market. This was the first drove of slaves I had ever seen, and being a little excited, I made a remark to the

Quaker which the landlord overheard, and touching my shoulder, he beckoned me to go with him. We went aside, and he said to me, "You are going to Kentucky, and I advise you to beware how you speak of these things. There are men in this place, who, had they heard that remark, would have had you in jail in a hurry. I hope you will heed my advice."

An incident that occurred on the U.G.R.R., not many months after, brought vividly to my remembrance the kind-hearted, unselfish landlord of the City Hotel of Wheeling. It was on a bitter cold day in December that a sleigh was driven into Fredonia, N.Y.; the driver had made some inquiries (this was his first trip as conductor), and turned his team down the creek in search of a depot. It was late in the evening, and the road was badly drifted, but the train went through and made connection as usual. The passenger came out from under the driver's seat, shook off the blankets and buffalo robes that had hid him and kept him warm. He was not inclined to talk at first, but a hearty welcome, a warm supper, and the assurance that he was safe from his pursuers, induced him to give a brief account of his adventures. He said:

"I have always lived in Loudoun County, Virginia. My mother was the cook, and I worked about the house, and sometimes traveled with master—went to Washington, Baltimore, Cumberland, and once to Wheeling, on horseback. One day, when mother gave me my dinner, she said, 'Charley, all my children gone but you, and Massa's done gone and sold you, and I'll never see you 'gin.' 'Guess not, mother, he promised you to keep me always;' but she said, 'I heard him tell the trader he'll send you to town Monday morning, and he must put you in jail.' Well, I was afraid to tell mother what I would do, because maybe somebody would hear, so I couldn't say good-bye to my poor old mother, but next morning master's best horse and I were 50 miles away towards Wheeling. Hid in the woods all day, at night left the horse loose in the woods, and went on as well as I could. Did not go through the towns, went round, then found the road and went on. Found corn in the fields, and some apples, and got to Wheeling in about fourteen or fifteen days. Was almost starved, went into the *City Hotel* before daylight. The landlord was up, and I asked him for some bread. He looked at me and said, 'You are a runaway.' I began to say 'no,' but he said, 'Go with me!' We went to the barn, and he said, 'Do you know whose horse that is!' Then I owned up, and begged him to let me go and not tell master. He then read to me an advertisement, offering five hundred dollars reward for me. Then I thought, it's no use trying—must go back, sold! Sold! Oh! I wanted to die; but the man said, 'See here! You see that house beyond that lot?' 'Yes, master,' I said. 'You go there and tell them I said they must take care of you, and give you something to eat.' Then he looked so happy, and I wanted to lie down and kiss his feet; but it was getting light. 'Hurry,' he said, 'go right in the back door.' When I got in I could see nobody but a sick woman on a bed. I told what the man said, and soon I heard horses running up the road, and looking out, saw my master and another man coming. I began to cry, but she told me to get under the bed and lie still, and when I had done so she took up her baby, and got it to screaming with all its might. Soon master opened the door and looked in, and asked if a negro boy had come in there. The baby cried and she pretended to try to stop it, and asked him what he wanted. He repeated the question. She tried to hush the baby, and finally said, 'Husband is at the barn; he can tell you if he has been here.' They went to the barn, and soon I heard them running their horses up the road. Then she said to me, 'Go up the ladder and lie down on the floor,' which I did, and when the man came in with his milk pail, he asked his wife who that man was, inquiring about a boy? She said, 'I don't know, but I know where the boy is.' 'Where is he?' 'He went up the ladder, and you must carry him something to eat, poor fellow, he's starved.' As soon as he could, he came to me with enough to eat, and then fixed a place for me to lie down, and said, 'You are tired and sleepy. Now go to sleep, and if you wake, don't stir nor make a noise until I come.' Having slept little since I started, I slept all day; it was dark when he roused me up and told me to go down. I found a good supper ready, and while I was eating the man and his wife said not a word. When I had done he said, 'Come out here.' Following him, I saw at the door three horses; there was a man on one of them; I was told to mount one, and he mounted the other. I was between them. Not a word was spoken, and passing round the edge of the town near the hill, we came to the road leading north near the bluff above the river. I didn't know what it all meant, but supposed they were going to give me up, and claim the five hundred dollars. We rode three miles maybe, hitched the horses in some bushes, and went down the steep bluff to the Ohio River. He pulled a stake and threw it into a boat that was tied to it, and motioned me to get in. We soon got across the river, then taking a little bundle, he directed me to go forward, and we were soon on a road. He then put two loaves of bread in my hand, and said to me, 'This is a free State, and there is the north star,' pointing to it; 'God bless you,' and I soon heard the splash of his pole in the river, and started northward.''

Charley found himself alone in the road, the river on his right hand, broad fields on his left, and no house in sight; as to the north star, he looked towards it when his friend pointed towards it, but did not know which it was; his education had been neglected. Smart negroes knew that star by sight. When a slave could find the north star, and show his mother how he knew it, and by what signs he found it, he was ready to graduate—he had finished his education—but Charley, poor fellow, had been having an easy time, riding about with his master, caring for the horses, blacking his boots, and brushing his clothes, and he had not thought of going north until his mother told him that he had been sold. Besides, Charley was terribly disappointed. He supposed he was to be delivered to his master; that a white man would feed him and help him on his way to freedom, when he could have five hundred dollars for less trouble and no risk, he had not supposed was possible. He began to feel dizzy and faint, went a few rods and sat down, and soon fell asleep. He dreamed that two men were putting him into jail; he struggled, and woke up finding himself alone, and darkness all around. He soon aroused sufficiently to understand the situation, and started along the road, not knowing whether he was going north or south, but kept going until it began to be light, when he saw a paper nailed to a board fence with a picture of a negro running, and looking like the advertisement that the landlord showed him in his barn. While he stood looking at it, a man came behind him, put his hand on his shoulder, and said, "What have we here?" He turned to run, but the man held on to him, speaking kindly, and said, "Don't be frightened, let us see what this is about," then he read the advertisement, and looking at Charley, said, "This means you; come with me, there is no time to be lost." He took him to a safe place far back in the woods, and seeing that he had bread with him, he said, "I will bring you more food tonight," and left him. When he came to bring food, he told Charley that he would have to stay a few days until the men that were looking for him were gone. He was soon taken to a comfortable place, but it was two or three weeks before his kind conductor felt safe in starting with him.

The route from Wheeling was supposed to be towards Detroit at that season of the year, and the hunters were able to trace Charley going that way. They met, all along the way, men who had seen him, and could describe him as well as if they had known him from his childhood. Those rascally U.G.R.R. conductors were putting him through Carroll, Starke, Wayne, Ashland, and Huron counties, toward Detroit, where he could cross over. There were plenty of men along this route that were waiting to show them the way he had gone.

Meanwhile, Charley was on the short route to Buffalo, by way of Meadville, Pa., and Westfield, N.Y., *though no man saw him on the way.*

DISTRICT OF COLUMBIA

Situated firmly in the South and surrounded by slave states, Washington was a paradox. Seat of a republic founded on the enlightenment principle of the equality of men, it had human slavery as a thriving local institution and slave pens and auction blocks within sight of the White House and Capitol. At the same time, a strong free black community provided the protection needed by runaways before they crossed Virginia or Maryland on their way to freedom.

Born of free parents in Leesburg, Virginia, Leonard A. Grimes operated as a hackman in Washington, D.C. The resourceful Grimes soon accumulated enough money to purchase a number of horses and carriages, which he used for Underground Railroad purposes. Once, while transporting a family of free blacks through Virginia, Grimes was apprehended, convicted, and sentenced to two years in the state prison in Richmond. Upon his release, Grimes returned to Washington for a short period. He later moved to Boston and became a pastor of the Twelfth Street Baptist Church, where he established a major station on the Underground. On several occasions, Grimes and his congregation purchased the freedom of individual slaves.

The Union Wesley Church in the city's black community also served as a major Underground station while under the leadership of Pastor J. W. Anderson.

Narrative of Solomon Northup

Perhaps the most celebrated fugitive slave narrative is that of Solomon Northup, who was rescued from a cotton plantation near the Red River in Louisiana. In 1853, Northup published *Twelve Years a Slave,* an account of his life as a free man and as a slave. It was so successful that twenty-seven thousand copies were printed within two years. This portion of his narrative (pages 42 to 44), in contrast to the other narratives, is a story of a man born free and kidnapped into slavery.

The building [in which the kidnapped writer found himself] was two stories high, fronting on one of the public streets of Washington. Its outside presented only the appearance of a quite private residence. A stranger looking at it would never have dreamed of its execrable uses. Strange as it may seem, within plain sight of this same house, looking down from its commanding height upon it, was the Capitol. The voices of patriotic representatives boasting of freedom and equality, and the rattling of the poor slave's chains almost comingled. A slave pen within the very shadow of the Capitol!

Such is a correct description as it was in 1841, of Williams' slave pen in Washington, in one of the cellars of which I found myself so unaccountably confined.

Northup discovered that one of his captors was a notorious slave-dealer whose real name was James H. Burch, who was connected in business, as a partner, with Theophilus Freeman of New Orleans. The person who accompanied him was named Ebenezer Radburn.

"Well, my boy, how do you feel now?" said Burch as he entered through the open door. I replied that I was sick, and inquired the cause of my imprisonment. He answered that I was his slave—that he had bought me, and that he was about to send me to New Orleans. I asserted, aloud and boldly, that I was a free man—a resident of Saratoga where I had a wife and children, who were also free, and that my name was Northup. I complained bitterly of the strange treatment I had received and threatened, upon my liberation, to have satisfaction for the wrong. He denied that I was free and, with an emphatic oath, declared that I came from Georgia. Again and again I asserted I was no man's slave, and insisted upon his taking off my chains at once. He endeavored to hush me, as if he feared my voice would be overheard. But I would not be silent and denounced the authors of my imprisonment, whoever they might be, as unmitigated villains. Finding he could not quiet me, he flew into a towering passion. With blasphemous oaths, he called me a black liar, a runaway from Georgia, and every other profane and vulgar epithet that the most indecent fancy could conceive.

After serving on various plantations in Louisiana, Northup escaped to the North, and experienced an emotional and joyful reunion with his wife and children in 1853.

Narrative of Thomas Smallwood

According to Thomas Smallwood, not much could be done in the way of Underground Railroad activities in Washington until 1842, when the Reverend Charles T. Torrey (referred to as Torry below) made his appearance there. This passage from the *Narrative of Thomas Smallwood*, 1851 (pages 18 and 22 through 25) gives great detail concerning operations.

I had heard of [Torrey's] arrest and trial at the seat of the Maryland government [Annapolis], to which he had gone to take notes of the proceedings of the slaveholders then assembled in convention, at that City, and I myself watched its progress with great anxiety. Although I was not at that time personally acquainted with him, yet immediately after his acquittal and return to Washington, the seat of the government of the Union, I formed an acquaintance with him through the agency of my wife, who took washing out of the house in which he then boarded; through her, I sought and obtained an interview with him. And be it spoken to the praise of the lady with whom he boarded, that she and my wife were the only assistance we had for some time in the execution of our plans. At our first interview he informed me of a scheme he had in view, and besides, there was great difficulty in meeting with teamsters to whom we could make propositions of that kind. We have paid for the conveyance of one person fifteen dollars, for the conveyance of three twenty-five, and for eight or nine fifty dollars, for a distance of only thirty-seven miles. I will relate one circumstance which took place during our operations which will serve to show how much justice there is in those charges before mentioned. About the latter part of August 1842, the beloved friend, Torry, who is now no more, was about to leave Washington for the North, and I desired he would take with him about fifteen persons—men, women, and children; but how that could be accomplished was a question of considerable importance, it was next to an impossibility to get a teamster to convey them at any price. So the only alternative left was to purchase a conveyance; and, then again, there was another obstacle in the way, almost insurmountable, which was the want of money. However, I got over this by the aid of a confidential friend who acted with me in all confidential matters relating to our operations, for though we had great difficulties to contend with, yet there were many things that worked in our favor. There happened to be a huckster who had a wagon for sale that just suited our purpose, and for which he asked fifty-three dollars; the bargain was closed by paying the money. The next point of difficulty which lay in the way was to obtain a span of horses; this, however, was got over by our calling on a teamster to whom we had given fifty dollars for one of those trips before alluded to, and who had a span for sale; although not very good, they answered our purpose. We therefore agreed to give him sixty-five dollars for them, paying twenty-five dollars down and I and my friend becoming responsible for the balance, which was forty dollars. Those obstructions were now overcome. . . .

We had to get a set of harness, and a pole made for the wagon, all which was to be done in one day, for until the morning of the day preceeding the night on which friend Torry was to start with the fifteen, we had strove to hire a conveyance, but could not succeed, notwithstanding those persons had all been notified to meet at a certain place on that night, which notice could not be revoked, therefore the people were on the spot at the appointed time. But we were not ready, therefore we had to conceal them in various places in the City; in the meantime morning arrived, and with it a terrible uproar. One had no one to get breakfast, Ann had absconded taking with her all her children; another had no one to black the boots, to set the table, and to wait breakfast, Bill had taken French leave, and gone about his business; and a third, had no one to drive the coach to church; others were also in as bad a fix, hence a general pursuit was instituted on all the roads leading North, but all to no purpose, for the people were yet in the City. One man, by name Gunnel, had a woman and two children whose husband desired to purchase them and for that purpose employed a gentleman while he was trying to bargain for them, so he would have no more to do with the matter. The only alternative then left for the husband was to seek deliverance by flight, and for that purpose he with another man called on me to see what I could do for him in the matter; after telling his story and stating to me the various difficulties he thought I would have to contend with which to me was a mere moonshine except the getting of a little girl, between five and six years of age; that child was required to set all night by the side of a cradle in its master's and mistress' bed chamber, in order that if their child should awake, she should rock it, to prevent it from disturbing their slumbers. To get that child was the work of its mother, and to do it required some skill and caution. However, she did it admirably; it seemed, as if by special providence of the Lord, a heavy sleep had come upon her master and mistress so that she went into their bed chamber as she informed me since and took her child from the side of the cradle, without a stir on their part, never to be placed there again, to spend a weary night for their comfort, for she with her children arrived safe in Canada, and she is now in Toronto. . . .

Mr. Torry then went to our first place of deposit, procured another waggon, and proceeded North with the people until he arrived at Troy, N.Y., without their owners hearing any thing of them. I received a letter from him dated at that place containing these words in substance, "I have arrived at Troy safe, with the chattels, and am now shipping them on board of a canal boat for Canada, and then I shall leave for Linn, Mass. . . ."

I turned my attention to laying plans for the performance of another; that I accomplished in some three or four weeks after, by sending off twelve or thirteen slaves, to the great annoyance of the slaveholders; notwithstanding there was a terrible uproar about that place, and a reward of two thousand dollars offered for the detection of the person or persons who were thus depriving them of their goods and chattels. But I continued to defy detection, and sent them off in gangs; never less than a dozen. I frequently had lots of slaves concealed about in Washington, who had fled to me for safety when they got wind that their masters were about to sell them to the slave traders, and when the united rewards for them would amount to from six to eight hundred, and a thousand dollars. These then were the times if I was a traitor to my brethren, with which my enemies have attempted to brand me, when I could have made my jack.

But on the contrary, I employed persons and furnished them with the means to purchase food for them until a convenient time should arrive for their departure, and then I would pack them off. For several reasons the entire arrangement, management and setting of those gangs forward, I had to attend to myself, but it was not practicable for me to travel with them always, because suspicion had already pointed to me, and I could not be absent from Washington without its being known; therefore my absence at the time of the departure of those gangs might have led to my arrest, and an investigation, resulted in my conviction. Besides, I was the sole proprietor of the so-called underground railroad in that section, it having been started without the assistance of an earthly being save Torry, myself, my wife, and the Lady with whom he boarded. Torry having gone North the burden and responsibility of consequences rested entirely on me, therefore I had to watch every moment as with an eagle's eye. I generally went out on the suburbs of the city previous to the night intended for their departure and selected the place at which they were to assemble, never selecting the same place a second time, nor were more than two allowed to come in company to the place selected, and that in different directions, according to the advice of Mr. Torry.

Narrative of Harrison Cary

This narrative from Still's *Underground Railroad Records* (pages 406 to 408) concerns an urban slave who was a skilled artisan, a bricklayer hired out by his owner for wages in much the same manner as Frederick Douglass.

The passenger bearing this name who applied to the Committee for assistance, was a mulatto of medium size, with a prepossessing countenance, and a very smart talker. With only a moderate education he might have raised himself to the "top round of the ladder," as a representative of the downtrodden slave. Seeking, as usual, to learn his history, the subjoined questions and answers were the result of the interview:

Q. "How old are you?"
A. "Twenty-eight years of age this coming March."
Q. "To whom did you belong?"
A. "Mrs. Jane E. Ashley."
Q. "What kind of a woman was she?"
A. "She was a very clever woman; never said anything out of the way."
Q. "How many servants had she?"
A. "She had no other servants."
Q. "Did you live with her?"
A. "No, I hired my time for twenty-two dollars a month."
Q. "How could you make so much money?"
A. "I was a bricklayer by trade, and ranked among the first in the city."

As Harrison talked so intelligently, the member of the Committee who was examining him, was anxious to know how he came to be so knowing, the fact that he could read being very evident.

Harrison proceeded to explain how he was led to acquire the art both of reading and writing: "Slaves caught out of an evening without passes from their master or mistress, were invariably arrested, and if they were unable to raise money to buy themselves off, they were taken and locked up in a place known as the 'cage,' and in the morning the owner was notified, and after paying the fine the unfortunate prisoner had to go to meet his fate at the hands of his owner."

Often he or she found himself or herself sentenced to take thirty-nine or more lashes before atonement could be made for the violated law, and the fine sustained by the enraged owner.

Harrison having strong aversion to both of the "wholesome regulations" of the peculiar institution above alluded to, saw that the only remedy that he could avail himself of was to learn to write his own passes. In possessing himself of this prize he knew that the law against slaves being taught, would have to be broken, nevertheless he was so anxious to succeed, that he was determined to run the risk. Consequently he grasped the boon with but very little difficulty or assistance. Valuing his prize highly, he improved more and more until he could write his own passes satisfactorily. The "cage" he denounced as a perfect "hog hole," and added, "it was more than I could bear."

He also spoke with equal warmth on the pass custom, "the idea of working hard all day and then being obliged to have a pass," etc.—his feelings revolted against. Yet he uttered not a disrespectful word against the individual to whom he belonged. Once he had been sold, but for what was not noted on the record book.

His mother had been sold several times. His brother, William Henry Cary, escaped from Washington, D.C., when quite a youth. What became of him it was not for Harrison to tell, but he supposed that he had made his way to a free state, or Canada, and he hoped to find him. He had no knowledge of any other relatives.

In further conversation with him, relative to his being a

single man, he said, that he had resolved not to entangle himself with a family until he had obtained his freedom.

He had found it pretty hard to meet his monthly hire, consequently he was on the look-out to better his condition as soon as a favorable opportunity might offer. Harrison's mistress had a son named John James Ashley, who was then a minor. On arriving at majority, according to the will of this lad's father, he was to have possession of Harrison as his portion. Harrison had no idea of having to work for his support—he thought that, if John could not take care of himself when he grew up to be a man, there was a place for all such in the poor house.

Harrison was also moved by another consideration. His mistress' sister had been trying to influence the mistress to sell him; thus considering himself in danger, he made up his mind that the time had come for him to change his habitation, so he resolved to try his fortune on the Underground Rail Road.

Narrative of Francis Henderson

This narrative is from Drew's *A North-Side View of Slavery* (pages 154 to 160).

I escaped from slavery in Washington City, D.C., in 1841, aged nineteen. I was not sent to school when a boy, and had no educational advantages at all. My master's family were Church of England people themselves and wished me to attend there. I do not know my age, but suppose thirty-three.

I worked on a plantation from about ten years old till my escape. They raised wheat, corn, tobacco, and vegetables— about forty slaves on the place. My father was a mulatto, my mother dark; they had thirteen children, of whom I was the only son. On that plantation the mulattoes were more despised than the whole blood blacks. I often wished from the fact of my condition that I had been darker. My sisters suffered from the same cause. I could frequently hear the mistress say to them, "you yellow hussy! you yellow wench!"

etc. The language to me generally was, "go do so and so." But if a hoe-handle were broken or any thing went wrong, it would be every sort of a wicked expression—so bad I do not like to say what—very profane and coarse.

Our houses were but log huts—the tops partly open—ground floor—rain would come through. My aunt was quite an old woman, and had been sick several years; in rains I have seen her moving from one part of the house to the other, and rolling her bedclothes about to try to keep dry—every thing would be dirty and muddy. I lived in the house with my aunt. My bed and bedstead consisted of a board wide enough to sleep on—one end on a stool, the other placed near the fire. My pillow consisted of my jacket—my covering was whatever I could get. My bedtick was the board itself. And this was the way the single men slept—but we were comfortable in this way of sleeping, *being used to it*. I only remember having but one blanket from my owners up to the age of nineteen, when I ran away.

Our allowance was given weekly—a peck of sifted corn meal, a dozen and a half herrings, two and a half pounds of pork. Some of the boys would eat this up in three days—then they had to steal, or they could not perform their daily tasks. They would visit the hog-pen, sheep-pen, and granaries. I do not remember one slave but who stole some things—they were driven to it as a matter of necessity. I myself did this—many a time have I, with others, run among the stumps in chase of a sheep, that we might have something to eat. If colored men steal, it is because they are brought up to it. In regard to cooking, sometimes many have to cook at one fire, and before all could get to the fire to bake hoe cakes, the overseer's horn would sound: then they must go at any rate. Many a time I have gone along eating a piece of bread and meat, or herring broiled on the coals—I never sat down at a table to eat except in harvest time, all the time I was a slave. In harvest time, the cooking is done at the great house, as the hands they have are wanted in the field. This was more like people, and we liked it, for we sat down then at meals. In the summer we had one pair of linen trousers given us—nothing else; every fall, one pair of woollen pantaloons, one woollen jacket, and two cotton shirts.

My master had four sons in his family. They all left except one, who remained to be a driver. He would often come to the field and accuse the slaves of having taken so and so. If we denied it, he would whip the grown-up ones to make them own it. Many a time, when we didn't know he was anywhere round, he would be in the woods watching us—first thing we would know, he would be sitting on the fence looking down upon us, and if any had been idle, the young master would visit him with blows. I have known him to kick my aunt, an old woman who had raised and nursed him, and I have seen him punish my sisters awfully with hickories from the woods.

The slaves are watched by the patrols, who ride about to try to catch them off the quarters, especially at the house of a free person of color. I have known the slaves to stretch clothes lines across the street, high enough to let the horse pass, but not the rider; then the boys would run, and the patrols in full chase would be thrown off by running against the lines. The patrols are poor white men, who live by plundering and stealing, getting rewards for runaways, and setting up little shops on the public roads. They will take whatever the slaves steal, paying in money, whiskey, or whatever the slaves want. They take pigs, sheep, wheat, corn—any thing that's raised they encourage the slaves to steal: these they take to market next day. It's all speculation—all a matter of self-interest, and when the slaves run away, these same traders catch them if they can, to get the reward. If the slave threatens to expose his traffic, he does not care—for the slave's word is good for nothing—it would not be taken. There are frequent quarrels between the slaves and the poor white men. About the city on Sundays, the slaves, many of them, being fond of dress, would appear nicely clad; which seemed to provoke the poor white men. I have had them curse and damn me on this account. They would say to me, "Where are you going? Who do you belong to?" I would tell them—then, "Where did you get them clothes? I wish you belonged to me—I'd dress you up!" Then I have had them throw water on me. One time I had bought a new fur hat, and one of them threw a watermelon rind, and spoiled the hat. Sometimes I have seen them throw a slave's hat on the ground, and trample on it. He would pick it up, fix it as well as he could, put it on his head, and walk on. The slave had no redress, but would sometimes take a petty revenge on the man's horse or saddle, or something of that sort.

I knew a free man of color, who had a wife on a plantation. The patrols went to his house in the night time—he would not let them in; they broke in and beat him: nearly killed him. The next morning he went before the magistrates, bloody and dirty just as he was. All the redress he got was, that he had no right to resist a white man.

An old slaveholder married into the family, who introduced a new way of whipping—he used to brag that he could pick a "nigger's" back as he would a chicken's. I went to live with him. There was one man that he used to whip every day, because he was a foolish, peevish man. He would cry when the master undertook to punish him. If a man had any spirit, and would say, "I am working—I am doing all I can do," he would let them alone—but there was a good deal of flogging nonetheless.

Just before I came away, there were two holidays. When I came home to take my turn at the work, master wanted to tie me up for a whipping. Said he, "You yellow rascal, I hate you in my sight." I resisted him, and told him he should not whip me. He called his son—they both tried, and we had a good deal of pulling and hauling. They could not get me into the stable. The old man gave up first—then the young man had hold of me. I threw him against the barn, and ran to the woods. The young man followed on horseback with a gun. I borrowed a jacket, my clothes having been torn off in the scuffle, and made for Washington City, with the intention of putting myself in jail, that I might be sold. I did not hurry, as it was holiday. In about an hour or so, my father came for me and said I had done nothing. I told him I would return in the course of the day, and went in time for work next morning. I had recently joined the Methodist Church, and from the sermons I heard, I felt that God had made all men free and equal, and that I ought not to be a slave—but even then, that I ought not to be abused. From this time I was not punished. I think my master became afraid of me; when he punished the children, I would go and stand by, and look at him—he was afraid, and would stop.

I belonged to the Methodist Church in Washington. My master said, "You shan't go to that church—they'll put the devil in you." He meant that they would put me up to running off. Then many were leaving; it was two from here, three from there, etc.—perhaps forty or fifty a week. . . . I heard something of this: master would say, "Why don't you work faster? I know why you don't; you're thinking of running off!" And so I was thinking, sure enough. Men would disappear all at once: a man who was working by me yesterday would be gone today—how, I knew not. I really believed that they had some great flying machine to take them through the air. Every man was on the lookout for runaways. I began to feel uneasy, and wanted to run away too. I sought for information—all the boys had then gone from the place but just me. I happened to ask in the right quarter. But my owners found that I had left the plantation while they had gone to church. They took steps to sell me. On the next night I left the plantation. At length I turned my back on Washington, and had no difficulty in getting off. Sixteen persons came at the same time—all men—I was the youngest of the lot.

There is much prejudice here against us. I have always minded my own business and tried to deserve well. At one time, I stopped at a hotel and was going to register my name, but was informed that the hotel was "full." At another time, I visited a town on business, and entered my name on the register, as did the other passengers who stopped there. Afterwards I saw that my name had been scratched off. I went to another hotel and was politely received by the landlady: but in the public room—the bar—were two or three persons, who as I sat there, talked a great deal about "niggers"—aiming at me. But I paid no attention to it, knowing that when "whiskey is in, wit is out."

DELAWARE

Delaware was the only state in the South where a black was considered to be free unless proved to be a slave. The black population in Delaware in 1860 totaled 21,627, of which 19,829 were free and 1,798 slaves. The great majority of these blacks, both free and slave, engaged in domestic or agricultural work. According to the records of the state of Delaware, the slave population was distributed as follows in the three counties in the state: Kent, 203; New Castle, 254; and agricultural Sussex, 1,341.

There is unmistakable evidence that blacks were living in Delaware among the original European settlers, some of whom were not adverse to owning slaves. In his article "The Negro in Delaware" (page 436) John A. Munroe wrote that the slave trade received first attention in the colonial assembly of 1775, when Delaware acted to ban further importation of slaves. However, the English governor, John Penn, William Penn's son, applied his veto.

By 1816 many Delaware citizens favored manumission of slaves and joined the American Colonization Society, whose goal was to establish free blacks in a land of their own in Africa. Many of these free blacks in America were beginning to present problems to slaveholders, as their presence increased other slaves' desire for freedom.

With total abolition by law barely spoken of, men of various faiths joined together in organizing such groups as the Delaware Society for Promoting the Abolition of

144

Slavery and the Sussex County Abolition Society. Although they were opposed to slavery, the two groups also worked hard to ameliorate the condition of free blacks within the state. Nevertheless, Delaware's newspapers continued to carry advertisements for runaway slaves, offering rewards for their apprehension.

The Underground Railroad seemed to meet a more sympathetic response in the northern portion of the state; the southern portion was distinctly proslavery in economy and in mind. Numerous fugitive slaves swarmed into Wilmington and vicinity, often being instructed by Thomas Garrett and by certain helpers in the free black community. Prominent among these helpers were Samuel Burris, Benjamin Webb, William Webb, Isaac Flint, Evan Lewis, George Wilmer, Ezekiel Jenkins, Joseph G. Walker, Joseph Hamilton, Severn Johnson, and Abraham Shadd. Shadd was a prosperous free black businessman who had espoused the abolitionist cause as early as 1830 while attending the first black political convention held in Philadelphia. He and his family assisted fugitive slaves for many years. Shadd's activist daughter, Mary Ann, was well known for her indifference to danger. When the family moved to West Chester, Pennsylvania, and later to Canada, they continued their forceful attack against slavery. Mary Ann Shadd Carry published the *Provincial Freeman* in Canada from 1854 to 1858, with headquarters first at Toronto and later at Chatham.

The African Union Protestant Church of the Reverend Peter Spencer in Wilmington was also a haven for journeying fugitive slaves. His congregation provided food and shelter to scores of freedom seekers.

An old black named Davey Moore, who sold peaches, fish, and other produce in Wilmington, was an important link on the Underground Railroad route that ran from Wilmington into Chester County, Pennsylvania. He was connected with Garrett and Dr. Bartholomew Fussell.

Much of the success of Delaware's Underground Railroad can be credited to the state's location at the headwaters of the seventeen rivers of the Eastern Shore of Maryland. Many slaves from further south came as stowaways up these waterways and landed in the state of

Delaware where they were given passage to stations in Pennsylvania.

Some of these fugitives escaped into Wilmington, but the prospect of absorption into a protective free black community had to be balanced against the risk of betrayal. Some were transported at night across the Delaware River from the vicinity of Dover, in boats marked by a yellow light hung below a blue one, and were met some distance out from the New Jersey side by boats showing the same light. Others crossed that same open bay without help, as the narrative below makes clear.

Harriet Tubman made numerous rescue trips through Delaware after her escape from Maryland. She described her route to Siebert in Boston on April 8, 1897, including how she made use of stations at Camden, Dover, Blackbird, Laurel, Millsborough, Concord, Seaford, Georgetown, Lewes, Milford, Frederica, Smyrna, Delaware City, Middletown, and New Castle on her way to Wilmington and Philadelphia.

During my investigation of Delaware's Underground Railroad routes, I located stations in Frederica, Smyrna, and Odessa. At Odessa, fugitive slaves often stayed at the old red brick Friends Meeting House on the south side of Main Street, sheltered in the loft under the roof. But Delaware's most important waystation was that of Tubman's close friend and great coconspirator Thomas Garrett, at 227 Shipley Street in Wilmington.

A Quaker, Garrett wore no pistol and carried no knife. Born in Upper Darby, Pennsylvania, on August 21, 1789, he was rugged, was called indestructible, and was spoken of as a humorist.

Garrett had come to Wilmington in 1822. Though he lived in a community that was antiabolitionist and though his Shipley Street home was often under close surveillance, he cunningly operated his Underground Railroad station for years and was said to have helped about twenty-seven hundred fugitive slaves to escape, with help from Delaware's free black community and from other sympathetic whites. Once, the Maryland State legislature offered ten thousand dollars for him as a "slave stealer," and he wrote to the parties saying it was not enough; if they would send twenty thousand, he said, "I'll show up in person."

Garrett worked for forty years sheltering fugitives and pleading their cause. In 1848, after he helped a freed man carry his enslaved family from Delaware to Philadelphia, a court in Wilmington tried him and assessed damages at five thousand dollars.

Garrett was not deterred by physical threats or financial penalties. He told the court defiantly: "I have assisted over fourteen hundred in twenty-five years on their way to the North, and I now consider the penalty imposed might be as a license for the remainder of my life. If any of you know of any slave who needs assistance, send him to me." After declaring that he had always been fearful of losing what little he possessed, he added, "but now that you have relieved me, I will go home and put another story on my house, so that I can accommodate more of God's poor." Harriet Beecher Stowe stated that she used the experiences revealed in the trial of Thomas Garrett as the basis for Simeon Halliday in *Uncle Tom's Cabin*.

On another occasion, a slaveowner from the southern region of the peninsula met Garrett in Wilmington and threatened: "If we ever catch you in our part of the world, we'll tar and feather you." "All right," said Garrett, "the first time I am in thy part of the world, I will call and see thee." Shortly thereafter, finding himself near the slaveowner's home, Garrett boldly drove up to the house and asked for him. When the man appeared, Garrett declared, "Thee said thee wanted to see me when I was in this part of the world and here I am." The shocked slaveowner waved him away, saying, "Go along, Mr. Garrett, no one could do harm to you."

It is reported that if he knew a party of slaves coming north was in danger, he would send his agents to intercept them before they entered Wilmington. His agents would ferry them across the Christiana River, where Garrett would sometimes lead them through underbrush and swamp to the next station.

While Thomas Garrett, Delaware's most famous conductor, was diligently helping hundreds of fugitive slaves to freedom in the North, his diametrical opposite, Patty

Cannon, "put the Underground Railroad into reverse," kidnapping both slaves and free blacks and selling them into slavery. She was a robust, tall woman with auburn hair. Coarse and salty language was her trademark. It is said that she had the strength of a man and could wrestle most men of her day to the ground.

She was born Lucretia Hanly, according to most historical accounts, in Canada. About 1802 she arrived on the Eastern Shore of Maryland and married Jesse Cannon. After three short years of marriage, her husband died a mysterious death. Later she would confess to this crime. Soon after, she relocated to Johnson's Crossroads, where Dorchester and Caroline counties, Maryland, join Sussex County, Delaware. Here she established a tavern and set up her notorious kidnapping ring with an accomplice, Joe Johnson. Apparently she was able to command strong loyalties, as her gang became legendary along the eastern seacoast. Mayor Joseph Watson of Philadelphia was alerted by the authorities that Patty's gang was kidnapping blacks in his city as late as 1826.

In a small room above her tavern, she kept a chamber where she was reputed to commit the most brutal and inhuman crimes, torturing and maiming her victims. Her tavern was referred to as the "Fort of Borgia" after one of history's most celebrated poisoners, Lucretia Borgia. Cannon employed several blacks in the area to inform fugitive slaves that their homes were station stops on the Underground Railroad and allow the trusting runaways to be entrapped by Cannon's gang. Standing today at Reliance, bordering Delaware and Maryland, is a historical marker documenting Patty Cannon's former home and the place of her foul deeds.

Narrative of Jacob Blockson

This narrative is from William Still's *Underground Railroad Records,* revised edition, 1833 (pages 488 to 491). It lacks the dramatic details that distinguish later narratives of escape, but it does represent the incentive to

A wagonload of fugitive slaves arrives at Levi Coffin's. Detail from *The Underground Railroad*, by Charles T. Webber. *Courtesy Cincinnati Art Museum.*

John Jones, a successful black businessman and agent on the Underground Railroad. *Courtesy Chicago Historical Society.*

Former home of Josiah Henson (Uncle Tom) in Dresden, Ontario, Canada. *Courtesy Uncle Tom's Cabin Museum.*

Robert Purvis, president of the Philadelphia Underground Railroad and abolitionist leader. *From the Blockson Afro-American collection.*

**Frederick Douglass, a fugitive slave, Underground
Railroad station master, and skilled abolitionist
orator.** *From the Blockson Afro-American collection.*

Thomas Garrett, prominent Quaker of Wilmington, Delaware, businessman, and Underground Railroad station master. *From the Blockson Afro-American collection.*

William Still, indefatigable agent in the Philadelphia Underground Railroad. *From the Blockson Afro-American collection.*

**William Lloyd Garrison, prominent antislavery
agitator and editor of the *Liberator*.** From the Blockson
Afro-American collection.

John Brown, from a
life-sized oil portrait
by Nathan B. Ontbank,
painted on an en-
larged photograph
of John Brown taken
in Boston by
J.W. Black.

Henry David
Thoreau, celebrated
Concord, Massa-
chusetts, author and
antislavery reformer.
*From the Blockson Afro-
American collection.*

Levi Coffin, the reputed president of the
Underground Railroad in Indiana and Ohio.
From Reminiscences *by Levi Coffin.*

Harriet Tubman, Moses of her people.
From the Blockson Afro-American collection.

Lucretia Coffin Mott, Quaker antislavery orator and station keeper on the Underground Railroad.
Courtesy Historical Society of Pennsylvania.

William and Ellen Craft, fugitive slaves.
From William Still, Underground Railroad Records.

**Thaddeus Stevens,
Underground Railroad
station keeper, served as
counsel in fugitive slave
cases.** *Courtesy Pennsylvania
Historical and Museum Commission.*

Lewis Hayden, fugitive slave and well-known agent in the Boston Underground Railroad.
From the Boston Afro-American collection.

Reverend Henry Highland Garnet, a militant antislavery orator who hid fugitives in his Troy, New York, church and home. *From the Blockson Afro-American collection.*

William Wells Brown, a former slave who became a well-known antislavery agent, author, and orator. *From the Blockson Afro-American collection.*

Still standing at Ripley, Ohio, Reverend John Rankin's former home sheltered hundreds of fugitive slaves. *Photo by C.L. Blockson.*

Sojourner Truth, unlettered former New York State slave. She wandered the land assisting the Underground Railroad and speaking against the institution of slavery. *From the Blockson Afro-American collection.*

William Lambert, co-founder of the African Mysteries and a leading agent on the Detroit, Michigan, Underground Railroad. *Courtesy of the Lambert family, Detroit.*

The Slave Auction by sculptor **John Rogers,** who expressed his abolitionist sentiments in his works. *Courtesy Pennsylvania Collection of Fine Arts, William Penn Memorial Museum and Archives.*

Escape of Henry Box Brown. *From the Blockson Afro-American collection.*

Thomas Wentworth Higginson, prominent Massachusetts abolitionist and author. He participated in the Anthony Burns rescue. *From the Blockson Afro-American collection.*

Salmon P. Chase, known as the attorney-general for fugitive slaves. He later served as Chief Justice of the United States Supreme Court. *From the Blockson Afro-American collection.*

escape posed by the threat of being sold, usually farther south, farther from freedom. It is also the narrative of my great-grandfather's cousin.

Jacob was a stout and healthy-looking man, about twenty-seven years of age, with a countenance indicative of having no sympathy with Slavery. Being invited to tell his own story, describe his master, etc., he unhesitatingly relieved himself somewhat after this manner; "I escaped from a man by the name of Jesse W. Paten [Layton]; he was a man of no business, except drinking whiskey, and farming. He was a light complected man, tall, large, and full-faced with a large nose. He was a widower. He belonged to no society of any kind. He lived near Seaford, in Sussex County, Delaware.

"I left because I didn't want to stay with him any longer. My master was about to be sold out this Fall, and I made up my mind that I did not want to be sold like a horse, the way they generally sold darkies then; so when I started I resolved to die sooner than I would be taken back; this was my intention all the while.

"I left my wife, and one child; the wife's name was Lear [Leah], and the child was called Alexander. I want to get them on soon too. I made some arrangements for their coming if I got off safe to Canada."

Jacob Blockson, after reaching Canada, true to the pledge that he made, wrote back as follows:

Saint Catharines. Canada West, Dec. 26th, 1858

Dear Wife:—I now inform you I am in Canada and am well and hope you are the same, and would wish you to be here next August. You come to suspension bridge and from there to St. Catharines, write and let me know. I am doing well working for a Butcher this winter, and will get good wages in the spring. I now get $2.50 a week.

I Jacob Blockson, George Lewis, George Alligood and James Alligood are all in St. Catharines, and met George Ross from Lewis Wright's. Jim Blockson is in Canada West,

and Jim Delany, Plunnoth Connon. I expect you my wife Lea
Ann Blockson, my son Alexander & Lewis and Ames will all
be here and Isabella also. If you can't bring all bring Alexander surely. Write when you will come and I will meet you in
Albany. Love to you all, from your loving Husband,

                                                    Jacob Blockson

Letters of Thomas Garrett

James A. McGowan's *The Life and Letters of Thomas
Garrett,* 1977, includes this letter written to Sarah Elizabeth (Hopkins) Bradford, biographer of Harriet Tubman.
Garrett's friend Tubman was probably the most frequent
visitor to his house. A conductor who made nineteen
dangerous excursions into the South and never lost a
passenger, her narrative appears under "Maryland." These
letters (from pages 153, 39, and 75) make clear the
close cooperation between white and black workers on
the Underground Railroad.

                                        Wilmington, 6 mo. 1868
My Friend:
    Thy favor of the 12th reached me yesterday, requesting
such reminiscences as I could give respecting the remarkable
labors of Harriet Tubman, in aiding her colored friends from
bondage. May I begin by saying, living as I have in a slave
State, and the laws being very severe where any proof could
be made of anyone aiding slaves on their way to freedom, I
have not felt at liberty to keep any written word of Harriet's
or my own labors, except in numbering those whom I have
aided. For that reason I cannot furnish so interesting an
account of Harriet's labors as I otherwise could, and now
would be glad to do; for in truth, I never met with any
person, of any color, who had more confidence in the voice
of God, as spoken direct to her soul. She has frequently told
me that she talked with God, and he talked with her every day
of her life, and she has declared to me that she felt no more

fear of being arrested by her former master, or any other
person, when in his immediate neighborhood, than she did in
the state of New York, or Canada, for she said she never
ventured only where God sent her, and her faith in the
Supreme Power truly was great.

I have been confined to my room with indisposition more
than four weeks, and cannot write too much; but I feel so
much interested in Harriet, that I will try to give some of the
most remarkable incidents that now present themselves to my
mind. The date of the commencement of her labors, I cannot
certainly give; but I think it must have been about 1845; from
that time till 1860, I think she must have brought from the
neighborhood where she had been held as a slave from sixty
to eighty persons, from Maryland, some eighty miles from
here.

Biographer Sarah Bradford gives the following footnote
to this statement by Garrett: "Friend Garrett probably
refers here to those who passed through his hands.
Harriet was obliged to come by many different routes on
her journeys, and though she never counted those whom
she brought away with her, it would seem by computa-
tion of others, that there must have been somewhat over
three hundred brought by her to the Northern States,
and Canada."

No slave who placed himself under her care, was ever
arrested that I have heard of; she mostly had her regular
stopping places on her route; but in one instance, when she
had several stout men with her, some thirty miles below here,
she said that God told her to stop, which she did; and then
asked him what she must do. He told her to leave the road,
and turn to the left; she obeyed, and soon came to a small
stream of tide water; there was no boat, no bridge; she again
inquired of her Guide what she was to do. She was told to go
through. It was cold, in the month of March, but having
confidence in her Guide, she went in; the water came up to
her armpits; the men refused to follow till they saw her safe
on the opposite shore. They then followed, and, if I mistake
not, she had soon to wade a second stream, and soon after

which she came to a cabin of colored people, who took them all in, put them to bed, and dried their clothes, ready to proceed next night on their journey. Harriet had ran out of money, and gave them some of her underclothing to pay for their kindness.

When she called on me two days after, she was so hoarse she could hardly speak, and was also suffering with violent toothache. The strange part of the story was found to be, that the masters of these men had put up the previous day, at the railroad station where she had left, an advertisement for them, offering a large reward for their apprehension; but they made a safe exit. She at one time brought as many as seven or eight, several of whom were women and children. She was well known here in Chester County and Philadelphia, and respected by all true abolitionists. I had been in the habit of furnishing her, and those who accompanied her, as she returned from her acts of mercy, with new shoes; and on one occasion, when I had not seen her for three months, she came into my store. I said, "Harriet, I am glad to see thee! I suppose thee wants a pair of new shoes." Her reply was: "I want more than that." I, in jest, said, "I have always been liberal with thee, and wish to be; but I am not rich, and cannot afford to give thee much." Her reply was: "God tells me you have money for me." I asked her "if God ever deceived her?" She said, "No!" "How much does thee want?" After studying a moment, she said, "About twenty-three dollars." I then gave her twenty-four dollars and some odd cents, the net proceeds of five pounds sterling, received through Eliza Wigham of Scotland, for her. I had given some accounts of Harriet's labors to the Anti-Slavery Society of Edinburgh, of which Eliza Wigham was Secretary. On the reading of my letter, a gentleman said he would send four pounds if he knew of any ways to get it to her. Eliza Wigham offered to forward it to me for her, and that was the first money ever received by me for her. Some twelve months after, she called on me again, and said that God told her I had some money for her, but not so much as before. I had, a few days previous, received the net proceeds of one pound, ten shillings, from Europe for her.

To say the least, there was something remarkable in these facts, whether clairvoyance, or the divine impression on her mind from the source of all power, I cannot tell; but certain it

was she had a Guide within herself other than the written
word, for she never had any education. She brought away her
aged parents in a singular manner. They started with an old
horse, fitted out in primitive style with a *straw collar,* a pair
of old Chaise wheels, with a board on the axle to sit on,
another board, swung with ropes, fastened to the axle, to rest
their feet on. She got her parents, who were both slaves
belonging to different masters, on this rude vehicle to the
railroad, put them in the cars, turned Jehu herself, and drove
to town in a style that no human being ever did before or
since; but she was happy at having arrived safe. Next day, I
furnished her with money to take them all to Canada. I
afterward sold their horse, and sent them the balance of the
proceeds. I believe that Harriet succeeded in freeing all her
relatives but one sister and her three children.

> Thy friend,
> Thomas Garrett

Garrett recalls one of his trips in a letter quoted by
Harriet Beecher Stowe in her *Key to Uncle Tom's Cabin*
(page 54).

> Wilmington, Delaware,
> 1st month, 18th, 1853

My Dear Friend, Harriet Beecher Stowe:
    I have this day received a request from Charles K. Whip-
ple, of Boston, to furnish thee with a statement, authentic and
circumstantial, of the trouble and losses which have been
brought upon myself and others of my friends from the aid we
had rendered to fugitive slaves, in order, if thought of sufficient importance, to be published in a work thee is now
preparing for the press. . . .
    I will now endeavor to give thee a statement of what John
Hunn and myself suffered by aiding a family of slaves a few
years since. I will give the facts as they occurred and thee
may condense and publish so much as thee may think useful
in thy work, and no more:
    In the 12th month, year 1846, a family, consisting of
Samuel Hawkins, a freeman, his wife Emeline, and six chil-

dren, who were afterwards *proved slaves*, stopped at the house of a friend named John Hunn, near Middletown, in this state, in the evening about sunset to procure food and lodging for the night. They were seen by some of Hunn's proslavery neighbors, who soon came with a constable, and had them taken before a magistrate. Hunn had left the slaves in his kitchen when he went to the village of Middletown, half a mile distant. When the officer came with a warrant for them, he met Hunn at the kitchen door, and asked for the blacks; Hunn, with truth, said he did not know where they were. Hunn's wife, thinking they would be safer, had sent them up stairs during his absence, where they were found. Hunn made no resistance, and they were taken before the magistrate, and from his office direct to Newcastle jail, where they arrived about one o'clock on 7th day morning.

The sheriff and his daughter, being kind, humane people, inquired of Hawkins and wife the facts of their case; and his daughter wrote to a lady here to request me to go to Newcastle and inquire into the case, as her father and self really believed they were most of them, if not all, entitled to their *freedom*. Next morning I went to Newcastle: had the family of colored people brought into the parlor, and the sheriff and myself came to the conclusion that the parents and four youngest children were by law entitled to their freedom. I prevailed on the sheriff to show me the commitment of the magistrate, which I found was defective, and not in due form according to law. I procured a copy and handed it to a lawyer. He pronounced the commitment irregular, and agreed to go next morning to Newcastle and have the whole family taken before Judge Booth, Chief Justice of the state, by habeas corpus, when the following admission was made by Samuel Hawkins and wife: They admitted that the two eldest boys were held by one Charles Glaudin, of Queen Anne County, Maryland, as slaves; that after the birth of these two children, Elizabeth Turner, also of Queen Anne, the mistress of their mother, had set her free, and permitted her to go and live with her husband, near twenty miles from her residence, after which the four youngest children were born; and that her mistress during all that time, eleven or twelve years, had never contributed one dollar to their support, or come to see them. After examining the commitment in their case, and consulting with my attorney, the judge set the whole family at liberty. The day was wet and cold; one of the children, three years old, was a cripple from white swelling, and could not walk a step; another, eleven months old, at the breast; and the parents being desirous of getting to Wilmington, five miles distant, I asked the judge if there would be any risk of impropriety in my hiring a conveyance for the mother and four young children to Wilmington. His reply, in the presence of the sheriff and my attorney, was there would not be any. I then requested the sheriff to procure a hack to take them over to Wilmington.

The following letters written to the Edinburgh Ladies Emancipation Society are published in McGowan's biography of Garrett (pages 126 to 131).

Wilmington, 9, 12, 1856

My dear Friend,
Thy kind note of 6 mo. 26th came to hand by the kindness of our friend, Sarah Pugh—& I can truly assure thee that it gave me a great pleasure to receive a note from thee. Since the receipt of them, I had not known of the colored heroine thou inquired for till the 8th of the month, when she very unexpectedly came to my store. She says she went to Canada some four months since, to pilot two fugitives, & was taken ill there, & is now just able to travel again. She is to leave this day for Baltimore, to bring away two slave children. When she returns, if successful, she will set out for her sister & two children, a distance of eighty miles on the coast of Maryland, near where her legal master now lives. She is quite feeble, her voice much impaired from a cold taken last winter, which I fear has permanently settled on her lungs.

While sick in Canada, the colored man with whom she had made her house in Philadelphia, died; she had left in his care her clothes & ten dollars. His widow had broken up housekeeping and returned to Harrisburg, 120 miles distant—she yet hopes to get all her [assets?] sometime. She told me, if she should be successful in getting the two from Baltimore, & the sister & two children from the eastern shore, she would be satisfied to remain at home till her health should be restored.

The name this noble woman is now known by is Harriet Tubman, & she requests me to inform thee that if the friend still feels disposed to send the five pound sterling to aid her in trustworthy calling, it may be sent to the care of Wm. Still, a clerk in the Anti-Slavery Office, Philadelphia, where our friend J. Miller McKim is employed. She will continue to report herself in the office whenever she is in the city.

The Anti-Slavery Cause is progressing with rapid strides. I think in this country the friends of the slave have more cause than ever to hope that the days of slavery are numbered. The North is becoming alarmed at the arrogance of 350,000 Slave-owners undertaking to rule 20,000,000 of freemen—I never had knew the country so aroused politically as the present time. I cannot *vote* myself, or take part further than cannot be avoided in such a tyrannical government, being a firm believer in *disunion* being the only certain & effectual remedy for abolishing slavery. Should *that* take place, the slaves will soon be free; at least that is my opinion. . . .

Thy friend,
Thomas Garrett

Wilmington, 10–24–56

My dear friend, E. Wigham,

Thy esteemed favor of 9th month 11th was handed to me by J. M. McKim on the 18th of this month, also five pounds designated for that noble woman, Harriet Tubman, forwarded by thee. As I had not heard [from] her for several weeks past, I left a letter at the Anti-Slavery office with Wm. Still, informing her of the handsome donation I had just received for her. On sixth day last, less than a week after I received thy letter and money, Harriet came into my office and addressed me thus—"Mr. Garrett I am here again, out of money, and with no shoes to my feet, and God has sent me to you, for what I need."—I said—"Harriet, art thou sure thou art not deceived? I cannot find money enough to supply all God's poor. I have five here last week and had to pay eight dollars to clothe and forward them." She said, "Well, you have got enough for me to pay for a pair of shoes, and to pay for my own and a friend's passage to Philadelphia." Then she said, "I must have twenty dollars more to enable me to go down to Maryland for a woman and three children.'' She said she had paid her last copper that morning to a coloured man that had brought her, and a delicate female—a house servant— some thirty odd miles in his carriage. I then told her that the Good Spirit had put it into the heart of a kind friend in England to send, especially for her, five pounds, so that she would have enough for all her present wants without calling on her Philadelphia friends for aid. She said, ''I thank you very much. I was sure I could get money from you, but I did not expect so much.''—The history of this trip was remarkable, and manifested great shrewdness. This girl was a slave in Baltimore, and was engaged to be married to a slave eight years since. For some reason his master determined to sell him to go South. A friend very kindly informed him of [this] fact. He went to see the object of his affections, bid her farewell, and left. He arrived safe in the interior of New York, and after being absent more than seven years, furnished Harriet with some money, and she went to Baltimore in pursuit. After considerable search she found the woman and brought her away. She had gone to Philadelphia with the captain of a steam boat, trading through the Delaware, and Chesapeake canal, and had taken precaution to get from him a certificate of her being a resident of Philadelphia, and free. She knew she could not bring a strange woman from Baltimore to Philadelphia, either by railroad or steamboat, without giving bonds in five hundred dollars, and therefore took passage for herself and companion to [Seaford], on the eastern shore of Maryland, in the steam boat and showing the Captain her passport from Philadelphia to Baltimore, and he, knowing the captain of the boat that took her to Baltimore, was on to give her a certificate also.

When the boat arrived at Seaford, she boldly went to the Hotel and called for supper and lodging. Next morning, when they were about to leave, a dealer in such stock attempted to arrest them, but on showing the captain's certificate, the landlord interfered. The woman went to the railroad and paid their passage to Camden, some fifty miles below here, and then came up in private conveyance.

I asked her if she was not frightened [when] arrested. ''Not a bit,'' she said. She knew she would get off safe. And now I hope by this time she has taken the girl to her long lost lover, but the strangest thing about this woman is, she does not know, or appears not to know, that she has done anything worth notice! May her Guardian continue to preserve her through many perilous adventures.

The piece cut out of the Trenton, New Jersey *Gazette*, giving a history of the slave heroine who returned to a slave state and rescued seven of her children and grandchildren is not the person I have given you a history of. I happened to be in Philadelphia when that woman was there with her children. She was also a noble woman. Harriet's health [has] much improved since I last saw her. She now looks as though she might be able to perform good service in the cause for years to come. . . .

Thomas Garrett

Narrative of Alexander Ross

This narrative makes it clear that deadly weapons were very much a part of this dangerous enterprise. Such Delaware conductors as Isaac Flint, John Hunn, Benjamin Webb, William Webb, and Evan Lewis were running grave risks as they delivered their passengers to the Underground Railroad stations in Chester County, Pennsylvania, even though it was a hotbed of abolitionism. Dr. Alexander Ross, the bold Canadian conductor, describes the dangers in his interesting *Recollections,* 1875 (pages 67 to 71).

During the summer of 1859, I was engaged in efforts to aid the oppressed people of the State of Delaware.

On one occasion I visited Wilmington, Delaware, for the purpose of liberating the young wife of a refugee who the year previous had made his escape to Canada from the little town of Dover. I learned that the object of my visit was owned by a widow lady, who had but recently purchased the poor slave, paying the sum of twelve hundred dollars for her. I also learned that the widow was disposed to sell the girl, in fact that it was her intention to take her to New Orleans in the fall for the purpose of offering her for sale in that market, where prices ranged in proportion to the beauty and personal charms possessed by these victims of man's inhumanity. . . .

Returning to the house of my friend I obtained a horse and small wagon, and at twelve o'clock that night drove up and down the street on which the house of the widow was situated, several times before I caught sight of the object of my search. She was standing near a fence, well shaded from the light of the moon. I drove near the sidewalk, and taking her into the carriage drove rapidly away on the road to Kennett Square, Pennsylvania. I kept the horse at a rapid gait until I got out of sight of Wilmington. After four o'clock in the morning I heard the sound of a carriage rapidly following me. Upon reaching the top of a small hill I looked back, and saw a horse coming at full gallop—behind him a buggy with two men in it. I directed the girl to crouch down in the bottom of the vehicle. I then put my horse to its utmost speed, hoping to cross the Pennsylvania line before my pursuers came up to me.

The piteous sobs and stifled cries of the poor slave at my feet, made me resolve to defend her to the last extremity. I had two good navy revolvers with me, and got them ready for action.

Looking back I saw that my pursuers were gaining upon me. They were not more than two hundred yards distant, and I could hear shouts for me to stop; but the more vigorously I urged on my horse. In another moment I heard the report of fire arms, and the whizzing sound of a bullet near my head. I then drew a revolver, and fired four times in quick succession at my pursuer's horse. I saw their horse stagger and fall to the ground. One of my pursuers then fired several times at me without effect. I was soon out of danger from them, and safe with my charge at the house of kind Hannah Cox. After a few hours' rest I went to Philadelphia, where I remained for a fortnight, until the excitement had quieted down. I then returned and conveyed the poor fugitive to Clifton, and from thence to Chatham, where she joined her husband.

Narrative of William Thomas Cope, John Boice Grey, Henry Boice, and Isaac White

Still's *Underground Railroad Records* includes this narrative (pages 481 to 485). It shows that the Underground also ran over water. These fugitives chose to row twenty miles in an open boat in choppy water rather than remain as slaves or take the more traditional but equally dangerous overland route.

These young bondmen, whilst writhing under the tortures heaped upon them, resolved, at the cost of life, to make a desperate trial for free land; to rid themselves of their fetters, at whatever peril they might have to encounter. The land route presented less encouragement than by water; they knew but little, however, concerning either way. After much anxious reflection, they finally decided to make their Underground Railroad exit by water. Having lived all their lives not far from the bay, they had some knowledge of small boats, skiffs in particular, but of course they were not the possessors of one. Feeling that there was no time to lose, they concluded to borrow a skiff, though they should never return it. So one Saturday evening, toward the latter part of January, the four young slaves stood on the beach near Lewes, Delaware, and cast their longing eyes in the direction of the Jersey shore. A fierce gale was blowing and the waves were running fearfully high; not daunted, however, but as one man they resolved to take their lives in their hands and make the bold adventure.

With simple faith they entered the skiff; two of them took the oars, manfully to face uncertain dangers from the waves. But they remained steadfast, oft as they felt that they were making the last stroke with their oars, on the verge of being overwhelmed with the waves. At every new stage of danger they summoned courage by remembering that they were escaping for their lives.

Late on Sunday afternoon, the following day, they reached

their much desired haven, the Jersey shore. The relief and joy were unspeakably great, yet they were strangers in a strange land. They knew not which way to steer. True, they knew that New Jersey bore the name of being a Free State; but they had reason to fear that they were in danger. In this dilemma they were discovered by the captain of an oyster boat whose sense of humanity was so strongly appealed to by their appearance that he engaged to pilot them to Philadelphia. The following account of them was recorded:

WILLIAM THOMAS was a yellow man, twenty-four years of age, and possessing a vigorous constitution. He accused Shepherd P. Houston of having restrained him of his liberty, and testified that said Houston was a very bad man. His vocation was that of a farmer, on a small scale; as a slave-holder he was numbered with the "small fry." Both master and mistress were members of the Methodist Church. According to William Thomas' testimony his mistress as well as his master was very hard on the slaves in various ways, especially in the matter of food and clothing. It would require a great deal of hard preaching to convince him that such Christianity was other than spurious.

JOHN stated that David Henry Houston, a farmer, took it upon himself to exercise authority over him. Said John, "If you didn't do the work right, he got contrary, and wouldn't give you anything to eat for a whole day at a time; he said a 'nigger and a mule hadn't any feeling.' " He described his stature and circumstances somewhat thus: "Houston is a very small man; for some time his affairs had been in a bad way; he had been broke, some say he had bad luck for killing my brother. My brother was sick, but master said he wasn't sick, and he took a chunk, and beat on him, and he died a few days after." John firmly believed that his brother had been the victim of a monstrous outrage, and that he too was liable to the same treatment.

John was only nineteen years of age, spare built, chestnut color, and represented the rising mind of the slaves of the South.

HENRY was what might be termed a very smart young man, considering that he had been deprived of a knowledge of reading. He was a brother of John, and said that he also had been wrongfully enslaved by David Houston, alluded to above. He fully corroborated the statement of his brother, and declared, moreover, that his sister had not long since been sold South, and that he had heard enough to fully convince him that he and his brother were to be put up for sale soon.

Of their mistress John said that she was a "pretty easy kind of a woman, only she didn't want to allow enough to eat, and wouldn't mend any clothes for us."

ISAAC was twenty-two, quite black, and belonged to the "rising" young slaves of Delaware. He stated that he had been owned by a "blacksmith, a very hard man, by the name of Thomas Carper." Isaac was disgusted with his master's ignorance, and criticized him, in his crude way, to a considerable extent. Isaac had learned blacksmithing under Carper. Both master and mistress were Methodists. Isaac said that he "could not recommend his mistress, as she was given to bad practices," so much so that he could hardly endure her. He also charged the blacksmith with being addicted to bad habits. Sometimes Isaac would be called upon to receive correction from his master, which would generally be dealt out with a "chunk of wood" over his "no feeling" head. On a late occasion, when Isaac was being *chunked* beyond measure, he resisted, but the persistent blacksmith did not yield until he had so far disabled Isaac that he was rendered helpless for the next two weeks. While in this state he pledged himself to freedom and Canada, and resolved to win the prize by crossing the Bay.

FREE
MIDWEST

Iowa had been settled as a free state primarily by easterners who were naturally connected to the antislavery cause over the slavery question. Author Ora Williams vividly describes a conversation with John Brown, as it was told to her by a Des Moines citizen, Isaac Brandt, in an article in the *Annals of Iowa,* April 1946:

"The last time I saw John Brown was at this gate," said Mr. Brandt. "As we leaned over it, he took my hand and held it a long time, then spoke a few words of kindness and courage and went on. This was in 1859, in the early part of the year, only a short time before he went on to Harpers Ferry. I had met him on other occasions. It was a winter day, but I was out in the yard when I saw a covered wagon drawn along the rough road with a man walking at the side whom I recognized at once. He halted at my place and I called him to the gate. I saw that he had a load in his wagon and gave him the signal for safety and he understood. I asked him how many, and he held up four fingers of his hand. It was early in the day and he went on eastward with his 'fodder' as we would have said. But in the few words exchanged he showed his passionate earnestness in the cause to which he had dedicated his life. Not far away there were places where he might have hid away for a night or a day those whom he was helping. But it was better to go on to places not so conspicuous.

"How did Brown know I could be trusted? Well, even if he had not met me before he knew it when I said 'hello,' much as we now do at the telephone. That was a pretty well established Underground Railroad signal for all's well. In response, he lifted his right hand to his ear and grasped the rim firmly between thumb and finger. That meant he understood. If he had held up his hand with palm extended outward it would have been different. I do not know how these signs or signals originated, but they·had become well understood. Without them the operation of the system of running slaves into free territory would not have been possible. Not only was the traffic illegal, but in every community, even in Iowa, and Ohio, there were some who opposed. Brown knew by the signals that I was a friend. I went to the wagon and peeked under the hay and cornstalks and saw four negroes keeping very quiet as they journeyed to they knew not where.

"No, John Brown did not tell me any of the details of his plans that had long before seen matured. But he let me know he had plans and that nothing could turn him aside. I learned that the party put up at the next station, the country tavern of Tom Mitchell, and remained until the following day."

Professor L. E. Parker of Grinnell, Iowa, wrote on August 30, 1894, to Siebert that "along this line Quakers and Oberlin (Ohio) students were the chief nameable group whose houses were open to such travelers more certainly than to white men." According to Parker, the experience of the Oberlin students did not come amiss later when they established themselves in Iowa. One of these former students, John Todd, became the moving spirit on the Underground Railroad at Tabor, Iowa, where his home was a prominent station. Todd was associated with Brown in the movement in Kansas and Nebraska. Although Brown and his followers were not men of peace,

to the Quakers they embodied the struggle against human slavery in which the Quakers so firmly believed.

The Underground station in Denmark, Iowa, was operated by a member of the Congregational Church, the
Reverend Asa Turner, who helped found the church
when his antislavery stand forced him to leave Quincy,
Illinois. Slaves were brought to Denmark in any way
possible, usually by wagon, in which they lay on the floor
covered with hay, sacks, or whatever was available.
Several Denmark homes were used as hiding places.
There the slaves could rest and find food before they
were taken to the eastern part of the state, to the village of
Augusta on the Skunk River or to the Ward Avery farm
north of Augusta, the present side of an ordnance plant.

Deacon Theron Trowbridge of the Congregational
Church in Denmark was also a noted conductor on the
Underground Railway. His home was a haven for hundreds of escaping slaves. It is said that once a slave girl
arrived in Denmark weeping uncontrollably because she
had been forced to abandon her baby when she fled a
farm near Kahoka, Missouri, about fifty miles southwest
of Fort Madison. "Any mother is entitled to keep her
baby," Trowbridge said as he strapped on his gun. He
mounted his horse and rode away. Two nights later he
returned with the baby and gave it to the mother.

Deacon Trowbridge is said to have originated the term
"hush puppies," for the corn dodgers he spiced heavily
with strychnine to be fed to the bloodhounds that led
slave-hunters to his home. Trowbridge often voiced his
opinion that the best bloodhound was a dead blood-
hound, because that dog couldn't trail fugitive slaves.

The Underground Railroad operation at Denmark did
not have the approval of all. The Fort Madison *Plain
Dealer* of May 27, 1857, warned citizens who openly and
defiantly aided fugitive slaves:

> To the disgrace of the County and State, Den-
> mark has the name of being a rendezvous of men,
> who occasionally engage in negro-stealing, at the
> same time professing the religion of the gospel.
> Men of less shrewdness have been hanged—have

received their just desserts—for engaging in practices of which respectable citizens of Denmark have
been accused.

The Underground Railroad began in southwest Iowa
and ran in a northeasterly direction across Adair County
to what is now the town of Stuart, then east down the
Raccoon River Valley to Adel or Redfield, thence to Des
Moines and through Grinnell to Muscatine. It is reported
that John Brown supervised this section of the railroad.
Cherry Place, east of the present Iowa Historical Building, was one of the main stations in Des Moines, but the
original building no longer exists.

Runaways were also hauled by night to Columbus City
in Lewis County or to Iowa City in Johnson County,
where the conductors were William Penn and Dr. Jesse
Bowen. John Brown was concealed during his last night
in Iowa City in Bowen's home. From here Brown and his
men were forwarded to West Liberty and harbored at an
old grist mill.

While Wilbur Siebert names only William Maxson as
an operator in Cedar County, other names are now known:
James Townsend, John Painter, Moses Varney, Dr. May-
nard, John Safely, Samuel Yule, Mr. Lundy, and Jonathan Casebeer. The Underground entered Cedar County
from Iowa City. Stations were approximately twelve miles
apart—the distance a team of horses could travel at
night without tiring or attracting attention. A station might
not be used twice in succession, also to avoid attention.
From West Branch and Springdale the route fanned out
north and east. Some of the station buildings still exist in
West Branch, others have been lost during the past 130
years.

All Quakers were suspect because of their opposition
to slavery, but many non-Quakers were also involved in
the system. The Maxon family members were Methodists of Amity, now College Springs, which was the first
town across the border from Missouri. Amity became
known by the fugitives as the "Stop and Start," as they
stopped to rest there after escaping slave territory. Amity
College, established in 1853, was closed for one year
during the Civil War when there were not enough stu-

dents to maintain classes, but during that year college buildings were used to house black refugees.

There was a relay station in Fayette County, Auburn Township, just on the outskirts of the old town of Auburn, now named Douglas. The relay station during the time of slavery was a farm just across the Turkey River from Auburn, owned by a family named Billmeyer. There was a tunnel from the barn down to the river. When slaves were hiding in the barn, a lookout was posted for slaveowners or other authorities in the vicinity.

United States Congressman Josiah B. Grinnell, John Brown's friend, is considered the most prominent station master among Iowa's Underground Railroad workers. Like Brown, Grinnell was an ardent abolitionist. (Grinnell College is named in his honor.) They frequently spoke from the same platform, along with William Lloyd Garrison, Wendell Phillips, Owen Lovejoy, and the Reverend Henry Ward Beecher.

Grinnell had a chamber in his house that he called the "liberty room." John Brown, while on his way to Canada in the winter of 1858–59, stacked his arms in the room, and his company of fugitive slaves slept there. "They came at night, and were the darkest, saddest specimens of humanity I have ever seen, glad to camp on the floor, while the veteran was a night guard, with his dog and a miniature arsenal ready for use on alarm," according to Grinnell's account (page 207).

Other important trails on the Underground Railroad in Iowa began west of Tabor. The line ran east to Madison and Dallas counties and proceeded through Earlham, a Quaker settlement, on to Des Moines, Grinnell, Washington, Crawfordsville, and Muscatine. A narrative written by Herman Cook, who was a conductor on the system, tells of another route that started from Tabor in Fremond County and crossed Adair County diagonally, striking Summit Grove, where the town of Stewart is today. From here one line proceeded east to Quaker Divide, a meeting house sometimes called Bear Creek, five miles northwest of Earlham. The other line crossed the Coon River near Redfield, then went through Adel, both lines joining together in Des Moines.

*   *   *

In comparison with other free states in the Midwest, Minnesota had very few black settlers, although blacks engaged in fur-trading in Minnesota in the early nineteenth century. Dred Scott, the subject of the celebrated Supreme Court decision, was perhaps the most famous black in Minnesota during this period. He was brought to Fort Snelling from Illinois.

Abolitionism was not a household word among the settlers. As historian Theodore Christian Blegan described them in his *Minnesota: A History of the State* (page 237):

> The Minnesota people were not all agreed in their attitude toward slaverey. Most of them were opposed to the extension of slavery, but few were abolitionists. Sometimes southerners came to Minnesota to be at the northern lakes in the summertime and brought Negro slaves with them. In 1860 a few abolitionists helped one of the slaves to escape to freedom, and there was much excitement. A mob formed: its sympathy was all on the side of the master, and only a sudden rainstorm prevented it from tarring and feathering the abolitionists.

Blegan is referring to Minnesota's most widely publicized slave case. A Tennessee slaveowner, Colonel Christmas, on vacation in Minnesota, was stopping at the popular Winslow House in St. Anthony in the summer of 1860 accompanied by his wife and a Negro servant named Eliza Winston. At some time in the past, Winston had been promised her freedom, but the promise had not been kept. In St. Anthony, with aid from an abolitionist, she petitioned for and secured a writ of habeas corpus on the grounds that she was "restrained of her liberty." Her case was heard in court.

Colonel Christmas appealed to Judge William D. Babbitt for help, but Babbitt had been a conductor on the Underground Railroad, helping fugitives toward freedom in Canada. He decided to take the slave to Judge Vanderburg's court, where an immense and unruly crowd had gathered to see if the slaveowner would lose his property. Judge Vanderburg's decision was to set her free on the grounds that her owner had forfeited his title by bringing her into a free state. The decision was in direct conflict with the Dred Scott decision. Most northern judges who supported the antislavery cause overlooked that decision, for they felt that the law of God took precedence over laws made by man dealing with human bondage.

The general public, however, especially those merchants who profited from the slaveholders, became angry and supported the rights of the master. Judge Babbitt took Eliza to his home and prepared for a siege. A shot fired by Babbitt forced the mob to retreat. As more antislavery men came to the rescue with their weapons, they outnumbered the proslavery people five to one and carried the day.

In a few days Eliza was sent to Windsor, Canada, where she stayed for a few months, finally coming back to Detroit, Michigan. There she began to write letters to those who had helped her in Minnesota, asking them to purchase her free papers and give her enough money to take her back to Memphis, Tennessee, where she could get possession of the house and lot left by her husband, and where she would have the opportunity to work in white homes for fifteen dollars a month or else return to her old master's family. The citizens who had risked their lives for her became disgusted and refused to help her. It is reported that shortly before the Civil War she returned to her master's home in Tennessee.

The Underground Railroad was active in Wisconsin as early as 1840. Few slaves came through Wisconsin compared to other midwestern states, but those who did were seldom caught. Strong abolitionist sentiment was brought here by settlers from the East, especially New York. Some blacks were brought into the territory by southern slaveholders, but they were usually given their freedom when they arrived.

In the spring of 1854, the abolitionist spirit of resistance among the most responsible citizens rose to a pitch when the following incident occurred, according to Siebert (*The Underground Railroad,* pages 327 and 328):

On March 10, 1854, Joshua Glover, who was living near Racine, Wisconsin, was arrested as a fugitive slave by United States deputy marshals and the claimant, B. W. Garland, of St. Louis. After a severe struggle Glover was knocked down, placed in a wagon, driven to Milwaukee, and there lodged in jail. The news of the capture reached Racine in a few hours, and a popular meeting, larger than ever before held in the town, assembled on the court-house square to take action. At this meeting, it was resolved to secure Glover a fair trial in Wisconsin; and it was voted, "That inasmuch as the Senate of the United States has repealed all compromises adopted by the Congress of the United States, we, as citizens of Wisconsin, are justified in declaring, and do declare, the slave-catching law of 1850 disgraceful and also repealed." This was but one of many nullifying resolutions adopted about this time in various parts of the North, although most of the resolutions were somewhat less extreme in statement.

At an afternoon meeting the deliberations ended in the decision of about a hundred citizens of Racine to take boat at once for Milwaukee. Upon arrival this delegation found the latter city in an uproar. A meeting of five thousand persons had already appointed a Committee of Vigilance to see that Glover had a fair trial, and this demonstration had led the authorities to call for the local militia to preserve order; but the militia did not appear. Such was now the temper of the crowd that it could be satisfied with nothing less than the immediate release of the prisoner. Glover was therefore demanded, but, as he was not forthcoming, the jail door was battered in, the negro brought out, placed in a wagon and forwarded to Canada by the Underground Railroad.

Sherman M. Booth, abolitionist editor of the *Daily Free Democrat,* was arrested for his participation in the daring rescue. Booth had ridden through the streets of Milwaukee crying, "Free men to the rescue! Slave-catchers in our midst! Be at the courts at two o'clock." Booth was tried and found guilty and committed to jail. He became the subject of a drawn-out legal battle with the government, as he was prosecuted under the Fugitive Slave

Law of 1850. Byron Paine, Booth's attorney, appealed to the state's supreme court, which ruled that the Fugitive Slave Law was unconstitutional. Booth, who had been freed pending the court decision, was rearrested by federal marshals on March 2, 1860, and was confined in the customs house at Milwaukee. He was declared guilty, sentenced to a month's imprisonment, and fined one thousand dollars by Chief Justice Roger Taney, who had issued the Dred Scott decision. After pressure was brought to bear upon President James Buchanan, Booth was finally pardoned two days before Lincoln's inauguration.

Probably the most important Underground Railroad station in Wisconsin was the Tallman house in Janesville, built specifically to accommodate the movement of fugitive slaves, with hiding places in both the basement and the attic and a special lookout on the roof. It was a brick structure with twenty rooms, erected between 1855 and 1857. When fugitives approached the house, a bell was rung to alert the servants and then a signal was given to the fugitives from a large stained-glass window. When the slaves saw the dim light, they proceeded to enter the cellar door that was always left open. The ingenious Tallman led his charges through a secret stairway in the maid's closet and finally through an underground tunnel, which led to the Rock River, where an Underground Railroad agent took them by riverboat to Milton.

Joshua Goodrich, founder of Milton's old Stage Coach Inn, now called Milton House, was a sympathetic supporter of Underground Railroad activities. He provided sanctuary for runaways by digging a tunnel between the inn and a log cabin in the rear of his property. Slaves entered and exited through a concealed trapdoor in the floor of the cabin to be hidden in a secret basement under the inn. Still standing today, the Tallman House and Milton Inn are documented reminders of Wisconsin's role in the Underground Railroad.

Under the provisions of the Ordinance of 1787, Michigan was admitted into the Union as a free state. This state's proximity to Canada made it a principal terminus for fugitive slaves. By 1838, an Underground Railroad network had been established and was in full operation. Levi Coffin, the dedicated Cincinnati agent, is generally given credit for establishing many of Michigan's Underground Railroad routes.

Due to Michigan's long border with Canada, the state soon became a natural thoroughfare for fugitive slave traffic. Windsor, Ontario, just across the river from Detroit, was a major center of entry. By 1860, there were sixty thousand blacks in upper Canada, forty-five thousand of them escaped slaves, of whom more than forty thousand had been forwarded across the Detroit and St. Clair rivers. Michigan, like its neighbor Ohio, held strong antislavery sentiments, since most of its early settlers were from New England.

These sentiments cost some Michigan residents dearly in the Crosswhite case. Adam Crosswhite, his wife, and their four children were fugitive slaves from Kentucky who escaped and settled in Marshall, Michigan, in 1846. Fearing that he might be sought by his former master, Crosswhite arranged with his neighbors to fire a signal shot in case that happened. One fall morning this shot was heard and the neighbors came running to find four Kentuckians and Deputy Sheriff Henry Dixon at Crosswhite's door.

Frank Troutman, the agent and nephew of the owner of the Crosswhites, led the group that had come to Marshall to return them to custody. Troutman and his friends found themselves facing a hostile crowd of Marshall residents who were opposed to their plan. As the crowd surrounded the Kentuckians, Troutman, unperturbed, spent his time jotting down their names and their comments. County officers soon arrived on the scene with warrants charging the Kentuckians with exhibiting weapons in a rude and threatening manner, assault and battery, breaking into houses, and various other offenses. When the "slave-catchers" were arrested and removed, the Crosswhites were left unguarded and lost no time in taking the Underground Railroad to Canada.

In May of the next year, Troutman returned to Marshall to secure evidence, to retain counsel, and to seek prosecution of the men who had prevented his capture of the Crosswhite family. On June 1, 1847, a suit was filed in

the Circuit Court of the United States for the District of
Michigan charging trespass against Charles T. Gorham,
Oliver C. Comstock, Jr., Asa B. Cook, Jarvis Hurd, John
M. Easterly, George Ingersoll, Herman Camp, Randal
Hobart, Platner Moss, William Parker, Charles Berger,
and John Smith. The suit claimed large damages.

On June 12, 1847, the first jury could not reach a
verdict and was discharged. The second trial was held in
Detroit, beginning on November 10, 1848. On December
5, 1848, a verdict was reached in favor of the Kentuckians and the defendants were assessed the sum of $1,926
damages plus the costs of the suit.

In the latter part of the eighteenth century, slaves had
begun escaping through Detroit in order to settle in Canada, and they were often harbored in the homes of free
black settlers. Many of these early free black settlers had
been emancipated by their French masters. Leaders who
emerged from among the black pioneers were Jean de
Baptiste, George de Baptiste, Joseph Ferguson, John G.
Reynolds, William Webb, William C. Moore, and William
Lambert, all managers of the black Underground Railroad in Detroit.

Among the lesser known black conductors on the Underground Railroad who recorded accounts of their secret activities, none were more outstanding in their
achievements than William Lambert and George de
Baptiste. According to historian Katherine DuPre Lumpkin,
neither Lambert nor De Baptiste was a native of Detroit.
Nor was either man a fugitive slave; both were born free,
around 1815, Lambert in Trenton, New Jersey, De Baptiste
near Fredericksburg, Virginia.

Lambert became the leader of the Michigan black Underground, and during the thirty-one years of his devo-
tion to the Freedom Train, he assisted thousands of
escaped slaves from Detroit into Canada. Early in his
career on the Underground, Lambert employed the
McKensyites, a band of renegades who would steal slaves
from their owners and resell them. Sometimes they sold
slaves three or four times before bringing them north.
The Underground Railroad had all types as conductors.
Lambert said of these men: "We used the scoundrels,

but after long debate we had concluded that the ends justified the means."

Later, under the leadership of Lambert and De Baptiste, members of Detroit's black Underground organized a more thorough and less sensational method of rescuing slaves. They devised passwords, handgrips, and a ritual for identification known as the African American Mysteries: the Order of the Men of Oppression. The following account appeared in an article on De Baptiste published on May 15, 1870, in the *Detroit Post*. The reporter wrote:

> Of course, in those days, the greatest secrecy and caution had to be maintained. The law severely punished such as were convicted of assisting fugitive slaves to escape, to say nothing of the yet more dreadful dangers of mob violence in a country strongly tinctured with Southern prejudices. Fugitive slaves generally started upon their long journey at night, and, until they were well advanced toward the Northern frontier, they traveled either at night or in disguise. All sorts of cunning tricks were resorted to for the purpose of concealing their movements. From the Ohio River, a chain of stations, a short distance apart, extended to White Pigeon in this State, whence it was easy to reach Detroit. The fugitive slaves were generally the most intelligent Negroes of the South. Frequently they were nearly white, so that they could, with the aid of wigs, and other disguises, pass as white people. Agents of the Road were constantly traveling in all the Southern states. It was their business to convey passengers as far as the Ohio River. On the arrival of a fugitive near the Ohio, notice was sent to agents on this side of the river. As it was not safe to write in any letter any intimation of the business of the road, secret, and yet open, means of communication were devised.
>
> Under the management of De Baptiste, the stations did a thriving business. De Baptiste's horses knew their business so well that, in the darkest night they needed no guiding. They went straight to the next station, which was at what was called the New England settlement, twelve miles north of Madison.

The New England families of Hickin, Tibbits, Nelson, and Hoyt, were staunch anti-slavery people. De Baptiste's horses, however, were never known to be out. More than once, he had them shod with carpets, and carefully led to the door of the stables of Wright Roy, a noted slave-catcher. On receiving notice of a job requiring the use of a wagon, De Baptiste's wagon always broke down the day before. He would take it to a wagon-maker's shop, whose owner was "in the ring." The wagon-maker would take off one or more wheels or the tongue, and put them in the shop. At night he would lock his shop, and go home. In the night, the U.G.R.R. men would enter the shop, by means of false keys, take out the wheels or tongue, put the wagon together, lift and carry it bodily to the door of Wright Roy's stable, where the horses would be, and start the expedition from there. Before morning, the team would drive back to Wright Roy's stables, where the horses would either have their feet muffled, and be led home, or, perhaps, be lifted bodily and carried home. Then the wagon would be carried back to the wagon-maker's shop, be taken apart again, and the parts returned to the inside of the locked shop. Thus, in case of any arrest, the wagon-maker could swear to facts that would avert suspicion.

The agents of the U.G.R.R. had to be always on their guard. Of course, those who were prominent in the business of the road, like De Baptiste, at Madison, were not only strongly suspected, but almost certainly known by many of the enemies to be engaged in the business of running off fugitive slaves. Still, they were so cautious that such a thing could not be proved against them in any court. For several years a reward of one thousand dollars was offered in Kentucky for the apprehension of De Baptiste.

William Breyfogle states in his book *Make Free* (page 79) that some fugitives had their choice between the long journey by land across the foot of the lower peninsula of Michigan, or the much longer voyage by schooner up Lake Michigan, through the straits, and then down

Lake Huron. Usually, a number of lake captains could be persuaded for a fee to deliver fugitives to Underground Railroad terminals in Canada, but some of these Great Lake barges and other vessels transported fugitives without charge. Researchers at the Detroit Public Library traced the route to freedom from Cass County to Canada (in a letter to C. L. Blockson, April 6, 1970).

An established route through Michigan started in Cass County, the main entrance into the state, and went through Cassopolis, Schoolcraft, Climax, Battle Creek, Marshall, Albion, Jackson and other stations along the route of the Michigan Central Railroad, leading to Detroit or farther north, from which points the slaves could be ferried across the Detroit River into Canada. Grand Rapids was a minor station on the Underground, where some fugitive slaves were harbored in a mission house, which later became St. Luke A.M.E. Zion Church operated by the black community.

The routes from the south appear to have led through Toledo, Ohio, and such Indiana towns as Angola, Goshen, South Bend, and Michigan City. Some fugitives however, were transported by the Great Lakes steamers, which carried them from Chicago, Racine, or Milwaukee to Sarnia.

An account of the fugitive slave network in Michigan could scarcely be called complete without some notice of the kidnapping of free blacks and fugitive slaves. Blacks in Michigan and elsewhere, after the passage of the infamous Fugitive Slave Law of 1850, found it extremely difficult to live in the North. Much Underground Railroad activity was directed at combatting this law.

Many citizens in Illinois were publicly committed to the antislavery cause and the Underground Railroad freedom movement. Furthermore, according to historian Larry Gara, while some abolitionists seemed to find work in the Underground Railroad merely an exciting diversion, Negroes in Illinois took a more sober view of the matter. Free Negroes were often involved in fugitive rescues, and frequently such rescues were attributed in the press to the work of a "Negro mob." Gara concludes that both free Negroes and fugitive slaves had a more vital and personal interest in the fugitive slave question than did the abolitionist, who viewed it partly as an indirect method of attacking the institution of slavery.

John Jones was a free black man who took a leading role in the fight against slavery. Jones's prosperous tailoring establishment, at 119 Dearborn Street in Chicago, enabled him and his wife, Mary, to expand the abolitionist activities they had begun in Alton, Illinois, and establish a station in their spacious home, where scores of escaped slaves were sheltered. Jones's home also served as a meeting place for local and national abolitionist leaders. He numbered Alan Pinkerton, Frederick Douglass, and John Brown among his many friends, and Douglass generally stayed with him when he visited Chicago.

When Brown's caravan of eleven slaves rescued from Missouri arrived in Chicago, they were met by the celebrated detective Alan Pinkerton, who invited them into his home, where his wife fed them. Pinkerton later distributed the slaves to other trustworthy friends of the city's Underground Railroad and directed Brown and his men to his black friend John Jones. With a pistol under his coat, the cigar-smoking Scottish detective later placed Brown, his men, and their fugitive slave caravan on a train bound for Detroit, with the help of C. G. Hammond, superintendent of the Illinois Central Railroad. Pinkerton gave Brown nearly six hundred dollars that he had raised from political allies and faithful Underground supporters.

Among all the methods used to support the Underground Railroad, none were more powerful than the antislavery presses. Elijah Lovejoy, a transplanted New England abolitionist, in 1833 had become editor of the *Observer,* a Presbyterian weekly in St. Louis. His antislavery views became extremely unpopular and in 1836 he moved to Alton, Illinois, near the Missouri border. There, Lovejoy continued to advocate immediate abolition in his new paper, the *Alton Observer.* Mobs destroyed three of his presses, and on November 7, 1837, while guarding another new press, he was killed. His martyrdom helped advance the cause of the abolitionist and the Underground Railroad in the North. Lovejoy aroused the attention of hundreds of citizens throughout the region who had previously been indifferent on the subject of slavery.

Following the establishment of the American Anti-Slavery Society in 1833, the Illinois State Anti-Slavery Society was organized at Upper Alton on October 26, 1837. Its activities consisted of distributing antislavery literature, collecting money, circulating petitions, holding prayer meetings and bazaars, and assisting fugitives. Citizens throughout the state were members of this society, and some were also members of other national and local societies. One of the state's most respected antislavery societies, the Galesburg Anti-Slavery Society, was formed at Galesburg on Independence Day, 1837, as an auxiliary of the American Anti-Slavery Society. In addition to its adult membership, this society organized a juvenile antislavery society to teach children the evils of slavery.

Numerous passengers on the Freedom Line were harbored by Galesburg conductors George Davis and Samuel Hitchcock, who with the assistance of the Blanchards and other families forwarded fugitives through Andover to Ontario to conductors Wycoff Wright and W. W. Webster.

Herman R. Muelder states in his book, *Fighter for Freedom* (page 62), that along the more than one hundred miles from Quincy to Galesburg there were Yankee villages or neighborhoods that would help the escaping Negroes travel north and east through Hancock, McDonough, and Fulton counties. Among the stations that have been remembered are those in Mendon, Round Prairie, Plymouth, Roseville, Canton, and Farmington.

Illinois historian Verna Cooley describes how important the geography of Illinois was in its Underground Railroad network. Bordered by Missouri, Kentucky, and Tennessee, and with its boundaries increased by the windings of the Mississippi and Ohio rivers, Illinois was easy of access for the slave. The rivers served as channels of escape, especially through regions hostile to the fugitive.

The Underground Railroad in Illinois was not a single

passageway along which escaped slaves were forwarded. There were a number of routes that ran northward at irregular intervals. One of these lines extended into Ogle County. Here fugitives were delivered from Sugar Grove to Buffalo Grove, and from these two villages forwarded to Byron. Among the early pioneers in Ogle County was Solomon Shaver, known for his radical abolitionist views, whose rambling stone house was a "safe house."

Fugitive slaves were also harbored in La Salle County, where the American folk hero Wild Bill Hickock was born in Troy Grove. There was a slave station at Troy Grove when he was a boy. From there to Lindwood, the Underground Railroad followed a stagecoach route that ran north and south along Kilbuck Creek. Among the operators were the Reverend George Gammell, pastor of the Byron Congregational Church, Lucius Reed, Charles Tanner, and Elijah Dresser.

According to a study prepared by Emma Scott in 1934, Illinois had five lines of the Underground Railroad, all leading to Chicago or the Illinois River. One ran direct from Chester; another from Alton; yet another from Quincy through Galesburg, Toulon, and Princeton; one from west of the Illinois River to Peoria and on north to Tazewell and Woodford counties; and the fifth from Sparta to Reno, through Springfield, Delavan, Dillon, Elm Grove, Tremont, Deacon Street, Groveland, Morton, Washington, Metamora, Crow Creek, Magnolia, Work Ford, and Greenville to Chicago.

In Chicago, there is a historical marker on Beverly Avenue that reads: "Refuge for Slaves. On this site, then in the midst of the prairie, stood the Gardner Home and Tavern. Built in 1836, it was bought by William Wilcox in 1844 and became a refuge for slaves during the Civil War. Erected by Chicago Charter Jubilee, authenticated by the Chicago Historical Society, 1937."

Fugitive slaves felt reasonably safe once they arrived in the city, for they were assured protection by certain abolitionists and by an activist free black community. On several occasions members of the slave protection network did not hesitate to resist officers of the law and southern bounty-hunters.

Elgin was another center of abolitionism. The Free-

Soil Party received more votes there than the Democrats and Whigs in 1848. The town's founder was on the state central committee of the Liberty Party as early as 1842, and his son-in-law, Dr. Charles V. Dyer, was considered the "president" of the Underground Railroad in the area. Elgin is thirty-eight miles northwest of Chicago and was therefore on the main line from Princeton through Aurora, twenty-five miles south of the lake terminus. Dr. Anson Root of Elgin was known to be an active agent as well as a leader in the Kane County Anti-Slavery Society.

The Underground Railroad existed in every state north of the border slave states and had a particularly extensive network in the states of Ohio, Indiana, and Illinois. The Ordinance of 1787, adopted to create and govern the Northwest Territory, stated that "there shall be neither slavery nor involuntary servitude, in the said Territory, otherwise than in the punishment of crimes whereof the party shall have been duly convicted." It was this feature, introduced into the great ordinance by New Englanders, that frustrated the many attempts subsequently made by Indiana Territory to have slavery admitted within its own boundaries by congressional enactment, according to Siebert. "It is probable," wrote James Ford Rhodes, "that had it not been for the prohibitory clause, slavery would have gained such a foothold in Indiana and Illinois that the two would have been organized as slaveholding states" (cited in Siebert, The Underground Railroad, page 338).

Considering the geographical location of Indiana, between the Ohio River and Lake Michigan, it was natural for the Underground Railroad network to be established in the region early. Indiana had its share of men and women who were staunchly opposed to slavery and regarded the system as an unmitigated evil. This viewpoint was expressed not only by the abolitionists, but by less passionate antislavery citizens.

Among Indiana's residents was Quaker Levi Coffin, the reputed president of the Underground Railroad. Harriet Beecher Stowe's characters Simeon and Rachel Halliday were based on Levi and Catherine Coffin. She also described a station stop on Eliza's journey as "A Quaker settlement in Indiana." Coffin had helped the real-life model for Stowe's Eliza during her flight to freedom, for Coffin's house at Newport, now Fountain City, was on the direct line between Canada and Cincinnati, where probably the greatest number of fugitives crossed the Ohio River from bordering slave territory. Coffin's house was often called the "Grand Central Station of the Underground Railroad."

During the summer of 1983, while on my tour of Underground Railroad sites, I had the opportunity to visit the Coffin homestead. It is a two-story brick house with a basement that was used as a hiding place. The interior has been kept simple in the Quaker tradition. Coffin kept a horse and wagon in his barn constantly ready for emergencies connected with the Underground.

It is impossible to ascertain the number of fugitive caravans. Siebert located 244 conductors in his study of the Underground Railroad in this state. In both Indiana and Michigan, women's societies were formed as auxiliaries, and the Female Anti-Slavery Association, formed at Jefferson in Henry County, organized a Committee of Vigilance "to seek out such colored females as are not suitably provided for, who may now be, or shall hereafter come, within our limits, and assist them in any way they may deem expedient, either by advice or pecuniary means."

At Diamond Island near West Franklin, Posey County, many runaway slaves were helped over the Ohio River and then taken by one of two routes. One route crossed the Wabash River at Webb's Ferry near the southern line of Gibson County and continued up along the Wabash or near it in Illinois to a rendezvous from which friends carried them on to a point near Lake Michigan either in Lake, Porter, or LaPorte counties. There was a place in each county where they could be secreted and smuggled on board a lumber bark owned and operated by antislavery people. This boat was not much to look at but was built for strength and speed. Anyone not acquainted with it would think the boat not fit to venture far from shore. The boat cruised along the shore, landing at different points in the three counties, loading and unloading the freight that was offered but carrying no passengers. The Negroes were kept secreted in the holds until a number were gathered together. Then they were taken along the Michigan shore on up into Canada. The other route from Diamond Island was to a point in Vangerburg County then known as the Calvert neighborhood, thence north to various rendezvous.

Near the city of Evansville was another place where the runaways crossed the Ohio. This was a very popular route as there were many free Negroes in the city among whom the refugees could be easily hidden. A third route was a short distance above the mouth of Little Pigeon. The refugees crossed here by skiff and were carried up and turned over to friends between Boonville and Lynnville in Warrick County, Indiana.

A fourth place for crossing the Ohio River was at a point midway between Owensboro, Kentucky, and Rockport, Indiana. There used to be a little fisherman's hut on the south bank of the river at this point. Two fishermen lived in that shack. They sold their catch to steamboats, flatboats, and coal fleets passing down the river and made good money this way, but their real business was to carry across the Ohio River the refugees that were brought to their shack at night.

A few miles east, at Rockport, Indiana, was another crossing over the Ohio River. The next regular crossing place was near the mouth of Indiana Creek in Harrison County. Refugees were ferried across, then conveyed to friends near Corydon who carried them farther north into Wayne, where they had a host of friends among the Quakers. They were then piloted through western Ohio and on to Lake Erie.

Probably more Negroes crossed over the Ohio River at two or three places above Louisville than at any other place from the mouth of the Wabash to Cincinnati. The reason for this was that the three good-sized cities at Clifty Falls (Greensburg, Westport, and Clarksburg) furnished good hiding places for the runaways. Those crossing at these places were all conveyed to Wayne County, Indiana, and thence on to Lake Michigan.

Ohio was a heavily used avenue of escape, for the right-of-way to freedom led by way of the Great Lakes via Detroit or Buffalo to Canada. E. Delorus Preston, Jr., wrote in his article "The Underground Railroad in Northwest Ohio" (pages 409 and 410):

Environmental factors such as location, nearness to rivers, types of soils along with other geographic conditions, have from the earliest times played most important roles in the affairs of mankind. The importance of Ohio's geographical location can be seen here from several angles. In the first place, the location has determined the history of the Underground Railroad in the State. As far back as 1815, Underground lines had been established, and there is a report of one rescue in 1812. After the War of 1812 soldiers from Virginia and Kentucky, returning home, carried back the news that there was freedom beyond the lakes. Many of the slaves, catching at these vague items of information, made them the basis of plans of escape which, "in entire ignorance of the distance and dangers of the way, but with marvellous faith for which that race is so remarkable, they proceeded to put into execution." Considering the "geographic situation of Ohio, we do not find it strange that the Underground Railroad was established in this region earlier than in most of the other free states.

The location of Ohio made it possible for emigrants to migrate to her shores and settle within her borders, who, because of their impoverished and impecunious condition, could have ill afforded to go elsewhere at a longer distance. These were the "poor whites" who left the slave States on account of slavery and the hindrances it interposed in the way of their success in life. They found the Ohio River a welcome balm, for it afforded no barrier at all, but conversely it served as a connecting link, thus enabling them to come cheaply into a land where free labor was not frustrated by the evils of slavery.

The Ohio River "flowing in sinuous curves from the point at which it crossed the Pennsylvania border to the Indiana line, was throughout almost its entire course an inviting objective to slaves escaping from their masters." Once the slaves had crossed the Ohio River, they were not only in free territory, but had placed that river between themselves and their pursuers. Most important, however, they were in a region where, for the most part, they could find white citizens who sympathized with the fugitives. Because of "its geographical location between the slave states and Canada" and the character of the early settlers from New England and from the Quaker settlements of North Carolina and Pennsylvania, then, the number of slaves escaping through Ohio was larger than in the case of other states.

As early as 1815, there were evidently organized efforts toward aiding fugitives in direct violation of state and federal laws. During that year fugitive slaves were crossing the Western Reserve to reach the Great Lakes ports for crossing to Canada. By 1817 Kentucky slave-owners were protesting over the escape of their slaves in appreciable numbers into Ohio and other free states.

While many Ohio citizens were in sympathy with the effort to aid fugitive slaves, it is probable that the majority were opposed to the Underground Railroad. In the face of this opposition, local conductors and station keepers were prepared to receive fugitives at any time, and they harbored them in houses, churches, livery stables, store rooms, and in all sorts of unusual places. Fugitives were disguised and sometimes nursed through serious illnesses by their temporary protectors.

Perhaps the most impressive account of the relationship between a station master and the fugitive slaves he harbored comes from Levi Coffin (pages 298 through 301):

When slave-hunters were prowling around the city we found it necessary to use every precaution. We were soon fully initiated into the management of Underground Railroad matters in Cincinnati, and did not lack for work. Our willingness to aid the slaves was soon known, and hardly a fugitive came to the city without applying to us for assistance. There seemed to be a continual increase of runaways, and such was the vigilance of the pursuers that I was obliged to devote a large share of time from my business to making arrangements for the concealment and safe conveyance of the fugitives. They sometimes came to our door frightened and panting and in a destitute condition, having fled in such haste and fear that they had no time to bring any clothing except what they had on, and that was often very scant. The expense of providing suitable clothing for them when it was necessary for them to go on immediately, or of feeding them when they were obliged to be concealed for days or weeks, was very heavy. Added to this was the cost of hiring teams when a party of fugitives had to be conveyed out of the city by night to some Underground Railroad depot, from twenty to thirty miles distant. The price for a two-horse team on such occasions was generally ten dollars, and sometimes two or three teams were required. We generally hired these teams from a certain livery stable, sending some irresponsible though honest colored man to procure them, and always sending the money to pay for them in advance. The people of the livery stable seemed to understand what the teams were wanted for, and asked no questions. It was necessary to use every precaution, and I thought it wise to act, as the monkey did, take the cat's paw to draw the chestnut from the fire, and not burn my own fingers. I generally gave the money to a second person to hand to the colored man. We had several trusty colored men—who understood Underground Railroad matters, and we generally got them to act as drivers, but in some instances white men volunteered to drive, generally young and able-bodied. Sometimes the depot to which the fugitives were consigned was not reached until several hours after daylight, and it required a person of pluck and nerve to conduct them to their stopping-place. If the party of fugitives were large they were soon scattered among the abolitionists in the neighborhood, and remained in safe concealment until the next night.

While the fugitives were resting and sleeping, their friends provided suitable wagons and drivers for the next night's travel to another depot, perhaps twenty-five or thirty miles distant. After our drivers had breakfasted, fed their horses, and rested a few hours, they would return home.

Learning that the runaway slaves often arrived almost destitute of clothing, a number of the benevolent ladies of the city . . . provided suitable clothing for the fugitives. After we came to the city, they met at our house every week for a number of years, and wrought much practical good by their labors.

Our house was large and well adapted for secreting fugitives. Very often slaves would lie concealed in upper chambers for weeks without the boarders or frequent visitors at the house knowing anything about it. My wife had a quite unconcerned way of going about her work as if nothing unusual was on hand, which was calculated to lull every suspicion of those who might be watching, and who would have been at once aroused by any sign of secrecy or mystery. Even the intimate friends of the family did not know when there were slaves hidden in the house, unless they were directly informed. When my wife took food to the fugitives she generally concealed it in a basket, and put some freshly ironed garment on the top to make it look a basketful of clean clothes. Fugitives were not often allowed to eat in the kitchen, from fear of detection. . . .

Throughout the nation, some who helped the runaways were important figures in American history, such as United States Respresentative Thaddeus Stevens of Pennsylvania; David Paul Brown and William S. Pierce, well-known Philadelphia lawyers; Richard Henry Dana, celebrated Boston attorney and author; and Charles Sumner, Senator from Massachusetts, who championed the cause of the fugitives, offering no compromise and asking only for liberty for the slaves.

In Ohio, Rutherford B. Hayes and Salmon P. Chase donated time to represent fugitives in court. In August 1892, former President Hayes wrote in a letter to Wilbur

Siebert that "as a young lawyer, from the passage of the Fugitive Slave Law until the war, I was engaged in slave cases for fugitives, having an understanding with Levi Coffin and other directors of the Underground Railroad that my services would be freely given" (see Siebert's *The Underground Railroad,* page 282).

Salmon P. Chase, at that time a young attorney soon to become prominent in the Liberty Party, later became Secretary of the Treasury and Chief Justice of the Supreme Court. Upon settling in Cincinnati, Chase generously contributed funds needed to support the clandestine work, along with such other local professional and business men as Thomas Emery, John J. Jolliffe, and Charles Hammond, editor of the *Cincinnati Gazette.*

In Congress, Joshua R. Giddings passionately appealed to his colleagues to denounce and abolish slavery. Fearless and loud-voiced, he was sent to the House of Representatives from the Ohio Western Reserve. A conductor on the Underground, Giddings kept a room in his house in Jefferson for fugitives. He once declared in a speech to the Thirty-sixth Congress, "Gentlemen will bear with me when I assure them and the President that I have seen as many as nine fugitives dining at one time in my house. I fed them. I clothed them, gave them money for their journey, and sent them on their way rejoicing." (See Dumond, page 339.)

In Cincinnati lived Harriet Beecher Stowe and her husband, Calvin, whose home in Walnut Hills served as a station on the Underground. Long noted for her antislavery sentiments, Stowe was the daughter of Lyman Beecher, president of Cincinnati's Lane Theological Seminary. Her eighteen years in Cincinnati gave her the background for her most famous novel, *Uncle Tom's Cabin.*

From its early days, Cincinnati was seen as an outpost of freedom, as opposed to Covington and Newport, Kentucky, fortifications of slavery. Within the city, many conflicts developed between pro- and antislavery groups as slaves were encouraged to escape to the North and to Canada, in spite of laws passed by the federal government and the state of Ohio making it illegal to assist them.

John Parker, a black conductor, was the owner of a

large iron foundry in Ripley, Ohio. It is reported that he took an active role in removing over one thousand slaves from bondage. Possessed of an inventive mind, Parker was also among a limited number of blacks who obtained patents in the United States during that period. He began his career as a conductor on the Underground Railroad in 1845.

When Margaret Burleigh and Mary Grew visited Ohio in 1855, they wrote back to William Lloyd Garrison and his wife that "here we find ourselves in a thoroughly antislavery atmosphere. Salem, we are told, has the honor to be a place especially feared and hated by the South, as one from which it is useless to attempt the recovery of a fugitive slave." (The quote is from a letter in a collection owned by this author.) Among the most enterprising conductors in this predominately Quaker community was a free black named George W. Lucas. He transported numerous fugitives from distant stations and delivered them to lake ports.

The city of Cleveland was a notorious stop on the Underground. Fugitives who arrived in the area from Ripley, Ohio, and other points often came by locomotive with tickets and written messages to be given to a free black man by the name of Bynum Hunt, who helped them to find employment for a short time around the docks. When the time was right he placed them on a steamboat named the *May Queen* sailing for Detroit, where the fugitives made it to freedom across the river into Canada. Elijah Anderson, another black conductor of Cleveland, is said to have taken hundreds of fugitives to a depot in Detroit.

Alfred Greenbrier, a free black conductor, devoted much of his spare time to helping his fellow blacks by harboring them on his farm near Cleveland. Greenbrier had a reputation as an outstanding breeder of horses, and he was also a member of the Abolitionist Party in Cleveland. His farmhouse contained secret rooms and was a known station on the Oberlin, Richfield, and Cleveland line of the Railroad.

The movement for black equality in Ohio was set upon stronger foundations when Oberlin College opened its doors to black students. Many of the students were antislavery activists calling for immediate emancipation. Some were taught by the fiery antislavery orator Theodore Weld, who spoke against slavery in Ladies' Hall, Oberlin. Most Oberlinites refused from the beginning to honor the rights of slaveholders. John Brown's father, Owen, was one of the trustees of Oberlin College and a station master on the Underground Railroad. In effect, the whole town was a station. In 1858 a fugitive slave named John Price was seized on the outskirts of Oberlin and the news of his arrest spread like wildfire. Hundreds of citizens followed him and his captors to nearby Wellington, stormed the hotel where he was confined, and freed him. Later they helped Price north toward Canada and safety. The case became known nationally as the Oberlin Wellington Rescue.

It was the boast of the people of Ashtabula County that no runaway slave was ever captured within its borders. The following statement appeared in the *Ashtabula Sentinel* on December 21, 1850: "The voice of the people is, Constitution or no Constitution, law or no law, no fugitive slave can be taken from the soil of Ashtabula County back to slavery. If anyone doubts this real sentiment, they can easily test it." The town was known in Underground Railroad code as "Mother Hubbard Cupboard" and as the "Great Emporium." Colonel William Hubbard, an ardent abolitionist who had a large brick house on a corner of Walnut Street and Lake Avenue, was in a major position of authority on the Underground and hundreds of fugitives found shelter in his home. Stationkeeper Hubbard had a tunnel dug from his barn to the edge of Lake Erie so that rowboats could deliver fugitives to waiting vessels whose trusted captains could transport their human cargo to Buffalo or the Canadian shore.

The impact of Ohio's Underground Railroad on fugitive slave transit can be seen from the number of routes in its network. Historian E. Delorus Preston, Jr., described the operation, listing town after town in his article "The Underground Railroad in Northwest Ohio."

An examination of the black communities in the state shows that in nearly every case they were active on the road to freedom. Blacks in Seneca County in northwestern Ohio as early as 1825 were assisting fugitives from the South. In the southeastern portion of the state, Burlington, a small Ohio River town, was an important station, and many of the residents of the town today are descendants of conductors and station keepers. The practice of free blacks concealing fugitives evidently persisted regardless of the danger, so they can properly be called an important link on the Underground Railroad.

Border warfare flared up again and again, with slavecatchers making raids into free states only to be driven back by outraged abolitionists and agents of the Railroad. A slaveowner complained about Painesville, Ohio, "Might as well hunt the devil there as to hunt a nigger!"

Narrative of the Slave Girl and the Soldiers

This narrative from Levi Coffin's *Reminiscences* (pages 606 to 608) concerns the escape of a fugitive during wartime.

Among the regiments that collected at Cincinnati, during the time of Kirby Smith's threatened raid into Ohio, was one from Racine, Wisconsin, which, from the well-known anti-Slavery sentiments of the commander, Colonel Utley, and the men composing it, had received the name of the Abolition regiment. While they were in camp near Nicholasville, Kentucky, a young mulatto slave girl, about eighteen years old, of fine personal appearance, was sold by her master, for the sum of seventeen hundred dollars, to a man who designed placing her in a house of ill-fame at Lexington, Kentucky. As soon as the poor girl learned of the fate in store for her, she fled from her master, and making her way to the camp of the Twenty-Second Wisconsin volunteers—the regiment referred to—told her story, and asked protection. The true-hearted men, to whom she applied for help, resolved to aid her, though the law did not then allow Northern troops to protect fugitive slaves who came within their lines.

Her master soon came to the camp in pursuit of her, but the men secreted her, and he did not find her. The colonel now wished to send her to a place of safety, and two soldiers volunteered to conduct her to Cincinnati. One of their officers told them that he knew me personally, and recommended them to bring the fugitive to my house. She was dressed in soldier's clothes and hidden in a sutler's wagon, under some hay. The two men dressed themselves in citizen's clothing, and having learned the password that would open a way for them through the picket lines, took their seats in the wagon, and drove out of camp about one o'clock at night. They traveled almost without stopping until the distance—more than a hundred miles—was traversed, and they reached Cincinnati in safety.

They came immediately to my house, and were ushered into the sitting-room, accompanied by their charge, who presented the appearance of a mulatto soldier boy. As there was other company present, they called me to one side and related their story. The "soldier boy" was given into my wife's care, and was conducted up-stairs to her room. Next morning he came down transformed into a young lady of modest manners and pleasing appearance, who won the interest of all by her intelligence and amiable character.

The party remained a day or two, to recover from the fatigue of their journey, and during the interval visited a daguerrean gallery, where they had their pictures taken, the lady sitting, the soldiers standing, one on either side, with their revolvers drawn, showing their readiness thus to protect her, even at the cost of their own lives. Not content with escorting her to a free State, these brave young men telegraphed to Racine, Wisconsin, and made arrangements for their friends there to receive her, and I took her one evening in my carriage to the depot, accompanied by her protectors, and put her on board the train with a through ticket for Racine, *via* Chicago. She was nicely dressed, and wore a veil, presenting the appearance of a white lady. I conducted her to a seat in a first-class car, her soldier friends having previously taken leave of her in the carriage. As the train moved off they lifted their hats to her, and she waved her handkerchief in goodbye. They afterward remarked to me, that it seemed one of the happiest moments of their lives when they saw her safely on her way to a place beyond the reach of pursuers. They had done a noble unselfish deed, and were rewarded by that approval of conscience which contains the most unalloyed joy of life.

Narrative of Levi Coffin

This narrative from Coffin's *Reminiscences* (pages 110 to 114) concerns his own activities as a conductor. Born in North Carolina in 1799, Coffin moved in 1826 to the Quaker settlement of Newport, now Fountain City, Indiana, where he kept a store until 1847. His home in Newport became a center at which three distinct lines of the Underground Railroad converged. A southerner from Kentucky, passing Coffin's home in pursuit of his slaves, reportedly said, "There's an Underground Railroad around here and Levi Coffin is its president."

The Underground Railroad business increased as time advanced, and it was attended with heavy expenses, which I could not have borne had not my affairs been properous. I found it necessary to keep a team and a wagon always at command, to convey the fugitive slaves on their journey. Sometimes, when we had large companies, one or two other teams and wagons were required. These journeys had to be made at night, often through deep mud and bad roads, and along by-ways that were seldom traveled. Every precaution to evade pursuit had to be used, as the hunters were often on the track, and sometimes ahead of the slaves. We had different routes for sending the fugitives to depots, ten, fifteen, or twenty miles distant, and when we heard of slave-hunters having passed on one road, we forwarded our passengers by another.

In some instances where we learned that the pursuers were ahead of them, we sent a messenger and had the fugitives brought back to my house to remain in concealment until the bloodhounds in human shape had lost the trail and given up the pursuit.

I soon became extensively known to the friends of the

slaves, at different points on the Ohio River, where fugitives generally crossed, and to those northward of us on the various routes leading to Canada. Depots were established on the different lines of the Underground Railroad, south and north of Newport, and a perfect understanding was maintained between those who kept them. Three principal lines from the South converged at my house; one from Cincinnati, one from Madison, and one from Jeffersonville, Indiana. The roads were always in running order, the connections were good, the conductors active and zealous, and there was no lack of passengers. Seldom a week passed without our receiving passengers by this mysterious road. We found it necessary to be always prepared to receive such company and properly care for them. We knew not what night or what hour of the night we would be roused from slumber by a gentle rap at the door. That was the signal announcing the arrival of a train of the Underground Railroad, for the locomotive did not whistle, nor make any unnecessary noise. I have often been awakened by this signal, and sprang out of bed in the dark and opened the door. Outside in the cold or rain, there would be a two-horse wagon loaded with fugitives, perhaps the greater part of them women and children. I would invite them, in a low tone, to come in, and they would follow me into the darkened house without a word, for we knew not who might be watching and listening. When they were all safely inside and the door fastened, I would cover the windows, strike a light and build a good fire. By this time my wife would be up and preparing victuals for them, and in a short time the cold and hungry fugitives would be made comfortable. I would accompany the conductor of the train to the stable, and care for the horses, that had, perhaps, been driven twenty-five or thirty miles that night, through the cold and rain. The fugitives would rest on pallets before the fire the rest of the night. Frequently, wagon-loads of passengers from the different lines have met at our house, having no previous knowledge of each other. The companies varied in number, from two or three fugitives to seventeen. . . .

Sometimes fugitives have come to our house in rags, foot-sore, and toil-worn, and almost wild, having been out for several months traveling at night, hiding in canebrakes or thickets during the day, often being lost and making little headway at night, particularly in cloudy weather, when the north star could not be seen, sometimes almost perishing for want of food, and afraid of every white person they saw, even after they came into the free State, knowing that slaves were often captured and taken back after crossing the Ohio River.

Such as these we have kept until they were recruited in strength, provided with clothes, and able to travel. When they first came to us they were generally unwilling to tell their stories, or let us know what part of the South they came from. They would not give their names, or the names of their masters, correctly, fearing that they would be betrayed. In several instances fugitives came to our house sick from exhaustion and exposure, and lay several weeks. One case was that of a woman and her two children—little girls. Hearing that her children were to be sold away from her, she determined to take them with her and attempt to reach Canada. She had heard that Canada was a place where all were free, and that by traveling toward the north star she could reach it. She managed to get over the Ohio River with her two little girls, and then commenced her long and toilsome journey northward. Fearing to travel on the road, even at night, lest she should meet somebody, she made her way through the woods and across the fields, living on fruits and green corn, when she could procure them, and sometimes suffering severely for lack of food. Thus she wandered on, and at last reached our neighborhood. Seeing a cabin where some colored people lived, she made her way to it. The people received her kindly, and at once conducted her to our house. She was so exhausted by the hardships of her long journey, and so weakened by hunger, having denied herself to feed her children, that she soon became quite sick. Her children were very tired, but soon recovered their strength, and were in good health. They had no shoes nor clothing except what they had on, and that was in tatters. Dr. Henry H. Way was called in, and faithfully attended the sick woman, until her health was restored. Then the little party were provided with good clothing and other comforts, and were sent on their way to Canada.

Narrative of Margaret Garner

This narrative is also in Coffin's *Reminiscences* (pages 557 to 564).

Perhaps no case that came under my notice, while engaged in aiding fugitive slaves, attracted more attention and aroused deeper interest and sympathy than the case of Margaret Garner, the slave mother, who killed her child rather than see it taken back to slavery. This happened in the latter part of January, 1856. The Ohio River was frozen over at the time, and the opportunity thus offered for escaping to a free State was embraced by a number of slaves living in Kentucky, several miles back from the river. A party of seventeen, belonging to different masters in the same neighborhood, made arrangements to escape together. There was snow on the ground and the roads were smooth, so the plan of going to the river on a sled naturally suggested itself. The time fixed for their flight was Sabbath night, and having managed to get a large sled and two good horses, belonging to one of their masters, the party of seventeen crowded into the sled and started on their hazardous journey in the latter part of the night. They drove the horses at full speed, and at daylight reached the river below Covington, opposite Wester Row. They left the sled and horses here, and as quickly as possible crossed the river on foot. It was now broad daylight, and people were beginning to pass about the streets, and the fugitives divided their company that they might not attract so much notice.

An old slave named Simon, and his wife Mary, together with their son Robert and his wife Margaret Garner and four children, made their way to the house of a colored man named Kite, who had formerly lived in their neighborhood and had been purchased from slavery by his father, Joe Kite. They had to make several inquiries in order to find Kite's house, which was below Mill Creek, in the lower part of the city. This afterward led to their discovery; they had been seen by a number of persons on their way to Kite's, and were easily traced by pursuers. The other nine fugitives were more fortunate. They made their way up town and found friends who conducted them to safe hiding-places, where they remained until night. They were then put on the Underground Railroad, and went safely through to Canada.

Kite felt alarmed for the safety of the party that had arrived at his house, and as soon as breakfast was over, he came to my store, at the corner of Sixth and Elm Streets, to ask counsel regarding them. I told him that they were in a very unsafe place and must be removed at once. I directed him how to conduct them from his house to the outskirts of the city, up Mill Creek, to a settlement of colored people in the western part of the city, where fugitives were often harbored. I would make arrangements to forward them northward, that night, on the Underground Railroad. Kite returned to his house at once, according to my directions, but he was too late; in a few minutes after his return, the house was surrounded by pursuers—the masters of the fugitives, with officers and a posse of men. The door and windows were barred, and those inside refused to give admittance. The fugitives were determined to fight, and to die, rather than to be taken back to slavery. Margaret, the mother of the four children, declared that she would kill herself and her children before she would return to bondage. The slave men were armed and fought bravely. The window was first battered down with a stick of wood, and one of the deputy marshals attempted to enter, but a pistol shot from within made a flesh wound on his arm and caused him to abandon the attempt. The pursuers then battered down the door with some timber and rushed in. The husband of Margaret fired several shots, and wounded one of the officers, but was soon overpowered and dragged out of the house. At this moment, Margaret Garner, seeing that their hopes of freedom were in vain seized a butcher knife that lay on the table, and with one strike cut the throat of her little daughter, whom she probably loved the best. She then attempted to take the life of the other children and to kill herself, but she was overpowered and hampered before she could complete her desperate work. The whole party was then arrested and lodged in jail.

The trial lasted two weeks, drawing crowds to the courtroom every day. Colonel Chambers, of this city, and two lawyers from Covington—Wall and Tinnell—appeared for the claimants, and Messrs. Jolliffe and Getchell for the slaves.

The counsel for the defense brought witnesses to prove that the fugitives had been permitted to visit the city at various times previously. It was claimed that Margaret Garner had been brought here by her owners a number of years before, to act as nurse girl, and according to the law which liberated slaves who were brought into free States by the consent of their masters, she had been free from that time, and her children, all of whom had been born since then—following the condition of the mother—were likewise free.

The Commissioner decided that a voluntary return to slavery, after a visit to a free State, re-attached the conditions of slavery, and that the fugitives were legally slaves at the time of their escape.

Early in the course of the trial, Lawyer Jolliffe announced that warrants had been issued by the State authorities to arrest the fugitives on a criminal charge—Margaret Garner for murder, and the others for complicity in murder—and moved that the papers should be served on them immediately. Commissioner Pendery wished that to be deferred until he had given his decision, and the fugitives were out of the jurisdiction of his court, but Jolliffe pressed the motion to have the warrants served—"For," said he, "the fugitives have all assured me that they will *go singing to the gallows* rather than be returned to slavery." He further said that it might appear strange for him to be urging that his clients should be indicted for murder, but he was anxious that this charge be brought against them before they passed from the jurisdiction of the Commissioner's Court, for the infamous laws of 1850 provided that no warrant in any event should be served upon the fugitives in case they were remanded to the custody of their owners. Not even a warrant for murder could prevent their being returned to bondage.

Jolliffe said that in the final argument of the case he intended not only to allege, but to demonstrate, conclusively, to the Court, that the Fugitive Slave Law was unconstitutional, and as part and parcel of that argument he wished to show the effects of carrying it out. It had driven a frantic mother to murder her own child rather than see it carried back to the seething hell of American slavery. This law was of such an order that its execution required human hearts to be wrung and human blood to be spilt.

"The Constitution," said he, "expressly declared that Congress should pass no law prescribing any form of religion or preventing the free exercise thereof. If Congress could not pass any law requiring you to worship God, still less could they pass one requiring you to carry fuel to hell." These ringing words called forth applause from all parts of the courtroom. Jolliffe said, "It is for the Court to decide whether the Fugitive Slave Law overrides the law of Ohio to such an extent that it can not arrest a fugitive slave even for a crime of murder."

The fugitives were finally indicted for murder, but we will see that this amounted to nothing.

Margaret Garner, the chief actor in the tragedy which had occurred, naturally excited much attention. She was a mulatto, about five feet high, showing one-fourth or one-third white blood. She had a high forehead, her eyebrows were finely arched and her eyes bright and intelligent, but the African appeared in the lower part of the face, in her broad nose and thick lips. On the left side of the forehead was an old scar, and on the cheekbone of the same side, another one. When asked what caused them, she said: "White man struck me." That was all, but it betrays a story of cruelty and degradation, and, perhaps, gives the key-note to Margaret's hate of slavery, her revolt against its thralldom, and her resolve to die rather than go back to it.

She appeared to be twenty-one or twenty-three years old. While in the court-room she was dressed in dark calico, with a white handkerchief pinned around her neck, and a yellow cotton handkerchief, arranged as a turban, around her head. The babe she held in her arms was a little girl, about nine months old, and was much lighter in color than herself, light enough to show a red tinge in its cheeks. During the trial she would look up occasionally, for an instant, with a timid, apprehensive glance at the strange faces around her, but her eyes were generally cast down. The babe was continually fondling her face with its little hands, but she rarely noticed it; and her general expression was one of extreme sadness. The little boys, four and six years old, respectively, were bright-eyed, woolly-headed little fellows, with fat dimpled cheeks. During the trial they sat on the floor near their mother, playing together in happy innocence, all unconscious of the gloom that shrouded their mother, and of the fact that their own future liberty was at stake. The murdered child was almost white, a little girl of rare beauty.

The case seemed to stir every heart that was alive to the emotions of humanity. The interest manifested by all classes was not so much for the legal principles involved, as for the mute instincts that mold every human heart—the undying love of freedom that is planted in every breast—the resolve to die rather than submit to a life of degradation and bondage.

A number of people, who were deeply interested in the fugitives, visited them in prison and conversed with them. Old Simon, his wife Mary, and their son Robert, while expressing their longing for freedom, said that they should not attempt to kill themselves if they were returned to slavery. . . .

But in spite of touching appeals, of eloquent pleadings, the Commissioner remanded the fugitives back to slavery. He said that it was not a question of feeling to be decided by the chance current of his sympathies; the law of Kentucky and of the United States made it a question of property. . . .

Margaret, her husband, and her youngest child were hurriedly sent off to the South. However, before reaching her destination she was involved in an accident aboard a sailing vessel. *The Liberator,* March 11, 1856, provides us with the following information:

When the accident occurred . . . ironed by coffles . . . they were heard calling for help and to be relieved of their handcuffs. Margaret had her child in her arms; but by the shock of the boat that came to the assistance of the Lewis, she was thrown into the river with her child. A black man and the cook on the Lewis sprang into the river, and saved Magaret who, it is said, displayed frantic joy when told that her child had drowned, and said she would never reach alive Ganies' Landing, the point to which she was shipped—thus indicating her intention to drown herself.

This account of her destination slightly differs from the account in the Philadelphia *Press,* March 14, 1870, which states that the couple were being shipped to New Orleans. According to this article, Robert and his wife hired themselves out in New Orleans until they were taken to Tennessee Landing, Mississippi, where they were sold to Judge Bonham and forced to labor on his plantation. Robert is quoted as saying that Margaret died in 1858 of typhoid fever. Her last words to her husband were never to marry again in slavery, but to live in hope of freedom, which she believed would come soon in some way. The account was reprinted from the Cincinnati *Chronicle*. Evidently Robert was then living in that city.

Narrative of Caroline Quarreles

John N. Davidson gives this account of the story of Caroline Quarreles (in some accounts spelled Quarles), one of the most celebrated in the annals of the Wisconsin Underground Railroad. Lyman Goodnow, born in Massachusetts, was a known agent on the Underground Railroad in Waukesha. He was eighty when he gave his account of the escape.

In the summer of 1842, a slave girl named Caroline escaped from St. Louis. She was so white that she went openly by steamboat to Alton, Illinois, mingling freely and unsuspectedly with some white girls who were on their way to an academy or school of some kind in Alton. There a colored man suspected her of being a fugitive, told her it was not safe to stay in Alton, and got her started by stage for Milwaukee. Before leaving her master's home Caroline became possessed— honorably, let us hope, but not take the trouble to ask—of one hundred dollars. A silver key unlocks many doors, and she got to Milwaukee. Here she found friends. Her pursuers also found helpers, one of whom was a Negro barber who, for a time, sheltered Caroline, but agreed to betray her. His treachery was baffled by a colored boy. An attorney, H. N. Wells, who had been approached by Caroline's pursuers, gave warning that they were in town. At night Asahel Finch, for many years a prominent attorney of Milwaukee, and a leading man in Plymouth Church, took the girl across the Milwaukee River. She was hidden all the next day under a hogshead, or something of the sort, near (what is now) Grand Avenue. Thence she was taken to the home of Samuel Brown. He took her to the home of Samuel Daugherty, a Baptist brother, living northward of Pewaukee. Thence she was taken by Ezra Mendall to Deacon Allen Clinton's near Prairieville. All this time a reward of three hundred dollars, a great sum for those days, was hanging over her head. So sure were her pursuers that she was somewhere in Prairieville that they watched the house of Rev. O. F. Curtis all one night.

Prairieville was then, in proslavery parlance, an "abolition hole." Of those who gave it that character none was more determined than Deacon Ezra Mendall of the Congregational Church. In something more than slang, though the words sound like it, he might be described as a "holy terror." He was a man of fervent piety, unflinching courage, and great physical strength. Before his conversion he had been, it is said, something of a pugilistic fighter. To him and to Lyman Goodnow, of the same church, was entrusted the duty of taking Caroline to a place of safety. They did not know where their journey would end. It proved to be one of thirty miles, and was made, of course, in the night. Conscientious scruples about keeping the Sabbath did not prevent these men from starting on a Sunday evening. At the first place to which they took Caroline, the home of a farmer, it was impossible to keep her, for the threshers were expected during the coming day.

The Reverend Solomon Ashley continues the tale:

Early of an August morning in the year 1842, a loud rap was heard on our door at Spring Prairie, Walworth County. I at once arose, and, upon opening the door, was accosted by Deacon Ezra Mendall, of Waukesha, and two associates, with a slave girl, apparently about eighteen years old, of fine figure and light yellow complexion. They said to me: "We have work here for you. This girl is hotly pursued, and a large reward is offered, and many are out hunting for her. We wish you to conceal her to-day, and to-night remove her to another place so that she cannot be tracked. We will come in a few days and take her. We must leave at once to avoid being seen here by daylight.''

As they rose to leave, the poor girl, looking at them anxiously, and with an expression of terror that I can never forget, inquired: "Are you leaving me with friends? Am I safe here?" Giving her an affirmative answer, they took leave.

This done, they were returning homeward when Mr. Goodnow, moving his feet in the straw with which the bottom of the wagon bed was covered, found therein a big butcher-knife. "Deacon, what's this?" "Oh," was the answer, "it's something I brought along to pick my teeth with." "You can guess," adds Mr. Goodnow, "what he intended to do if any one had attempted to capture us."

The girl was concealed during the day, and the following night was placed in care of Deacon J.C.P., at Gardner's Prairie. . . .

Accordingly, the Abolitionists who knew of the case made up a purse for traveling expenses, and sent Mr. Goodnow to take the fugitive to Canada. Others besides the friends at Waukesha interested themselves effectively in the same way. Among these were Dr. Edward G. Dyer and Rev. W. R. Manning, a Baptist clergyman. A minister of the Disciple denomination named Fitch accompanied Goodnow and Caroline into Illinois. "I was steering," says Mr. Goodnow, "for the house of a man named Russell, who was a Methodist, though not an Abolitionist. . . . but he was more than willing to assist any human being to freedom. If that was being an Abolitionist, he was one. [After a perilous journey of five weeks, Caroline crossed the Detroit River into Canada.]

FREE
MIDDLE
ATLANTIC

Antebellum Pennsylvania was a hub of the nationwide escape routes for several geographic and historical reasons. Unlike other states immediately north of the Mason-Dixon line, Pennsylvania had an international port at Philadelphia that was a natural meeting place for boats traveling north from Virginia, Maryland, and Delaware. At the busy Philadelphia port, there was a constant traffic of foreigners as well as indigenous blacks and whites. Thus fugitives and their helpers could blend into this cosmopolitan atmosphere with relative ease. Also, the Blue Mountains traverse south central Pennsylvania. Once runaways crossed this hazardous and unfamiliar terrain, the mountains proved to be a natural fortress that protected them from slave-catchers.

Smaller than Philadelphia, yet rich in churches and self-help institutions, were the free black communities of such cities as Lancaster, Carlisle, Meadville, and Pittsburgh. In western Pennsylvania, the Monongahela River was a main waterway from the South to Pittsburgh, and in the northwest Erie was a focal point for travel into Canada, either across the lake or up the shore to Niagara.

It took nearly sixty years from the foundation of the Pennsylvania Abolition Society in 1775 to the beginnings of organized Underground activity. The onset of antislav-

203

ery activity and fugitive aid in 1833 coincided with the beginnings of educational and social self-improvement movements in the black community in Pennsylvania. The leadership of the associated reform organizations was invariably composed of black abolitionists.

Black communities in Pennsylvania, especially in south-eastern Pennsylvania, outstripped all others in the United States in fostering black improvement. Nearly half of the adult black population of Lancaster, York, West Chester, Harrisburg, Columbia, Gettysburg, Chester, and Phila-delphia, for example, held membership in mutual-aid and self-help organizations during the 1840s. Philadelphia was the "antebellum capital" of America's northern free black population.

In 1837 the Pennsylvania Anti-Slavery Society was organized to coordinate the establishment of juvenile and adult antislavery societies in all parts of Pennsylva-nia. But even this society emphasized agitation against slavery to the neglect of fugitive aid, which irritated black abolitionists. By December 1840 the Pennsylvania Anti-Slavery Society, dominated by white abolitionists, had appointed a committee "to inquire into the cause of the diminution of interest among the colored people in re-spect to association with us."

It was not until the enactment of the Fugitive Slave Law of 1850 that the antislavery societies began to real-ize the practical value of helping escaping slaves. By 1852 the policies of the Pennsylvania Anti-Slavery Soci-ety had evolved sufficiently for it to coordinate the pass-ing along of fugitive slaves.

One of the popular versions of how the Underground Railroad got its name comes from Pennsylvania. Al-though he concedes that it is unverified, historian Robert C. Smedley relates it in his work on Chester County (page 25):

> In the early part of the Underground Railroad slaves were hunted and tracked as far as Columbia, Lancaster County. There pursuers lost all trace of them. The most scrutinizing inquiries, the most vig-orous search, failed to educe any knowledge of them. These pursuers seemed to have reached an

abyss, beyond which they could not see, the depths of which they could not fathom, and in their bewilderment and discomfiture they declared that "There must be an underground railroad somewhere." This gave origin to the term by which this secret passage from bondage to freedom was designated ever after.

Although there was a relatively substantial abolitionist segment in the Pennsylvania population, many of the state's whites felt toward free blacks and slaves much as did southern racists. But the majority of white Pennsylvanians were simply apathetic about the plight of blacks. Much Railroad activity went on in full view of whites who weren't supporters but didn't care enough to notify the authorities.

Even within the Underground Railroad, bigotry was a problem. Fugitives were frequently banned from entering the homes of conductors, or were forced to eat in a designated area. Shackles were sometimes put on slaves to control them while they were in conductor's homes, and spies of both races would sometimes sell out escaped slaves.

White churches, on the whole, did not participate in aid to fugitives. Indeed, they were often hostile to runaways. Most black churches, on the other hand, offered extensive assistance.

Thus, one cannot make the generalization that Pennsylvania was "friendly to the Negro." The immense burden of antislavery work and fugitive aid was carried by a relatively small contingent of citizens.

The Quakers have long enjoyed the reputation of having been the most active in the Underground Railroad. Various sources, however, belie this image; only a small minority of this religious community raised their voices against slavery and participated in the struggles to transport slaves to freedom.

The Reverend Samuel Ringgold Ward, a former fugitive slave, said, "They will give us good advice, they will aid in giving partial education—but never a Quaker school, beside their own children. Whatever they do for us savors of pity, and is done at arm's length" (see Quarles, page 172).

In fact, the Quaker majority were extremely uncomfortable with members who were active in the antislavery movement, and took both official and unofficial measures against activists. The Hicksites, a splinter group which named itself after Elijah Hicks, left the Society of Friends over this issue. However, even Quakers who deplored the Underground Railroad activities of their members did not betray fugitive slaves who sought their assistance.

The flights to freedom actually began before the Underground Railroad was known by that name. George Washington wrote in 1786 about fugitive slaves in Philadelphia "which a Society of Quakers in the city (formed for such purposes) have attempted to liberate." Washington, a slaveholder himself, was probably referring to the Pennsylvania Abolition Society, which included among its members at various times such non-Quakers as Benjamin Franklin, Thomas Paine, Dr. Benjamin Rush, and the Marquis de Lafayette.

The Constitution of the United States contained the genesis of the first Fugitive Slave Law, passed by Congress in 1793, which placed a fine on anyone rescuing, harboring, or hindering the arrest of a fugitive. This law was rendered ineffective by a decision of the U.S. Supreme Court in *Prigg vs. Pennsylvania* in 1842.

In the Prigg case, a fugitive from Maryland, Mary Morgan, had been seized in Pennsylvania by Edward Prigg, an agent of her owner. Prigg hadn't bothered to get a warrant for her arrest, believing himself within the rights conferred by the Fugitive Slave law of 1793.

However, the operators of the Underground Railroad had him arrested under the state law against kidnapping. He appealed to the U.S. Supreme Court, which ruled that the master need not be restrained by state laws from seizing his slaves, but that the state was not required to waive its laws or lend a hand. Therefore, it upheld his conviction under the state's kidnapping law.

Such early Philadelphia advocates of manumission as Francis D. Pastorius, Anthony Benezet, and George Bryant were all dead when the tracks of the Underground were laid by a new breed of fiery abolitionists. Yet it was they who first popularized and lobbied for total abolition in the white community.

Philadelphia's black community, as early as 1787, formed the Free African Society, an organization for mutual aid. Out of this society grew two important churches: the African Methodist Episcopal Church or "Mother Bethel," and the African Church of St. Thomas. These two churches became the centers of spiritual and political life in the antebellum black community of Philadelphia.

The churches' pastors, Richard Allen and Absalom Jones, were steadfast friends of the Underground Railroad. Allen's church, Mother Bethel, hid hundreds of slaves. Bishop Allen and his wife, Sarah, received fugitive slaves in their home, provided them with the necessary assistance, and rescued them from slave-hunters.

By the 1830s many of the black clergy in Philadelphia permitted abolitionists and fugitive aid meetings and activities in their buildings, and even joined these efforts themselves. For example, on April 16, 1838, the Zoar A.M.E. Church in Northern Liberties held a public meeting to solicit contributions and increase membership for the Vigilant [Fugitive Aid] Association and Committee. The Reverend Walter Proctor, an agent on the Underground Railroad and pastor of Mother Bethel Church, belonged to the Philadelphia Vigilance Committee. The Reverends Stephen H. Gloucester of the Central Presbyterian Church of Color, Daniel Scott of the Union Baptist Church, William Douglass, and Charles L. Gardiner all had an Underground connection in the city. Campbell African Methodist Church also established a reputation for helping escaped slaves. The Reverend John T. Moore, pastor of the Wesley African Methodist Episcopal Church, offered his church as a temporary headquarters for fugitives. Pastor Moore was born a slave, and his freedom was procured through the courageous efforts of his mother, who ran away from her owner and carried her son with her. Ministers were also instrumental in helping to organize the Free Produce Movement, by which concerned citizens throughout the North were urged to refrain from using the products of slave labor.

In general, black churchmen realized that organized assistance to fugitives and the overthrow of slavery directly challenged the prevailing religious dogma of many white churches that a truly religious person was one who was patient, even with slaveholders.

A veteran of the Revolutionary War, James Forten, was one of Philadelphia's most influential black residents. He established a successful business manufacturing sails, and his wealth exceeded one hundred thousand dollars. Active in numerous political causes, his commitment to the abolitionist movement was indicated by his contacts with William Lloyd Garrison and others. In fact Forten is given credit for convincing Garrison that African colonization was evil. When Garrison launched his newspaper, the *Liberator,* Forten encouraged him and contributed a considerable amount of money toward its publication.

Forten's daughter Harriet was one of the founders, in 1833, of the Female Anti-Slavery Society in Philadelphia. She married Robert Purvis, "president" of the Philadelphia Underground Railroad. Purvis, who might have passed as white, was of English, African, and Jewish extraction. His wealthy parents sent him at an early age to Philadelphia from Charleston, South Carolina. His knowledge of the antislavery movement was stimulated by his father, William Purvis, a native of Ross Country in Northumberland, England. Robert Purvis and his two brothers were brought to the North by their parents in 1819. His mother was a free-born woman of Charleston, South Carolina. "William Purvis, though resident in a slave state, was never a slaveholder, but was heartily an Abolitionist in principle," according to Still (page 711). Robert Purvis's inclination to join the crusade for slave freedom was confirmed in 1830 while attending Amherst College, where he met William Lloyd Garrison. The two men formed a warm and close friendship that lasted throughout their lives.

In 1833, Purvis became a charter member of the American Anti-Slavery Society and later served as president and vice president of both the Philadelphia Vigilance Committee and the Pennsylvania Anti-Slavery Society, organized in Harrisburg. For decades, Purvis was the only black member of the Pennsylvania Abolition Society. In 1838, he published his famous *Appeal of Forty Thousand Citizens, Threatened with Disfranchisement,*

To the People of Pennsylvania, when the state's legislature enacted a law depriving blacks of the right to vote.

In the home of their mother, Harriet Judah Purvis, at Ninth and Lombard streets, Purvis and his brother, Joseph, sheltered numerous fugitive slaves. When the two brothers inherited a large sum of money, they moved their families to a sprawling farm in Byberry, Bucks County, some fifteen miles from the city, where they used their large home and barn as a temporary shelter for fugitive slaves.

Underground Railroad lore provides modern readers with a vast amount of information on Robert Purvis; however, little is said of his brother, Joseph, who died at an early age. He also married one of James Forten's daughters, Sarah Louise, who was known for her literary talents and antislavery commitment. A short but revealing account of his Underground activities has been transmitted to us by the black agent William Whipper, as recorded by Still (page 738):

> The history of this brave and noble effort of Purvis, in rescuing a fellow being from the jaws of slavery, has been handed down, in Columbia, to a generation that was born since that event has transpired. He always exhibited the same devotion and manly daring in the cause of the flying bondman that inspirited his youthful ardor in behalf of freedom. The youngest of a family distinguished for their devotion to freedom, he was without superiors in the trying hour of battle. Like John Brown, he often discarded theories, but was eminently practical.

Robert Purvis said that he destroyed many of his records of the Vigilance Association of Philadelphia because he feared that its members might be prosecuted or those whom the committee assisted might be recaptured. Although Purvis's large home was demolished many years ago, his barn still offers evidence of its Underground Railroad history.

William Still, secretary of the Philadelphia Vigilance

Committee and Purvis's friend, wisely hid the committee's papers in the loft of a building that stood on the grounds of the Lebanon Cemetery. Still declared later that he kept the records to help him reunite relatives and friends. According to Still's journal, the committee assisted approximately 495 runaway slaves between December 1852 and February 1857. When he published his classic book covering eight years of assistance, he recorded accounts of approximately 800 escaped slaves, including 60 children, who had received aid from the committee.

As a deterrant against infiltration, Still and his co-workers in the Anti-Slavery Office rigidly questioned all escaped slaves and strangers who came to them for assistance. The Underground Railroad had to be protected from spies and imposters who would expose its secret operation for fame or money.

One of those questioned presumably was Mrs. Ellen Wells, a former slave from St. Louis, who later traveled throughout the nation soliciting money to purchase her mother, her children, and several other relatives from bondage. Upon leaving Philadelphia she traveled to Boston and, in that city, secured funds from religious conventions, members of the legislature, and other sources. When a prominent Boston abolitionist wrote for information about her, William Still answered that the woman was an imposter and a prostitute. Still's letter accidentally was given to Mrs. Wells, who immediately made a copy of it and sued Still for scandalous and malicious libel. Still pleaded guilty to having written the letter, while offering proof of his character. Nevertheless, the court sentenced him to ten days in prison and fined him one hundred dollars. A large number of his friends within the city and across the country expressed public sympathy for him, and Still's antislavery friends in Boston paid his fine from the treasury of the Massachusetts Anti-Slavery Society.

In August 1835, the more militant black and white abolitionists created the Philadelphia Vigilance Association "to fund aid to colored persons in distress." The association elected three black officers at its initial meeting: James McCrummel, president; Jacob C. White, secretary; and James Needham, treasurer. A few weeks later, it chose Charles Atkins, also a black, as the author-ized agent to solicit funds for the association. Philadel-phia's black community figured prominently in the formation and activities of the association. It is recorded that a secret room with a trapdoor was used by association members to hide fugitive slaves.

The minute books of the Philadelphia Vigilance Com-mittee for the period from 1839 to 1854 are recordings of more than meetings; each is a case book of its opera-tions as well. An example: one record of cases includes: "No. 10, July 17th, Man from Eastern Shore of Myd. Sent to P-S, Willow G[rove] expense 50 cts reported by Healy . . . No. 15, Woman from Del. reported J. G. Bias, sent to N.Y."

The Vigilance Committee of Philadelphia assisted des-titute fugitives by providing board and room, clothing, medicine, and money. It informed fugitives of their legal rights, gave them legal protection from kidnappers, and frequently prosecuted individuals who attempted to ab-duct, sell, or violate the legal rights of free blacks. More-over, it helped runaways set up permanent homes or gave them temporary employment before their departure to Canada. It send fugitives to the North via other con-tacts with the Vigilance Committee of New York, with which it maintained a close working relationship.

At every juncture of its history, a majority of the offi-cers of the Vigilance Association were black. In 1839, for example, nine of the sixteen members of the Vigilance Committee were black, including McCrummel, White, Needham, James Gibbons, Daniel Colly, J. J. G. Bias, Shephert Shay, and Stephen H. Gloucester. Other blacks included William Still, Robert Purvis, Charles H. Bustill, Charles Reason, and Joseph C. Ware. From 1840 on, the Vigilance Committee was composed almost entirely of blacks and reflected the critical stance of Philadel-phia's black community.

Sixty concerned black and white women organized the Philadelphia Female Anti-Slavery Society on December 9, 1833, under the leadership of Lucretia Mott. Among the black members, were three daughters of James Forten—Sarah, Harriet, and Margaretta—his wife, Char-lotte, Grace and Sarah Douglass, Hetty Burr, and Lydia

White. The Forten's granddaughter Charlotte was the society's youngest member. The society's influence was so profound that similar societies were organized all along the northeastern seaboard and throughout the Midwest. The women sponsored Anti-Slavery Fairs, held in the city from 1835 to 1861, usually the week before Christmas, to replenish the continually exhausted treasury of the society. One year the fair raised thirty-five thousand dollars. The fairs were occasions to publicize the antislavery cause and honor its heroes, who were invited to speak. In 1859, Robert Purvis and William Wells Brown, a well-known orator and author, were among the guest lecturers. Anti-slavery poet Frances Ellen Watkin Harper was another distinguished speaker. In addition to her frequent appearances at antislavery bazaars in Pennsylvania and in other areas, she provided aid to fugitive slaves in her home.

The efforts of the city's antislavery movement were enhanced also by singer Elizabeth Taylor Greenfield, called the "Black Swan," who supported the movement by giving benefit concerts. On November 9, 1855, she gave a concert at the Shiloh Church to raise money for Mary Ann Shadd Carry's newspaper, *The Provincial Freeman.*

Knowledge of Mary Meyers' Underground Railroad activities was common among the black students who attended the Lombard Street School, and frequently purchased cakes from her cake shop. On one occasion a fugitive slave woman was delivered to her shop in a box. After a conference with J. Miller McKim and William Still, a decision was reached to hide the woman in the store until arrangements could be made for her journey to Canada.

Henrietta Bowers Duterte was also active in the slave-hiding network. In 1858 she became the first black woman undertaker in the city, and on several occasions she cleverly concealed fugitives in caskets. She was also known to have included them in funeral processions until their safety was assured.

The Bustills were one of the most outstanding black families during this era. More than any other single family, the Bustills were responsible for bringing Philadel-

phia's free black community into political, social, and
cultural prominence. The family's ancestry was African,
Indian, and English, and they were members of the Society of Friends. Cyrus Bustill, born a slave in Burlington,
New Jersey, in 1732 bought his freedom and perfected
the art of baking. Later he moved to Philadelphia and
established a business. During the Revolutionary War he
transported bread to George Washington's army at Valley Forge. Bustill, with Richard Allen, Absalom Jones,
and James Forten, was one of the founders of the Free
African Society in 1787.

Bustill and his wife raised a family of eight children of
whom several became teachers, artists, and seamen.
Cyrus's grandson Joseph C. Bustill, while teaching
school in Harrisburg, served as an important conductor
on the Underground Railroad. His brothers, Charles
and James, were active members of the Philadelphia
Underground. Charles H. Bustill and his wife, Emily,
were members of the Philadelphia Vigilance Committee. Their daughter Maria Luisa married William Drew
Robeson, an escaped slave from North Carolina, who
within a few years had educated himself in the finest
classical tradition and graduated from Lincoln University
School of Divinity. Their illustrious son, Paul LeRoy
Robeson, stood as a monument to the Bustill family's
stability.

Joseph C. Bustill frequently wrote to his friend and
fellow agent William Still, and a number of his letters
were published in Still's *Underground Railroad Records.*
The following (from page 43) reveals a sample of Bustill's
activities:

Harrisburg, May 26 '56

Friend Still: I embrace the opportunity presented
by the visit of our friend, John F. Williams, to drop
you a few lines in relation to our future operations.
The Lightning Train was put on the Road on last
Monday, and as travelling season has commenced
and this the Southern route for Niagara Falls, I have
concluded not to send by the way of Auburn, except
in cases of great danger; but here after we will use

the Lightning Train, which leaves here at one
thirty and arrives at your city at five o'clock in the
afternoon, so it may reach you before you close.
These four are the only ones left. The woman has
been here some time waiting for her child and her
beau, which she expects here about the first of
June. If possible, please keep a knowledge of her
whereabouts to enable me to inform him if he
comes.

Yours as ever, Jos. C. Bustill

The Underground Railroad in Philadelphia, as elsewhere, had its tragedies as well as its triumphs. One of
these tragedies involved a Philadelphia Quaker by the
name of Passmore Williamson. He hid Jane Johnson
and her two sons, Daniel and Isaiah, slaves of the United
States Minister of Nicaragua, John H. Wheeler, who was
traveling through Philadelphia en route to New York
City on July 18, 1855. When Williamson refused to
reveal the location of the three, whom he persuaded to
escape, he was arrested and became involved in a notorious trial. During the four months Williamson was in the
Old Moyamensing Prison, he received widespread support from abolitionists, as evidenced by the following
account, which appeared in the *Anti-Slavery Advocate* of
November 1, 1855:

The Supreme Court of Pennsylvania has refused
to issue a writ of Habeas Corpus in behalf of Mr.
Williamson. He therefore lies in jail at the mercy of
Judge John K. Kane. A large spirited Anti-Slavery
Convention was held at Norristown, Pennsylvania,
on the 1st inst. The proceedings mainly had reference to the case of Passmore Williamson, the outrage of Judge Kane, and the supineness of the
Supreme Court of Pennsylvania, in protecting the
liberties of her citizens. A resolution was adopted,
commending to the friends of freedom everywhere,
the circulation of petitions to Congress for the im-
peachment of Judge Kane, and a committee was

appointed to prepare a form of petition and distribute it for signature through the state. Jane Johnson was present at the meeting, and by her presence and her simple narrative, produced a deep impression upon the audience.

Lancaster City, Columbia, and Christiana were sites of militant resistance to slave-hunters and kidnappers, resulting in armed conflicts and the deaths of whites and blacks alike. These communities possessed strong and active black communities, led by such famous Underground Railroad workers as William Whipper and Stephen Smith. For a time, Thaddeus Stevens resided in York, Gettysburg, and Lancaster and assisted the Underground Railroad in various ways, chiefly as an attorney, representing fugitive slaves in court and employing fugitives at his ironworks at Caledonia.

Blood was first shed in resistance to the Fugitive Slave Law in 1850 when slaves of Edward Gorsuch, a prominent Maryland farmer, were discovered in Christiana, Pennsylvania, in 1851 in the home of fugitive William Parker. They had fled to Lancaster County by means of the Underground Railroad. Gorsuch expressed his intention of "getting his property, or breakfast in hell." Threats were exchanged, shots were fired, the cry of "kidnappers" was raised, and neighbors arrived in numbers. Gorsuch was killed in the exchange and his son was wounded. Parker and thirty others were tried for treason, but Thaddeus Stevens so ably defended them that the jury returned a "not guilty" verdict in fifteen minutes. Parker, the subject of a national manhunt, made a daring escape to Canada with assistance from his boyhood friend Frederick Douglass and others. He was never apprehended. The Christiana Riot became one of the most famous events in the annals of the Underground Railroad.

In Montgomery County, a rural county adjacent to Philadelphia, most whites were lukewarm in regard to aiding escaping slaves. Some whites were sympathetic and willing to help in time of real need, but they did not want their involvement generally known. Consequently, here too blacks did most of the real fugitive-aid work, such as providing shelter and rescuing escaped slaves in trouble. Among the better known blacks involved were Ben Johnson, John August, and Dan Ross of Norristown.

A steadfast friend to the Underground Railroad in Montgomery County was Lucretia Mott, Quaker minister and leader in both the antislavery and women's rights movements. She was threatened by an angry crowd in Norristown in 1842 when she left an antislavery meeting at the First Baptist Church arm-in-arm with Frederick Douglass. When the evening came, the crowd outside stoned the church before being dispersed by antislavery sympathizers and members of the black community.

Berks County was the scene of substantial Underground Railroad activity. Among the important Underground Railroad stations were Reading, Pine Forge, and White Bar. Agents forwarded fugitive slaves from there to Philadelphia. Dauphin County, Berks County's neighbor, was also a center of the Underground Railroad. Among the three most important conductors in Harrisburg were William Jones, pastor of the Wesley A.M.E. Church, Dr. William Rutherford, and Joseph C. Bustill.

Bucks County was more conservative than Chester and Montgomery counties. Nevertheless a lively Underground route ran from Philadelphia through the towns of Bristol, Bensalem, Newton, Quakertown, Doylestown, Buckingham, and New Hope into Lambertville, New Jersey.

Delaware County did not have the heavy concentration of Underground Railroad stations found in neighboring counties. The main route ran along West Chester Pike from Philadelphia to Phoenixville. Stations were operated in Upper Darby, Manor, Newtown Square, and Media. The city of Chester was often the first stop for runaways coming from Wilmington, Delaware, and the Chesapeake Bay area.

The Underground Railroad entered Indiana County with conductors at Dixonville. From there the route stretched over to Clearfield County, near Burnside, and into the Grampian Hills. Williamsport, Muncy, and Peninsula in Lycoming County were stations where fugitives could be sheltered for a short time.

The substantial antislavery population of Johnstown, in

Cambria County, offered help to escaping slaves. In central Pennsylvania, Mifflin County's Lewisburg was a rendezvous point for operations around the state, and the home of celebrated black abolitionist the Reverend William Grimes. In neighboring Blair County, Hollidaysburg and Altoona—though not possessing large black populations—rendered service to any fugitives passing through.

In Pittsburgh, the largely black sections of Arthursville and Hayti were well known for aiding runaways. Such black leaders as the Reverend Lewis Woodson, John B. and George Vashon, John Peck, and the militant Martin R. Delaney were all agents and conductors in the city. Black community members formed the Pittsburgh Juvenile Anti-Slavery Society and the State Convention of Colored Freemen of Pennsylvania. The Pittsburgh Philanthropic Society was an all-black group that, like the Philadelphia Vigilance Committee, was active in spiriting slaves through Pennsylvania or into hiding in the neighborhood.

The counties of Crawford, Warren, Venango, Mercer, Butler, and Erie are quiet and distinctly rural in character. Nevertheless a vital segment of the Underground Railroad ran through this region. John Brown's home stood next to his tannery at New Richmond, Crawford County. His tannery and barn had a trapdoor leading into a partial cellar where slaves were hidden. Brown operated his station in conjunction with Richard Henderson, the well-known conductor at Meadville. Henderson is reported to have assisted over five hundred slaves.

The first specific allusion to black slavery in New Jersey was in a report made in 1680, which noted that Lewis Morris, of Shrewsbury, an iron master and plantation owner, had between sixty and seventy Negro slaves. (See C. A. Price, page 2.) The number in the colony increased continuously as slave ships delivered their human cargoes at the ports of Camden and Perth Amboy.

For a long period slavery proved difficult to eradicate in New Jersey. With the exception of its neighbor New York, no colony north of the Mason-Dixon line had so large a slave population.

The first major crusade against slavery was begun by

a Mt. Holly tailor named John Woolman. Woolman became an antislavery reformer when his employer asked
him to draw up a bill of sale for a slave woman. Woolman wrote in his journal, "I was so afflicted in my mind
that I said before my master, and thy friend, that I believed slavekeeping to be a practice, inconsistent with
the Christian Religion." Woolman devoted his life to humanitarian causes, traveling throughout the colonies
preaching and teaching. In 1754, he issued a pamphlet
entitled *Some Consideration in the Keeping of Negroes;
Recommended to the Professors of Christianity of Every
Denomination.*

The institution of slavery in New Jersey was weakened
when antislavery societies were organized at Trenton in
1786 and in Burlington in 1793. In 1794, the Abolition
Society of Salem was active in the defense of kidnapped
Negroes and committed to purchasing their freedom if
necessary.

In 1804, the General Assembly moved toward universal emancipation. Antislavery Governor Joseph Bloomfield signed an act which stated that every child born of a
slave was free, but must remain as a servant of the
mother's master until age twenty-five if a boy, twenty-one
if a girl. A state law of 1846 freed all slaves, though
leaving some apprenticed to their masters until they
reached a certain age. As a result, New Jersey soon
attracted hundreds of fugitive slaves.

The sentiment against slavery in New Jersey was traced
years after the event by Siebert:

> New Jersey was probably not behind southeast-
> ern Pennsylvania in point of time in Underground
> Railroad work. This is to be inferred from the fact
> that the adjacent parts of the two states were largely
> settled by people of a sect distinctly opposed to
> slavery, and were knitted together by those ties of
> blood that were known to have been favorable in
> other quarters to the development of underground
> routes. That protection was given to fugitives early
> in the present century by the Quakers of Southeast-
> ern New Jersey before 1818.

Among those in southern New Jersey who took the most active part in aiding escaping fugitives was a courageous Quaker woman named Abigail Goodwin, of Salem. With the assistance of her sister Elizabeth, Goodwin was active in the antislavery cause as early as 1836. A year later she wrote to an antislavery friend, Mary Grew, "I do feel at least a willing mind to encounter reproach and suffering to any extent, almost, to advance this great cause" of abolition (see Still, page 617).

Goodwin was one of the devoted Underground station keepers who suffered for her loyalties. Her clothes were often more ragged than those of the runaway slaves who knocked on her door. She saved and borrowed money and organized sewing societies to support the Underground Railroad.

On February 10, 1858, she sent the following letter to William Still.

Dear Friend: Thee will find enclosed, five dollars for the building fugitives, a little for so many to share it, but better than nothing; oh that people, rich people, would remember them instead of spending so much on themselves; and those who are not called rich, might if there was only a willing mind, give too of their abundance; how can they forbear to sympathize with those poor destitute ones—but so it is— there is not half the feeling for them there ought to be, indeed scarcely anybody seems to think about them. In as much as ye have not done it unto one of the least of these my brethren, ye have not done unto me. Thy friend A. Goodwin.

One of the most successful Underground routes in southern New Jersey led from Delaware Bay across Cumberland County through Woodbury and Westville in Gloucester County, Gloucester City and Camden in Camden County, south from Medford through Mt. Holly.

Trenton was an important stop on the Underground Railroad for fugitive slaves on a route from Philadelphia that led into Staten Island. From Trenton, another connection of the invisible train led overland into Jersey City, Newark, and finally New York City. Because of the great danger from the known presence of proslavery sympathizers and spies, a number of stations in Trenton were designated by letters of the alphabet, to protect the safety of the station keepers and their passengers.

The following account pertaining to the operations of the Underground appeared in the Trenton *Evening Times,* March 30, 1898, in the form of a letter by Edward Magill, President of Swarthmore College in Pennsylvania:

Some time about 1840–45, when residing at Langhorne, we had a party of six stout fugitives arrive, whose experience had been somewhat different from that of ordinary fugitives. They had escaped in a small boat, used in connection with the lighter service on Albemarle Sound. Their trusted leader, or captain, having a small compass and knowing something of the inlets of the coast, had piloted them slowly northward, having secured some provisions, before starting, and they succeeded in working their little craft up the Delaware bay and up the river, landing only for short periods until they passed Philadelphia, and then they accidently found a friendly adviser who directed them to our village. On arriving there they found shelter for the night among some colored people. The next day their case was made known to our Anti-Slavery friends and I was chosen to convey them to Trenton in a good covered wagon, in which all were placed. I was advised to report them to Benjamin Plumly, then a merchant there. On arriving at the store I spoke to Rush and he, seeing the situation, said drive them to the yard, and get them under cover of the barn, as there were slave agents then in town, looking for victims, and we might arouse suspicion. He furnished ample provision for the party, but advised me, if possible, after feeding the horses, although storming, to push right on to Princeton, where there was a safe rendezvous. Although the team was hired for Trenton only, considering the situation, I did not hesitate, and on reaching the suburb of Princeton I reported my party to a colored man,

who was on the regular line via New Brunswick and
the Raritan river steamer to New York.

New Jersey was closely allied with Pennsylvania and
New York as a center in the fugitive slave network. The
main route led across the Delaware River to Camden,
through Mt. Holly, Bordentown, Pennington, Hopewell,
Princeton, and New Brunswick, where slave-catchers carefully watched for runaways across the bridge over the
Raritan River to Jersery City. New Brunswick was considered one of the most dangerous branches on the system
because slave-hunters in search of runaways operated a
headquarters there. At the Raritan River bridge, east of
the city, railroad trains were sometimes stopped by these
hunters of slaves. To prevent the apprehension of fugitive slaves, local conductors served as lookouts, warning
their co-workers when to transport slaves in boats to
Perth Amboy. Some sea captains risked taking on fugitive slaves and hired them to pump water from their
canal boats. Others used their schooners to transport
runaways to ports in New England.

The American Revolution inspired a movement to end
slavery in New York, and in 1799 the state enacted a
gradual emancipation act. After that date slavery declined until complete emancipation, enacted by a state
law in 1817, became final on July 4, 1827.

During the same year, *Freedom Journal,* the first black
newspaper, was founded in New York by John Russwurm
and the Reverend Samuel E. Cornish, four years before
the publication of William Lloyd Garrison's *Liberator.* When
Russwurm left for Liberia, Cornish continued the paper
until 1830 under the name *Rights of All.*

As the intensity of the antislavery movement grew in
the 1830s, conventions, meetings, and written memorials
to state and federal governmental bodies regarding these
concerns abounded. A small but steady stream of fugitive slaves, primarily from the upper South, entered the
state seeking a less oppressive life, and New York State
soon became a focus for several routes which led overland from Pennsylvania and New Jersey.

As that steady stream of fugitive slaves filtered into

New York City, a small but persistent group of individuals assisted them. Possibly the best known of these was the Quaker Isaac T. Hopper, who had been active in assisting runaway slaves and free blacks in Philadelphia as early as 1787. One of those he had assisted was the Reverend Richard Allen, founder of the African Methodist Episcopal Church. Allen was a highly respected man in Philadelphia, but nonetheless was arrested by a slave-catcher as a fugitive slave. There was a trial, but it didn't last long when it was proved that the fugitive slave in question had been missing for more than twenty years. The case against Allen was dismissed and, upon the advice of Isaac Hopper, he sued the slaver-catcher, who was sent to jail when he could not pay the bail of eight hundred dollars. After three months, Allen had the charges dropped and the slave-catcher was released. In 1829 Hopper moved to New York City, where his sympathy for fugitive slaves was sustained with the financial help of Arthur and Lewis Tappan, two wealthy brothers. In 1835, Hopper attracted notoriety when he was falsely accused of harboring a fugitive slave in his store on Pearl Street.

Considering New York City's geographic location and its growing free black community, it is not surprising that the city became an important terminal of the Underground Railroad. Between 1800 and 1830 the city's black community grew steadily. A number of the new residents were runaways from the Gabriel Prosser Conspiracy of 1800 in Virginia, the Denmark Vesey Uprising of 1822 in South Carolina, the Nat Turner Rebellion of 1831 in Virginia, and other collective efforts to attain freedom.

A small group of black leaders organized the predominately black New York Committee of Vigilance on November 29, 1835, with David Ruggles as its secretary. The African Dorcas Society, an organization of black women, raised funds, fed the fugitives, and organized sewing circles.

Born free in Norwich, Connecticut, Ruggles later moved to New York City, where from 1829 to 1833 he operated a grocery business. Actively connected with the antislavery movement, he wrote articles and pamphlets, edited newspapers, and his home at 67 Lispenard Street became a major station on the Underground Railroad. Abolitionist Samuel May credited Ruggles with assisting at least six hundred runaway slaves. Among those he sheltered was Frederick Douglass. Ruggles led a dangerous existence. He narrowly escaped one attempt made on his life by the captain of a slave ship.

His acquaintances described Ruggles as a man of "ordinary size, with an athletic form and dark complexion," and "an intelligent and benevolent countenance." He encountered perils with the courage of a martyr and he commanded respect from all who knew him. Many persons owed their lives to him.

Ruggles's friend George Downing was another prominent station master on the Underground and there are many stories about the assistance given by him. Both escaping slaves and abolitionists found food and shelter in Downing's Oyster House at the corner of Broad and Wall Streets. He owned and operated his well-known restaurant for forty-six years, from 1820 to 1866, during many of these years serving fugitive slaves in the restaurant cellar.

Founded in 1796, the African Methodist Episcopal Zion Church was active in the city. Even though white ministers were in charge of the congregation at its founding, it was through the consistent efforts of the Reverend James Varick, who established "Mother Zion" Church in 1820, that it became a sanctuary for freedom-seeking slaves until all danger of discovery disappeared. A number of celebrated black personalities connected with the emancipation train worshipped there and delivered antislavery lectures from the pulpit. In 1829 a tall former slave woman from Hurley, New York, stood up in the middle of a service. She renounced her name of Isabella and said that henceforth she would be known as Sojourner Truth. "Sojourner," she explained, "because I am a wanderer, Truth because God is Truth so Truth shall be my abiding name until I die," (se W. J. Walls, page 151).

Later, with her head wrapped in a white turban, Sojourner Truth journeyed throughout the North raising funds to aid fugitive slaves. She preached from pulpits that "America owes my people some of the dividends," and further, "I shall make them understand that there is a debt to the Negro people which they can never repay. At least they must make amends." Sojourner Truth's two ubiquitous friends, Harriet Tubman and Frederick Douglass, on several occasions worshipped and lectured at Mother Zion.

One route from New York City is reported to have followed what is now Star Route 22, to Nassau and Brainerd, Rennselaer County, and then northward to Hoosick and Bennington, Vermont. The Reverend Garrett Van Hoesen was the principal conductor on this line. Another route led from Troy across the Hudson River to the Adirondacks and North Elba, where John Brown's farm and home are located. From this point slaves could travel toward Canada relatively unmolested.

Harriet Tubman was well acquainted with northern New York. In his biography of Tubman (page 59), Earl Conrad, a historian of the Underground Railroad, wrote: "In New York she called with her groups at the offices of the Anti-Slavery Society, where Oliver Johnson and others greeted her. From there Harriet and her gangs jumped to Albany."

From Albany, the escaped slaves pushed through several other small communities. Growing Underground Railroad sentiment prompted other black churches to open their doors to fugitive slaves. Tattered and anxious visitors from the South knew that they could receive aid in the Reverend Henry Highland Garnet's Presbyterian Church at Troy, for Garnet was one of the most prominent black activists on the Underground.

He was born a slave in New Market, Maryland, and when he was nine years old, his family escaped to New York City. Upon completing his education from several schools and a theological institute, he took up residence with his wife, Julia, in Troy, where he was licensed to preach. Garnet, who walked with a wooden leg, made his strong and vigorous personality felt on antislavery platforms whenever he spoke. This grandson of a Mandinga ruler spoke with fearful pride. While attending the National Negro Convention in 1843, held in Buffalo, Garnet delivered his celebrated "Call to Rebellion" speech, commanding that Negroes, both slaves and free, adopt a "motto of resistance" to slavery.

Garnet was more militant than most black leaders,

rejecting the idea of nonresistance, but it was becoming increasingly evident to many in the cause that only resistance could protect fugitives from the grasping hands of the slave-hunters. For example, Charles Nalle was a runaway slave from Culpeper County, Virginia, who was discovered in Troy, and was taken to the United States Commissioner's office. As news of Nalle's arrest spread, an angry crowd gathered. Sarah Bradford, Harriet Tubman's biographer, recounts the incident (pages 126 to 128):

When Nalle was brought from Commissioner Beach's office into the street, Harriet Tubman, who had been standing with the excited crowd, rushed amongst the foremost to Nalle, and running one of her arms around his manacled arm, held on to him without ever loosening her hold through the more than half-hour's struggle to Judge Gould's office, and from Judge Gould's office to the dock, where Nalle's liberation was accomplished. In the *meelee,* she was repeatedly beaten over the head with policemen's clubs, but she never for a moment released her hold, but cheered Nalle and his friends with her voice, and struggled with the officers until they were literally worn out with their exertions, and Nalle was separated from them.

True, she had strong and earnest helpers in her struggle, some of whom had white faces as well as human hearts, and are now in Heaven. But she exposed herself to the fury of the sympathizers with slavery, without fear, and suffered their blows without flinching. Harriet crossed the river with the crowd, in the ferry-boat, and when the men who led the assault upon the door of Judge Stewart's office were stricken down, Harriet and a number of other colored women rushed over their bodies, brought Nalle out, and putting him in the first wagon passing, started him for the West.

A lively team, driven by a colored man, was immediately sent on to relieve the other, and Nalle was seen about Troy no more until he returned a free man by purchase from his master. Harriet also disappeared, and the crowd dispersed. How she came to be in Troy that day, is entirely unknown to our citizens; and where she hid herself after the rescue is equally a mystery. But her struggle was in the sight of a thousand, perhaps of five thousand spectators.

The pursuit and forced return of escaped slaves was certain to meet resistance in Syracuse. No town in New York State is reported to have received a larger number of fugitive slaves than Syracuse. This town was the home of that great "Underground Railroad King," the Reverend Jermain Wesley Loguen. The *Weekly Anglo-African* newspaper reported on November 24, 1860, that Loguen attained this name through his daring escape to freedom and his unending war on slavery. There are few men whose history is so marked with stirring incidents, instructive lessons, and encouraging examples as Loguen's. He was intimate friends with Harriet Tubman and Frederick Douglass, and Douglass's son married Loguen's daughter. After Loguen escaped to Canada, he returned to New York and lived for short periods in Rochester, Utica, Ithaca, and Bath before settling in Syracuse. Loguen and his wife, Caroline, established two major Underground Railroad terminals in Syracuse, their home and his church. He is credited with helping some fifteen hundred fugitive slaves escape to Canada.

The Emancipation Train had a core of ardent supporters in Rochester, the last major stop in northeastern New York. After running a gauntlet of other towns, escaped slaves came to this city by railroad, by wagon, or on foot seeking shelter, food, money, and clothing. Through the Underground Railroad grapevine they were directed to the home of Frederick Douglass and other friends. Douglass's home became the most important "overflow" station in Rochester. The very first issue of his beloved *North Star* stated that its editor was involved in the operation of the Underground. On one occasion, Douglass had eleven fugitives at his house. He said: "It was the largest group I ever had and it was difficult for me to give shelter, food, and money for so many at once, but it had to be done so they could be moved on immediately to Canada." Harriet Tubman led her "passengers" to the home of Douglass and his wife, Ann, on several occasions.

Rochester was also the home of Susan B. Anthony. Raised to be self-supporting by a Quaker father, she spoke out for temperance, women's rights, and abolition, despite vehement prejudice against women in public affairs. When Harriet Tubman did not stay with the Douglasses or at the African Methodist Episcopal Zion Church at Spring and Favor streets, she stayed with the Anthonys, the Blosses, or the Porter family. In a letter dated August 29, 1868, Douglass wrote to Harriet Tubman:

> The difference between us is very marked. Most of what I have done and suffered in the service of our cause has been in public and I have received much encouragement at every step of the way. You, on the other hand, have labored in a private way. I have wrought in the day—you in the night. I have had the applause of the crowd and the satisfaction that comes of being approved by the multitude, while the most you have done has been witnessed by a few trembling, scared and footsore bondmen and women, whom you have led out of the house of bondage and whose heartfelt "God Bless You" has been your only reward. Excepting John Brown—of sacred memory—I know of no one who has willingly encountered more perils and hardships to serve our enslaved people than you have.

Frederick Douglass could count on the support of the Female Anti-Slavery Society, for the active Rochester group, formed in 1835, included such antislavery friends as Elizabeth Cady Stanton, Sojourner Truth, Sallie Holley, Amy Post, and Mrs. Samuel Porter. Stanton was a cousin of radical millionaire Gerrit Smith, who often donated money to that society.

In western New York, according to historian Arch Merrill, "A chain of underground stations wound through Warsaw, Sheldon, Arcade, Perry, Pearl Creek, Wyoming, and other places. The routes were flexible and the identity of the station master has been established." Merrill had in mind Warsaw's leading station keeper, William

Smallwood. He hid slaves in a nearby swamp, as well as in the cellar of his home. There is a tale that, when the slave-hunters came to the East Hill, Smallwood's wife, Elizabeth, would rock serenely on a chair placed on a rug squarely over the trapdoor that led to the cellar where slaves were secreted. Smallwood flaunted his abolitionist activities and it was his wish that on his tombstone these words be inscribed: "He was a friend of the slave."

Tompkins County was known as a major stop and start station. Tendai Mutunhu, a chronicler of the Tompkins County Underground, mentions a number of towns in addition to Ithaca as rendering valuable materials and monetary assistance to runaways making their way to Canada. Another Tompkins County historian, Sidney Gallwey, documents the Underground Railroad saga further.

> George A. Johnson, a Free Negro and a well-known Ithaca barber, was working in his father's barbershop during the 1830's and 40's. Whenever several fugitives came to him for aid, he would visit Ithaca lawyer Ben Johnson who would provide money for shoes, clothing, and passage on to Canada. Some of the other abolitionists who aided Johnson were Benjamin Halsey, John Murdock, and E. T. Tillotson.

Escaped slaves were often provided with a hiding place for the night in the steamboat *Simeon DeWitt*. On the following morning they would be transported to Cayuga Bridge at the northern end of Cayuga Lake. From there, they would continue their journey with the North Star as a guide to Canada. Cayuga Bridge was in operation for various periods of time until 1872. It was a wooden structure extending from Cayuga Village on the east to Bridgeport on the route to Geneva and was used to help fugitives cross from one side of Cayuga Lake to the other.

Farther east, near the Pennsylvania border, the town of Jamestown attracted escaped fugitives as they began to make pilgrimages by way of the Underground. *The*

Jamestown Journal of March 4, 1859, contained the following:

> Last week a passenger on the "Underground Railroad" reached this station in a needy condition and was promptly assisted by the Agents here. He was one of a party of nine, owned by a man in Southern Virginia, all of them having started for Canada together and doubtless reaching the Queen's domains before this. His master owned five hundred slaves; he had never been whipped or badly treated, and but for the increasing years of his master and the certainty of a "sell out" at his death they never would have left. One of the Agents states that the road is in good condition and doing a thriving business. Bueno!

Many of the escaping slaves who passed through Jamestown stopped at the home of Catharine Harris, where they were hidden in the basement. Cited by the New York State Historical Commission, this building still stands as a documented memorial of the Underground.

Narrative of Jerry McHenry

This celebrated fugitive slave's rescue received national attention. Conductor Eber Pettit vividly recalls the event in his *Sketches in the History of the Underground Railroad* (pages 50 to 53).

The fugitive slave, named Jerry, had been discovered by a detective employed by his master, a month or two previous to the Anti-Slavery Convention, which had been announced for the first of August, I think, though I am not certain as to the exact time, and the agent of the claimant had been several weeks making arrangements to carry out the programme that

was announced in Congress, and published and repeated by
the press all over the South. "That hot-bed of Abolitionism
has got to be humbled; Syracuse was to be taught that there was
a State known as 'Old Virginia,' 'The Old Dominion,' 'Mother
of Presidents,' " though even Virginia rejoiced in being able
to shirk the responsibility of having brought into the world the
accidental tenant of the White House [Millard Fillmore],
whom the chivalry were employing to do their dirty work.

I met Jo [Norton] early in the morning on the day of the
Convention. He said that many of the fugitives had left for
Canada, having heard rumors that one or more of them were
to be arrested on that day, but, said Jo, "I have a pleasant
home here, my children are going to school, and I have all
the work I can do. Besides all that," said he, "There are not
men enough in Virginia to carry *me* out of this city. If there is
to be any excitement of that sort here, I'm bound to have a
hand in it, and I shall stay and help fight it out."

The vague rumors that were afloat were not sufficient to
put Jerry and his friends upon their guard. The only persons
who *knew* what was going on were such as sympathized with
the slaveholder, for animals of the "genus copperhead," had
already become sufficiently numerous to consume a vast amount
of bad whiskey. A marshal was brought from Rochester to
make the arrest, for no citizen of Syracuse could be found
who dared to "face the music." Jerry, all unconscious of
danger, was busily employed, hammering away at a barrel in
a cooper shop, when about twelve o'clock he was seized,
and, after a brave fight, was ironed hand and foot, thrown
upon a cart that the marshal had pressed into his service, and
started for the office of the Commissioners.

The Convention had organized in Market Hall, and commenced business, when a man came in and interrupted the
proceedings by saying, in an excited manner, "Mr. President,
an officer from Rochester has arrested a fugitive, and is now
carrying him off; they are now on the canal bridge." In a
moment the Convention was broken up, men, women, and
children rushed into the street, and ran toward the bridge, but
before the crowd arrived the marshal had got Jerry into the
Commissioner's office.

The city was in an uproar; no such excitement had ever
been witnessed in Syracuse before. Thousands of people from
the country and adjacent towns were there to attend the

Convention. The fugitives and free colored men surrounded the building and they were surrounded on all sides by a dense mass of people. Some of the best lawyers in the State were present, and *volunteered* their services to defend Jerry, while one lawyer *sold* his services to the slave catchers. The Commissioner's office was on the second floor of a large brick building, one side of which fronted on the canal. The outside door was fastened with heavey bars, and the inner door securely locked to keep out the crowd, and it was with difficulty that Jerry's friends and counsel got into the room where the trial was to be held.

The trial was protracted and delayed until the court and counsel were tired and hungry, and adjourned for supper, leaving the prisoner in charge of the marshal and his deputies. The officer took pains to make the crowd understand that he was armed, and would shoot down any man who should attempt to rescue the prisoner. Meanwhile, Jo had organized a party, and had everything ready to storm the stronghold of the slave power in Syracuse. Although it was time to light the lamps in the streets, the crowd had not diminished nor the excitement abated. The court and counsel had just reached the hotel when Jo gave the signal to his men, and in an instant a stick of timber twenty feet long was mounted on the shoulders of as many stout negroes as could stand under it; at the word "Jo," with a shout and run, the battering ram was thrown upon the door, and carried all before it. Then Jo, at the head of his men, with a crow-bar in his hands, ran up stairs and attacked the inner door. The marshal was a brave man for so great a rascal—none but rascals of high grade would accept Fillmore's commission under the Fugitive Slave Law—and when the door gave way under the furious blows of Jo's crowbar, he fired at him, but Jo was too quick for him. The ball went into the floor, and the marshal's arm hung limp at his side, shattered by the crow-bar. The men rushed in and seized the deputies, but the marshal jumped through an open window, and fell thirteen feet to the tow-path of the canal; he managed to get away in the shadow of the building, and found his way to a surgeon's office.

Jerry was found lying on the floor, bloody, almost naked, and bound in chains. He had proved himself a hero by fighting the whole United States in the persons of the President's special Commissioners. He was provided with clothes and money, and the poor fellow never saw the city of Syracuse again by daylight. The next time we heard from him he was making barrels in Canada.

Narrative of William Henry Johnson

Johnson was a barber and an active agent and his house sheltered many fleeing bondmen. Born of free parents in Alexandria, Virginia, in 1833, Johnson's parents sent him to Philadelphia to learn his trade. When the city authorities began to question his Underground Railroad activities, he moved to Norwich, Connecticut, and later to Albany, New York, continuing his work on the Railroad. Johnson was the agent whose name appeared on the box in which Henry Box Brown made his daring escape from Richmond to Philadelphia. This brief sketch from Johnson's autobiography (pages 125 and 126) demonstrates that problems existed within the Underground Railroad network between co-workers. Note that William Still, the legendary Underground Railroad dispatcher, was accused of harboring an informer.

In 1857, with others, I was engaged in the performance of a very disagreeable duty. It was the explusion from the city of Philadelphia of a Negro, who claimed to be a gentleman; he was a slave-holder, and while visiting that city made his home with William Still, on South Street, below Ninth Street. It came about in this way: Joseph Venning then kept a cigar store on the other side of the street, above Ninth. His parents occupied the residence portion of the house. Many young fellows of my acquaintance made Mr. Venning's store a place of rendezvous. Among our latest associates was a young man that we would readily have taken for being white had we not also met his mother. She was a bright mulatto. This young fellow's name was George Steel. We saw him for the last time on a Sunday afternoon preceding the incident that followed. On Monday he was missing. His mother was troubled. On Tuesday morning the secret of her tribulation was unfolded. She, as well as her son, were escaped slaves from South Carolina. The son had left the city Sunday evening hastily; his mother on Monday morning. Steel was a waiter at the Continental Hotel, Ninth and Chestnut Streets. It soon developed that their master was in the city, with officers, looking for their apprehension, and that John Francis, also of Charleston, had been in secret conference with the master, and had imparted the information of the whereabouts of the mother and son. When these facts became public, the indignation of the colored people knew no bounds. A mass meeting was held the next evening on Sixth Street, near Lombard, in front of George W. Goines' store. Mr. Goines was chosen as chairman and Thomas Shonock as secretary. Many speeches were made and condemnatory resolutions adopted. A committee of three was appointed to see that Francis left the city or took the consequences of staying. The committee consisted of George E. Stevens, Parker T. Smith, and the writer of this. Backed up by the indignant people, we immediately repaired to Still's house. We were met at the door by him. He expressed great indignation of the action taken at the meeting, and declared his intention to defend to the bitter end his boarder and the sanctity of his domicile. This did not amount to much; he was pushed to one side, and the committee entered the house and Francis' room, confronting the base informer with the action of the meeting, which demanded his immediate expulsion from the house and city. He attempted to make a defense, but, upon looking out of the front window, and realizing the hostile attitude of the indignant and venturesome citizens gathered in the street, agreed, if safe conduct was guaranteed him across Gray's Ferry bridge, that he would leave the city before daylight. He evidently felt that his life was in danger if he attempted to stay. This was agreed to. The crowd was informed, and immediately dispersed, and Francis was well on his way South before the sun rose on Wednesday morning. He never was known to return to the good old Quaker City.

FREE
NEW
ENGLAND

On July 14, 1909, Aella Green published an article on the Underground Railroad in the Springfield, Connecticut, *Sunday Republican:*

Fugitives fleeing from slavery at the South and reaching New York and Westchester County were heartened there to resume their journey toward freedom in Canada; and then they fared on through the shore towns to New Haven. From thence two routes of the Underground system extended northward across Connecticut, one of them going through Southington and places north of it, and entering Massachusetts at Southwick and Westfield, the other one extending through North Guilford and Meriden to Hartford and Springfield. The two routes came together at Northampton. And at the corners of the triangular section of the Bay state described by these converging lines of the road were kept three principal stations of the system. The agents at these points were true men and brave, and the conductors making trips to and from these stations had both the wisdom and the intrepidity fitting them for the hazardous business in which they were engaged. Faring through Connecticut by either of the two routes, the fugitives found that which, had they dared to sing at all, would have caused them to sing, "Jordan am a hard road to trabbel, I believe." In every one of the towns on each route there were people of pronounced pro-slavery ideas, people glad to see the slaves sent back to the servitude from which they were fleeing, and some of whom were not adverse to aid in their rendition, at least not averse to putting the hunters on their track. Risky business, indeed, was it for the fugitives to traverse Connecticut, and hazardous for the agents of the road to do their work.

In one of those Connecticut towns there still lives a matron of pro-slavery notions, who was between thirty and forty years of age when the Underground people were the most active in their work, and she boasts, to this day, that "she didn't help the niggers— not she." Near by the farm on which she then lived and which she still holds as "her own probberty," lived then two men that afterward went to the South and worked plantations with slaves, and "didn't think niggers wuz fit fur ennythin, but fer be made ter wuk fer white folks"—and "she didn't nuther." This woman had other neighbors who held similar pro-slavery notions. But let her great age insure her protection from severity of criticism now that slavery is done away; let her and her neighbors and their like be forgiven.

Another element which enters into the computa-tion of the interest which some Connecticut people took in fostering "the institution" is the fact that the cotton-gin, which helped to make slavery profitable, was the invention of Eli Whitney, a Connecticut man. Sometimes, too, young men from that state went to the South and found places as slave-drivers, in which business some of them showed great aptness, and received great pay. Other young men from Connect-icut went to the South to teach in the families of the planters. Thus it came about that Connecticut Yan-kees not only sold the slaveholders clocks and cot-ton machinery, but also taught their children and tasked and flogged their "niggers." Connecticut Yan-kees might be said to have had a selfish interest in slavery at the South, and it would be natural for them to look with disfavor on those whose operations endangered the perpetuity of "the institution." And there were still others in Connecticut who opposed the operators of the Underground road. They disliked, or pretended to dislike slavery; but they thought that "seeing there was a law" against helping fugitive slaves on their way, the law should be obeyed. But the opposition in that state to the business of the Underground road also sprang from the inbred hatred of many of the people of the state for the negro. This hatred "had come down from former generations." It had been carefully kept through all the stages of its transmission; it had been fostered with the fondness given a favorite child; it had been guarded as a precious treasure; it had been prized as a sacred jewel. It was in this state that the negro prisoner "Cato" was for a long time kept chained to the cold, damp, rock floor of a noisome cell, below ground—kept there until the fastened leg rotted off, or wore off. Records do not mention the exact cause of the severing of the leg, but it was in the ancient prison in the "Copper Hill" neighborhood, near Simsbury.

Fugitive slaves who came through Canterbury probably were harbored on the family farm where Prudence Crandall had opened a "young ladies boarding school" whose pupils included a number of daughters of the town's best families. She also proposed to integrate her school with "little misses of color." During that year of 1833, Sarah Harris, a seventeen-year-old black girl, applied and was accepted for admission as a nonresident student. Although Harris lived on a small farm in the vicinity, owned by her respectable father, most of the white parents immediately withdrew their daughters in protest. The majority of the citizens of Canterbury and surrounding communities strongly denounced Crandall. However, maintained by her Quaker persuasion, she stood her ground, even though she was warned by a prominent minister's wife that, if she did not dismiss the young negro, her school would fail. Let it fail then, said

Crandall, "for I should not turn her out" and boldly declared that she would open a school exclusively for colored girls. Andrew T. Judson, proslavery spokesman and state senator, led the attack upon Crandall. True to her convictions, however, she opened the school to black girls who came from Philadelphia, Boston, Providence, and New York.

Black historian Horatio T. Strothers describes the town of Farmington as an important center of Underground Railroad activities where by 1836 an antislavery society was organized with seventy members. Strothers writes (page 166): "In the Spring of 1839, Cinque and Tami and other negroes from the [celebrated] Amistad incident came to Farmington to enjoy the hospitality of local abolitionists and win supporters all over the town by their constant good cheer. Their simple friendliness and almost childlike delight in the new sights about them did much to break down local prejudice against people of color."

In the Amistad incident referred to, Cinque, the son of an African ruler, led the revolt of fifty slaves en route by ship from Africa. They killed all but two of the crew, tied the remaining crew to the bridge, and demanded to be returned to Africa. However, the Spanish ship's mate tricked them by steering toward Connecticut. Upon landing, the Africans were charged with piracy and murder. Represented in court by former President John Quincy Adams, their case became a national sensation. Cinque became a hero, and his men were finally granted their freedom by the Supreme Court of the United States. Cinque later returned to Africa, only to become a slave trader himself.

Geographically, Farmington was located on a system of roads that led to Hartford. By 1828, a canal was constructed and was soon used to transport fugitive slaves along with other merchandise.

No story of the abolitionist cause in Connecticut would be complete without the name of Theodore Weld. Born in Hampton, Connecticut, on November 23, 1803, his father was Ludovicus Weld, a graduate of Harvard and pastor of the Congregational Church in Hampton, and his mother was the former Elizabeth Clark. A close friend of the poet John Greenleaf Whittier, Weld once described himself as a backwoodsman who "can grub up stumps, roll logs and burn brush heaps." He believed that the crusade against slavery should be carried to the populace in the North as well as the South, and moved among the cities, towns, seminaries, and colleges recruiting followers to the antislavery cause. His influence among the faculty and students at Lane Seminary and Oberlin College in Ohio made those institutions centers for social reform. His anthology, *American Slavery As It Is,* was widely circulated. Like his Connecticut-born contemporary John Brown, Weld believed in total equality of the races. He lived with black families and taught their children. After hundreds of speeches on the subjects of abolition and social reform, his voice failed him occasionally for long periods of time, but he lectured until his ninetieth birthday and died at the age of ninety-one on February 3, 1895.

The Underground Railroad developed in New Haven during the late 1820s and continued to serve fugitive slaves through the early years of the Civil War. Among the first fugitives to reach this city via "the freedom road" was William Grimes, a mulatto slave from Savannah, Georgia, who explained in his narrative how he escaped that southern city with help from friendly seamen who hid him among bales of cotton. After the vessel landed in New York City, Grimes became connected with Underground Railroad workers who directed him toward Connecticut. Trudging mile after mile through Greenwich and other coastal towns, he finally arrived in New Haven. His freedom was purchased shortly thereafter by a gentleman in Litchfield, on the promise that the fugitive would repay him. He held the deed to Grimes's home as security. Grimes became a barber and worked on the Underground Railroad.

At New Haven, the Reverend Simon S. Jocelyn and his brother, the artist Nathaniel Jocelyn, regarded blacks as friends from their boyhood days. Simon Jocelyn served as pastor of a local black church and established a school for black children. Also identified with Underground Railroad activities in the city was the Reverend Amos G. Beman, pastor of the Temple Street Church. He recorded a portion of his Underground activities in his diary, and later in *The Voice of the Fugitive,* Henry Bibb's antislavery newspaper. Before moving to New Haven, Beman served as an agent on the Underground while teaching school at Hartford.

Francis Gillette of Bloomfield and Hartford, a United States senator, was a prominent antislavery leader in that section of the state. His home is documented as a station on the Underground. Gillette and his abolitionist brother-in-law, John Hooker, were related through marriage to Harriet Beecher Stowe.

Slavery was abolished in Rhode Island in 1784. Nevertheless, Quaker Arnold Buffum of Rhode Island was read out of the Friends meeting for his Underground Railroad activities and is buried in the graveyard across the street from the Smithfield Meeting House in Rhode Island. Quakers who wished to evade the abolition issue spared no pains in disowning him. In 1832, Buffum became the first president of the Massachusetts Anti-Slavery Society. His father, William, was a member of the Rhode Island Society for the Gradual Abolition of Slavery.

Elizabeth Buffum Chace and her sister, Lucy Buffum Lovell, were daughters of Arnold, whose home at Valley Falls, now Central Falls, was an active Underground station. Elizabeth Buffum Chace wrote in *Two Quaker Sisters* (page 10): "I am ashamed to say that my early Quaker ancestors in Newport, Rhode Island, were interested in the slave trade and that ships came into the harbor direct from Africa and most of the human cargo was disposed of in that village and redistributed to other sections." She goes on to say that leading families engaged in the shipping trade considered the slave trade as a part of their business.

Due largely to the antislavery sentiment of the Buffum and Lovell family women, the Female Anti-Slavery Society of Rhode Island was organized in 1835. Chace narrates the following incident in *Two Quaker Sisters* (pages 119 and 120):

In the village of Fall River were a very few respectable young colored women who came to our meetings. One evening, soon after the Society was formed, my sister, Lucy, and I went to see one of these negro women and invited them to join. This raised such a storm among some of the leading members that, for a time, it threatened the dissolution of the Society. They did not think it at all proper to invite them to join the Society, thus putting them on an equality with ourselves. Lucy and I maintained our ground, however, and the colored women were admitted.

Chace and Lovell go on to state that several persons, in various parts of the country, were forcibly carried out of Friends meetings for attempting to urge upon them the duty "to maintain faithfully their testimony against slavery." They sadly relate that "we were few in number and the great body of Quakerism in the country was against us. Our lips were sealed in the meetings, and out of meetings we were in disgrace, despised, and rejected."

In Providence, Daniel Mitchell, a stern abolitionist, worked on the Underground Railroad along with Jethrom and Anne Mitchell from Newport, according to Siebert. Another noted Providence station was the home of the well-known philanthropist Moses Brown, who generously contributed moral support and financial aid to antislavery causes in New England.

Quaker station master Charles Perry operated a station in his home at Westerly. Perry forwarded fugitives at nightfall across the state line to his brother, Harvey, in North Stonington, who secreted slaves in "a well-concealed black hole." On one occasion, Charles Perry was greeted with hisses and pelted with eggs when he escorted Frederick Douglass to an antislavery meeting.

Touro Synagogue, dedicated in 1763 by Spanish Jews and thus America's oldest Jewish house of worship, used its quarters as a station on the Underground Railroad.

Let Southern oppressors tremble—let their secret abettors tremble—let their Northern apologists tremble—let all the enemies of the persecuted blacks tremble. I will be as harsh as truth, and as uncompromising as justice. On this subject I do not wish to think, or speak, or write with moderation. Tell a man whose house is on fire to give a moderate alarm . . . I am in earnest. I will not equivocate—I will not excuse—I will not retreat a single inch—AND I WILL BE HEARD!

There were the words with which twenty-six-year-old William Lloyd Garrison of Massachuestts concluded his "Manifesto" in the first issue of the *Liberator,* January 2, 1831. Squint-eyed, bespectacled, and lean, Garrison expressed his opinions against slavery so strongly that he was considered fanatical. Demanding immediate and complete emancipation, he was willing to cast away the Bible, the Constitution, and the Union to that end.

Prominent black Underground agents in Boston included John J. Smith, a barber born in Richmond, Virginia, whose shop served as a front for Underground activities, and Boston-born William C. Nell, who worked on the *Liberator* and the *North Star.* A self-taught historian, Nell published his classic *Colored Patriots of the American Revolution* in 1855. He lived at No. Five Meeting House, Beacon Hill. Joshua B. Smith, a former slave, also contributed considerably to the cause.

Erected in 1806, the venerable African Meeting House, also referred to as "The Abolition Church," is the site on which Garrison founded the New England Anti-Slavery Society in 1832. The church was used as a station stop for runaway slaves.

As steeped in tradition as any Underground Railroad station in Massachusetts was the home of Nathan Johnson in New Bedford. He offered his home to the escaped Maryland slave Frederick Augustus Bailey, whom the world soon knew as Frederick Douglass. It was Johnson who suggested his new name to twenty-one-year-old Bailey. Anna Murray, Douglass's wife, aided her husband in New Bedford and Lynn. Both towns were heavily used by fugitives who chose to escape by sea.

Siebert, writing on the Underground Railroad in Massachusetts for the American Antiquarian Society, reported:

The first recorded evidence of befriending the runaway in Massachusetts, in a manner often employed later by Underground operators, occurred shortly after the passage of the Fugitive Slave Law of 1793. This runaway had been apprehended, and Josiah Quincy appeared in court as his defender. Mr. Quincy tells us that he "heard a noise, and turning round he saw the constable lying on the floor, and a passage opening through the crowd, through which the fugitive was taking his departure without stopping to hear the opinion of the court."

New Bedford, as an Underground center, had terminals both in the South and the North. One of its terminals in the South was Portsmouth, Virginia. At that place lived a colored woman by the name of Eliza Bains, who worked for sea-captains. Thus she became conversant with the times of sailing, and the destinations of their vessels. Being also a hider of escaping slaves, she got numbers of them on board vessels bound for New Bedford and Boston. Among those attempting flight from Portsmouth in May 1854, were Clarissa Davis and her two brothers.

The brothers succeeded in reaching New Bedford, but Clarissa found it necessary to stay hidden for two months longer. Then she sailed for Philadelphia, whence the Vigilance Committee promptly forwarded her to join her brothers. Soon their father came and was reunited with his children. In fact, the Vigilance Committee of Philadelphia sent a number of fugitives to New Bedford, among them being Thomas Bayne, who became a dentist and a member of the city council there. For a couple of years Frederick Douglass was a member of the colony of fugitives at New Bedford.

The out-bound Underground routes radiating by land from Boston were not less than five in number. Curiously enough, one ran southeast to Plymouth, a distance of thirty-seven miles. This was the Plymouth and Middleboro (New York, New Haven, and Hartford) Railroad. A few slaves were also landed at Plymouth and sent up to Boston.

Midway between Reading and Medford lies Stoneham, where the house at No. 307 Main Street bears a tablet with the inscription:

UNDERGROUND RAILROAD
This House, the Home of Deacon Abijah Bryant,
Harbored Many Fugitive Slaves
In the Years Preceding the Civil War.

Located on Park Square in Boston is a duplicate of a casting by sculptor Thomas Ball called "Emancipation Group," donated by Moses Kimball. The model for the "kneeling slave" was Archer Alexander, a fugitive slave from Missouri.

In its Constitution of 1777, Vermont prohibited slavery, and on May 1, 1834, the Vermont Anti-Slavery Society was formed.

In his history *The Underground Railroad* (page 23), Siebert wrote:

> It is safe to say that there was no better soil in the United States for the antislavery movement to take root and develop in than that of Vermont. As a select committee of the State Senate said in 1855, Vermont was "born of a resistance to arbitrary power, her first breath was that of freedom, her first voice a declaration of equal rights of man. How then could her people be otherwise than haters of slavery." Furthermore, there were no conditions in Vermont, as there were in the New England States on the coast, to weaken the sentiments of her people on the subject of human bondage. They had practically no commercial dealings with the South, almost no social intercourse with that section, and no shipping interests to profit by the slave trade.

This does not mean that Vermont had no proslavery citizens. In Montpelier, Randolph, and a few other communities there were enough of these to break up antislavery meetings in 1835, and slave-hunters could find an occasional low fellow in certain localities to aid them in the attempt to capture a runaway slave.

The western trunk of the Vermont Underground ran from Bennington County to Burlington and then by St. Albans to Canada. In the southwestern corner of Vermont, in Pownal and Bennington, the principal families involved in the Underground were the Paddocks, Carpenters, Perkinses, and Hazzards.

The principal operator at Manchester, some twenty miles from Bennington, was Daniel Roberts, Jr., who was doubtless assisted by conductors Philbrook Barrows, Jr., D. E. Nicholson, and Lyman Batcheller at Wallingford, twenty-three miles from Manchester. Nine miles north at Rutland, T. T. Thrall was known as a zealous agent and, with the aid of other helpers, frequently placed fugitive slaves on steam cars.

At Castleton, a short distance from Rutland, lived Erastus and Harvey O. Higley. These workers sent their passengers onward to Fair Haven, where station keeper Zenas C. Ellis and some of his sympathetic neighbors participated in sheltering runaways. Ellis hid his charges in his fishing boats and transported them to Whitehall. There they were placed upon canal boats heading for Canada.

After the fugitives had eaten and rested at the homes of other conductors, they sometimes were forwarded to the home of Quakers Aaron and Dinah Rogers, near Whitehall. They entrusted their passengers along the Rutland County route to the editors of the *Telegraph*, Arian T. Ramsey, and his friend Rodney V. Marsh.

The eastern trunk of the Underground came from other New England states via Brattleboro and up the Connecticut River and its tributaries to Montpelier, or over the lower passes through the Green Mountains into the valley of Otter Creek; thence through Middlebury, Vergennes, Ferrisburg, and Charlotte to Burlington. Another entrance was from the Hudson Valley northward through Bennington and Rutland, joining the first at Middlebury. Middlebury became a major center for abolitionists when the anti-slavery society was founded in 1835 by fourteen men. By 1837, the society had increased its membership to one hundred and seventy-five.

Bellows Falls, located along the canal, served as a transportation depot for both lumber and fugitive slaves. Sanford Granger, a prominent Methodist, assisted in the transportation. Fugitive slaves who were not transported on lumber barges continued their journey by other means.

At West Windsor, according to local tradition, Bezalee Bridge concealed his southern friends behind a central chimney and later spirited them to Woodstock or Hartland Corners.

Abolitionist sentiment exploded in 1852 with a force that shook the world, in large part due to the writing of Harriet Beecher Stowe. Stowe had moved to Brunswick, Maine, in 1850 with her husband, Professor Calvin Stowe, who had accepted a teaching position at Bowdoin College. The Stowe family resided in the house where anti-slavery poet Henry Wadsworth Longfellow had lived as a college student.

Wilbur Siebert wrote (page 32):

> As it was the Fugitive Slave Law that brought the North face to face with slavery nationalized, so it was the Fugitive Slave Law that occasioned, in the spring of 1852, the production of *Uncle Tom's Cabin,* a novel the great political significance of which has been generally acknowledged. The observations and experience that made possible for Mrs. Harriet Beecher Stowe the writing of this remarkable book were gained by her while living at Cincinnati, where she was enabled to study the effects of slavery. While thus a resident of the borders of Kentucky, she numbered among her friends slaveholders on the one side of the Ohio River and abolitionists on the other. At the time of her first trip across the Ohio in 1833, she visited an estate, which is described as that of Colonel Shelby in *Uncle Tom's Cabin.* Her associations and sympathies brought home to her the personal aspects of slavery, and her house on Walnut Hills early became a station on the Underground Railroad, remaining so doubtless till 1850, when she removed to Maine.

In his autobiography (page 351), Frederick Douglass wrote of "the book known as *Uncle Tom's Cabin,* a work of marvelous depth and power" whose "effects were amazing, instantaneous, and universal."

Three thousand copies were sold in twenty-four hours. The first edition of five thousand copies was sold out within a week, a hundred thousand in eleven weeks, five hundred thousand in Great Britain in five months. Eight printing presses running continuously day and night could not supply the demand for copies. The book appeared in Germany, Italy, Russia, and France and soon was translated into other languages all over Europe, where it was the subject of conversation in bazaars, restaurants, and churches. Ironically, William Lloyd Garrison had rejected *Uncle Tom's Cabin* for serialization in the *Liberator,* but his rival publisher Gamaliel Bailey picked it up and ran it in the *National Era.*

Was there really an Eliza, an Uncle Tom? Indeed, Stowe had met the real-life "Uncle Tom," one Josiah Henson, who had told her of the real-life "Eliza,' whom he encountered in Canada after Levi Coffin helped her escape there.

Siebert concluded that "in Harriet Beecher Stowe, the thousands of fugitive slaves that had been unwittingly acting as missionaries in the cause of freedom through the earlier years found those words carried their story to the multitudes" (*The Underground Railroad,* page 323).

Maine was an ideal haven for smuggled fugitives, as sea captains forwarded their human cargo to agents waiting on the wharves to arrange for the next stop. U.S. Senator Henry Wilson wrote of a slave found secreted, in 1837, aboard the ship *Boston,* of Maine, homeward bound from Georgia. The captain was charged with slave-stealing and the governor of Georgia demanded him as a fugitive from justice. However, the governor of Maine refused to comply with the requisition, as the laws of his state considered slaves persons rather than property. Many other freedom-seeking travelers escaped as stowaways.

The prevailing sentiment in Portland was favorable to the temporary sojourn of fugitives, and Portland became a vital station for the "trackless train" as it moved toward New Brunswick and Lower Canada. Among the documented Underground Railroad stations serving other areas in Maine are the Episcopal Parish House in Gardiner and the Lamb House, located near the Kennebec River. The

Nason House in Augusta contained a secret room behind a large bookcase, large enough to contain fugitives.

Birthplace of Daniel Webster, John B. Hale, Salmon P. Chase, Horace Greenley, Charles A. Dana, and proslavery President Franklin B. Pierce, New Hampshire was also a state where friends of the Underground Railroad boldly directed their passengers to the "promised land."

The antislavery atmosphere in New Hampshire had evoked sympathy for runaway slaves as early as 1796. In that year, the citizens of Portsmouth defied President George Washington's request to return one of his female slaves. He wrote to Joseph Whipple, Collector of Customs at that town. Customs Collector Whipple declared in his letter to the President that the return of the slave would be impossible, public sentiment being too strong against it.

By 1835, several local, county, and state antislavery societies had been established. Some did little but talk; others offered more concrete forms of assistance to runaways.

Siebert wrote (page 36) that in New Hampshire there was a station at Canaan after 1830 and probably before that time. This information was received in a letter from Mr. Charles Lord dated July 6, 1896, stating: "My maternal grandfather, James Furber, lived for several years in Canaan, where his house was one of the stations of the Underground Railway. His father-in-law, James Harris, who lived in the same house, had been engaged in helping fugitive slaves on toward Canada ever since 1830." Furber is said to have transported fugitives to Lyme, New Hampshire, about once a fortnight.

While slaves were probably also smuggled by other routes within the state, we know for certain that they traveled up the east side of the Connecticut River, beyond Haverhill, then passed northeastward through Franconia and Littleton and across the Vermont boundary to Lunenburg.

Narrative of Charlotte Forten

Charlotte Forten was the granddaughter of abolitionist James Forten of Philadelphia. She went to Massachusetts to attend the Salem Normal School, and resided at the home of Underground Railroad agent Charles Lenox Remond and his sister, Sarah Remond. This account is from Billington's edition of her *Journal* (pages 43 to 46).

Thursday, May 25, 1854. Did not intend to write this evening, but have just heard of something which is worth recording—something which must ever rouse in the mind of every true friend of liberty and humanity, feelings of the deepest indignation and sorrow. Another fugitive from bondage has been arrested; a poor man, who for two short months has trod the soil and breathed the air of the "Old Bay State," was arrested like a criminal in the streets of her capital, and is now kept strictly guarded—a double police force is required, the military are in readiness; and all this done to prevent a man, whom God has created in his own image, from regaining that freedom with which he, in common with every other human being, is endowed. I can only hope and pray most earnestly that Boston will not again disgrace herself by sending him back to a bondage worse than death; or rather that she will redeem herself from the disgrace which his arrest alone has brought upon her. . . .

Saturday, May 27. Returned home, read the Anti-Slavery papers, and then went down to the depot to meet father; he had arrived in Boston early in the morning, regretted very much that he had not reached there the evening before to attend the great meeting at Faneuil Hall. He says that the excitement in Boston is very great; the trial of the poor man takes place on Monday. We scarcely dare to think of what may be the result; there seems to be nothing too bad for those Northern tools of slavery to do. . . .

Tuesday, May 30. Rose very early and was busy until nine o'clock; then, at Mrs. Putnam's urgent request, went to keep store for her while she went to Boston to attend the Anti-Slavery Convention. I was very anxious to go, and will certainly do so tomorrow; the arrest of the alleged fugitive will give additional interest to the meetings, I should think. His trial is still going on and I can scarely think of anything else; read again today as most suitable to my feelings and to the times, "The Run-away Slave at Pilgrim's Point," by Elizabeth B. Browning; how powerfully it is written! how earnestly and touchingly does the writer portray the bitter anguish of the poor fugitive as she thinks over all the wrongs and sufferings that she has endured, and of the sin to which tyrants have driven her but which they alone must answer for! It seems as if no one could read this poem without having his sympathies aroused to the utmost in behalf of the oppressed. After a long conversation with my friend on her return, on this all-absorbing subject, we separated for the night, and I went to bed, weary and sad.

Wednesday, May 31. Sarah and I went to Boston in the morning. Everything was much quieter—outwardly than we expected, but still much real indignation and excitement prevail. We walked past the Court-House, which is now lawlessly converted into a prison, and filled with soldiers, some of whom were looking from the windows, with an air of insolent authority which made my blood boil, while I felt the strongest contempt for their cowardice and servility. We went to the meeting, but the best speakers were absent, engaged in the most arduous and untiring efforts in behalf of the poor fugitive; but though we missed the glowing eloquence of Phillips, Garrison, and Parker, still there were excellent speeches made, and our hearts responded to the exalted sentiments of Truth and Liberty which were uttered. The exciting intelligence which occasionally came in relation to the trial, added fresh zeal to the speakers, of whom Stephen Foster and his wife were the principal. The latter addressed, in the most eloquent language, the women present, entreating them to urge their husbands and brothers to action, and also to give their aid on all occasions in our just and holy cause. I did not see father the whole day; he, of course, was deeply interested in the trial. Dined at Mr. Garrison's; his wife is one of the loveliest persons I have ever seen, worthy of such a husband. At the table, I watched earnestly the expression of that noble face, as he spoke beautifully in support of the non-resistant principles to which he has kept firm; his is indeed the very highest Christian spirit, to which I cannot hope to reach, however, for I believe in "resistance to tyrants," and would fight for liberty until death. We came home in the evening, and felt sick at heart as we passed through the streets of Boston on our way to the depot, seeing the military as they rode along, ready at any time to prove themselves the minions of the South.

Thursday, June 1st. The trial is over at last; the commissioner's decision will be given tomorrow. We are all in the greatest suspense; what will that decision be? Alas! that any one should have the power to decide the right of a fellow being to himself! It is thought by many that he will be acquitted of the *great crime* of leaving a life of bondage, as the legal evidence is not thought sufficient to convict him. But it is only too probable that they will sacrifice him to propitiate the South, since so many at the North dared oppose the passage of the infamous Nebraska Bill. . . .

Friday, June 2. Our worst fears are realized; the decision was against poor Burns, and he has been sent back to a bondage worse, a thousand times worse than death. Even an attempt at rescue was utterly impossible; the prisoner was completely surrounded by soldiers with bayonets fixed, a cannon loaded, ready to be fired at the slightest sign. Today Massachusetts has again been disgraced. Again has she shewed her submission to the Slave Power; and Oh! with what deep sorrow do we think of what will doubtless be the fate of that poor man, when he is again consigned to the horrors of Slavery. With what scorn must that government be regarded, which cowardly assembles thousands of soldiers to satisfy the demands of slaveholders; to deprive of his freedom a man, created in God's own image, whose sole offense is the color of his skin! And if resistance is offered to this outrage, these soldiers are to shoot down American citizens without mercy; and this by the express orders of a government which proudly boasts of being the freest in the world; this on the very soil where the Revolution of 1776 began, in sight of the battle-field, where thousands of brave men fought and died in opposing British tyranny, which was nothing compared with the American oppression of today. In looking over my diary, I perceive that I did not mention that there was on the Friday night after the man's arrest, an attempt made to rescue him, but although it failed, on account of there not being men enough engaged in it, all honor should be given to those who

bravely made attempt. I can write no more. A cloud seems
hanging over me, over all our persecuted race, which nothing
can dispel.

Narrative of James Mars

*The Life of James Mars, A Slave Born and Sold in
Connecticut,* written by himself, contains this account
(pages 4 to 6).

The treatment of slaves was different at the North from the
South; at the North they were admitted to be a species of
the human family. I was told when a slave boy, that some of the
people said that slaves had no souls, and that they would
never go to heaven, let them do ever so well.

My father was born in the State of New York, I think in
Columbia County. He had, I think, three different masters in
that State, one by the name of Vanepps, and he was Gen.
Van Rensallaer's slave in the time of the Revolution, and was
a solider in that war; he was then owned by a man whose
name was Rutser, and then was owned in Connecticut, in
Salisbury, and then by the minister in North Canaan.

My mother was born in old Virginia, in Loudon County; I
do not remember the name of the town. The minister of North
Canaan, whose name was Thompson, went to Virginia for a
wife, or she came to him; in some way they got together, so
that they became man and wife. He removed her to Canaan,
and she brought her slaves with her, and my mother was one
of them. I think there were two of my mother's brothers also.
The Rev. Mr. Thompson, as he was then called, bought my
father, and he was married to my mother by him. Mr. Thompson ministered to the people of Canaan in holy things; his slaves
worked his farm. For a short time things went on very well;
but soon the North and the South, as now, fell out; the South
must rule, and after a time the North would not be ruled. The
minister's wife told my father if she only had him South,
where she could have at her call a half dozen men, she would
have him stripped and flogged until he was cut in strings, and

see if he would do as she bid him. She told him, "You mind, boy, I will have you there yet, and you will get your pay for all that you have done." My father was a man of considerable muscular strength, and was not easily frightened into obedience. I have heard my mother say she has often seen her mother tied up and whipped until the blood ran across the floor in the room where she was tied and whipped. Well, as I said, the South and the North could not agree; the South seceded and left the North; the minister's wife would not live North, and she and her husband picked up and went South, and left my father and mother in Canaan to work the farm, and they lived on the farm until I was eight years old. My mother had one child when she came from the South; I was the first she had after she was married. They had five children born in Canaan—three died in infancy. I was born March 3d, 1790. Mr. Thompson used to come up from Virginia and talk about our going South.

He would pat me on the head and tell me what a fine boy I was. Once when he was in Canaan, he asked me if I would like to go with him and drive the carriage for my mistress.

Horatio T. Strother adds the following in his book on the Underground Railroad in Connecticut (page 15):

James' father, however, had other ideas. Though he was only "a slave without education," yet he was a vigilant man; and as a father, he was naturally greatly concerned for the welfare of his wife, his daughter, and his two sons. He saw and heard much, kept it to himself—and planned his family's escape. He knew there was some ill feeling between Canaan and Norfolk, so to Norfolk they would go. Accordingly, he hitched up the parson's team in the dark of night, put his few possessions and his family aboard the wagon, and set out. The trip was not without incident—among other things, they ran afoul of someone's woodpile in the darkness—but they reached Norfolk well before daylight. There they found refuge in Pettibone's tavern, whose owner, like his descendants, was a friend of fugitive slaves. He welcomed the Mars family, helped them unload, and gave them a resting place for the balance of the night. But the tavern obviously could not be a permanent refuge. Of what happened next, James wrote many years later, "It was soon known in the morning that we were in Norfolk; the first enquiry was where will they be safe. The place was soon found. There was a man by the name of Phelps that had a house that was not occupied; it was out of the way and out of sight. After breakfast, we went to the house; it was well located; it needed some cleaning and that my mother could do as well as the next woman. . . . Days and weeks passed on and we began to feel quite happy, hoping that the parson had gone South."

But Thompson had not gone, and after some time the word spread that he was planning to recapture his slaves—particularly James and his brother Joseph. Therefore a Mr. Cady, who lived next door to Phelps, volunteered to take the boys to a place where they would be safe. At twilight he led them over hills and through woods, over rocks and fallen logs. At one point they came out on top of Burr Mountain, in the north-west corner of the township. "We could look down in low grounds," said James, "and see logs that were laid for the road across the meadow; at every flash they could be seen, but when it did not lighten, we could not see any thing; we kept on, our pilot knew the way." He led them down the hills toward the center of town, and so to the Tibbals house.

Here the boys were welcomed by "an old man, a middle aged man and his wife and four children. . . . We had not been there long," James continued, "before it was thought best that my brother should be still more out of the way, as he was about six years older than I, which made him an object of greater search, and they were at a loss where to send him, as he was then about fourteen years of age." Fortunately for Joseph, a young man named Butler, who was visiting in the neighborhood, agreed to take him to Massachusetts.

James, meanwhile, remained with the Tibbals for "a few days," after which he rejoined his parents and sister at the Phelps house. But before he arrived there, Thompson had come and gone; he had left James' mother with this proposition: "If she would go to Canaan and see to his things and pack them up for him, then if she did not want to go [to Virginia], she need not." Since this was a bargain, James and his sister were obliged to return to Canaan with their parents. Still the parson, mindful of the profits from the Virginia auction block, was not satisfied—he wanted Joseph. Hence he demanded that James' father search for him and bring him back. Now was the time for the elder Mars to act, and again he plotted to rescue his family. With Thompson's team of horses, he slipped his family away along the familiar route to Norfolk. Reaching Captain Lawrence's tavern there about two in the morning, they were given lodging for the night; then, to make their recovery more difficult, the Captain advised them to disperse and hide in different houses in the neighborhood.

James, at the outset, was passed to the home of an old woman nearby. "I stopped with her a few days, with instructions to keep still. You may wonder why I was sent to such a place; most likely it was thought that she had so little room that she would not be suspected of harboring a fugitive." A man named Walter frequently stopped by "to see how his boy did"; he told James that, if anyone else came to the house, he "must get under the bed." After several days of this hole-and-corner life, James was moved again, spirited from house to house through a chain of hiding places. "I was sent to Mr. Pease, well nigh Canaan, and kept rather dark. I was there for a time, and then I went to stay with a man by the name of Akins, and stayed with him a few days, and went to a man by the name of Foot, and was with him a few days." Finally, he said, "I went to another man by the name of Akins, and was there some time."

While James was being whisked about in this fashion, Thompson decided to sell him and Joseph on the spot; and to encourage the boys to appear on the scene, he allowed their parents to select the persons to whom they might be sold. Thus, when they came home in September of 1798, their new owners had been decided upon. Mr. Munger of Norfolk agreed to pay Thompson $100 for James, while Mr. Bingham of Salisbury undertook to pay the same for Joseph. Had there been a well-organized underground system in the community, this transaction might never have materialized. At any rate, James' parents and sister were set free, while Joseph, it is supposed, remained a slave until he reached the age of twenty-five. James, on the other hand—after the death of Mr. Munger—became a freeman at twenty-one, married, and settled down in Norfolk for the balance of his fruitful life.

Narrative of Austin Bearse

Reminiscences of Fugitive Slave Law Days includes this narrative (pages 8 to 10 and 36 to 39).

I am a native of the State of Massachusetts. Between the years of 1818 and 1830, I was from time to time mate on board of different vessels engaged in the coasting trade on the coast of South Carolina. It is well known that many New England vessels are in the habit of spending their winters on the Southern coast, in pursuit of this business—for vessels used to run up the rivers for the rough rice and cotton of the plantations, which we took to Charleston. We often carried gangs of slaves to the plantations as they had been ordered. These slaves were generally collected by slave-traders in Charleston, brought there by various causes, such as the death of owners and the division of estates, which threw them into the market. Some were sent as punishment for insubordination, or because the domestic establishment was too large; or because persons moving to the North and West preferred selling their slaves to the trouble of carrying them. We had on board our vessels, from time to time, numbers of these slaves—sometimes two or three, and sometimes as high as seventy or eighty. They were separated from their families and connections with as little concern as calves and pigs are selected out of a lot of domestic animals. Our vessel used to lie at a place called Poor Man's Hole, not far from the city. We used to allow the relatives and friends of the slaves to come on board and stay all night with their friends, before the vessel sailed. In the morning it used to be my business to pull off the hatches and warn them that it was time to separate, and the shrieks and cries at these times were enough to make anybody's heart ache. . . .

There was a plantation at Coosahatchie, back of Charleston, kept by a widow lady who owned eighty negroes. She sent to Charleston and bought a quadroon girl, very nearly white, for her son. We carried her up. She was more delicate than the other slaves, so she was not put with them, but carried up in the cabin.

I have been on the rice plantations in the rivers, and seen
the cultivation of the rice. In the fall of the year, the plantation hands, both men and women, work above their knees in
water in the rice ditches, pulling out the grass to fit the
ground for sowing the rice. . . . I have seen slavery in the
Spanish and French ports. My opinion is, that American
slavery, as I have seen it in the internal slave trade, as I have
seen it on the rice and sugar plantations, and in the city of
New Orleans, was *full as bad* as any slavery in the world—
heathen or Christian. People who go for visits or pleasure
through the Southern States, cannot possibly know those
things which can be seen of slavery by shipmasters. . . .

In my past days, the system of slavery was not much
discussed. I saw these things as others did, without interfer-
ence. Because I no longer think it right to see these things in
silence, I trade no more south of Mason and Dixon's line.

In 1834, I first saw the *Liberator*. I read it with delight. In
July, 1847, I sailed with a loaded vessel bound to Albany,
N.Y. On my arrival there, I called on the Mott sisters, ladies
well known to the Anti-Slavery friends in Boston and else-
where. Miss Mott told me they had a slave secreted just out
of the city, who was in danger. His name was George Lewis.
A writ was out for him, and she wished me to take him to
Boston. As soon as I was ready to sail, she brought him to
my vessel at night, with his baggage, and I stowed him away.
In three days I passed New York, and on getting into Long
Island Sound, I told George Lewis he could safely show
himself on deck, which he was glad to do.

One night in September, 1854, Wendell Phillips, Jacob M.
Haskell, and J. B. Smith came to my house at nine o'clock,
telling me that a schooner lay down at Fort Independence,
from Wilmington, North Carolina, with a fugitive slave on
board. The schooner proved to be the "Sally Ann," from
Belfast, Maine, and was loaded with yellow pine lumber for
parties in Boston. They wished me to get my yacht under-
weigh. I did. Going past the vessel I hailed the schooner and
asked the captain if he was ready to give up the slave he had
aboard (having been told by Mr. Haskell that the man to
whom the schooner was consigned wanted to get rid of him).
The answer I got was this: "If you come alongside my vessel
I will send you into eternity—quick!" So I went on up to
Long Wharf and waited for three hours, and only got Mr.

Haskell. No other man came. Knowing it was soon coming daylight, I had to lay a plot. I took a dozen old hats and coats and fastened them up to the rail in my yacht, which gave me the appearance of having so many men; I then went down back alongside the schooner again, and told the captain I had now come prepared, and he had better give up the fugitive and save bloodshed. After parleying a little while he agreed to put the slave in my boat. My brother went under his bow with the boat and the slave jumped in, and they pulled alongside the yacht. Then I made sail for City Point, South Boston. I landed the slave and carried him up to my house, stripped off his old tow suit and dressed him in another, so he could not be known. By this time it was daylight. Had just got him ready when Mr. Samuel May, Jr., and Dr. S. Cabot drove up to my house with a carriage, took him and carried him to the Boston and Worcester depot, and Mr. May went on with him to Worcester, and from there he was sent on the Underground Railway to Canada.

The next day the vessel hauled into Boston Wharf, and the captain had a notice inserted in the papers that his vessel was boarded by a set of pirates in the night, the slave rescued, and offering $500 for the man who headed the gang. After President Lincoln's proclamation, in 1863, the man returned from Canada and came to see me. He shipped on board a vessel for the West Indies; I have never seen him since, and cannot recall his name. . . .

In October, 1854, at eleven o'clock, one night, Wendell Phillips, in company with the late Dr. Samuel G. Howe, came to my house at City Point, South Boston, with word that the brig "Cameo," of Augusta, Maine, from Jacksonville, Florida, with a cargo of pine lumber, for Boston, was below. Mr. Phillips also had learned of the secretion of a slave on board, with the intention of gaining his freedom, if possible. Mr. Phillips hearing that the vessel was off Boston Light at sunset the same evening, wished me to get my men together at once, as a part of the Vigilance Committee, and search the city to find the brig. I called my brother, and we both started for the city and summoned the men. I sent some to Charlestown, Chelsea, and East Boston, and some to the North End. I took City Point and Neponset for my route. I gave my brother Boston Wharf as far as Long Wharf, with the intention of examining every vessel lying in the city. The next morning, at eight o'clock, we were to meet at No. 21 Cornhill, which were the headquarters of the Vigilance Committee. At that time and place we met, and my brother had found the brig and slave. The vessel was lying at Boston Wharf. The slave had left the vessel, but the mate followed him and persuaded him to return to it. He had on his slave dress of tow cloth. As soon as possible the Vigilance Committee swore out a writ to search the vessel; and with it in a constable's hand, Mr. Emery B. Fay, Mr. Wendell Phillips, and myself and brother, took a hack and went to Boston Wharf, where the vessel lay. The constable then boarded her and informed the mate that he was about to execute the warrant. The mate in reply told him to go ahead and search. We made a thorough search, but found no slave; but I went down into the after-hatch and there on the lumber was the bed where the slave had rested, during the voyage of twelve days. While I was in the vessel's hold, Mr. Fay called to me to come to him at once. I jumped upon the wharf. He said, "Look at that vessel on the opposite side of the dock; I think the slave we want is there." I went there at once, and as I was getting aboard, the whole crew left, except the slave. The vessel proved to be the schooner "William," of Augusta, Maine, and belonged to the same owners as the "Cameo." The draw-tender was in the act of opening the draw to pass the vessel through. The slave's clothing had been changed, and he was put on board the schooner to go back South to his old master. When I asked him if he was a slave, he looked confused, but made no reply. Again I asked him if he came in the "Cameo"—pointing to that vessel. He said, "Yes, Massa," telling me then of the captain's threat to throw him overboard off Cape Cod, if he showed himself. I told him to leave the vessel and follow me, as he was among friends and was now a free man. This he gladly did. Mr. Phillips put him into a carriage, and we drove directly to Lewis Hayden's house, in Southac Street.

The constable returned his writ with the endorsement, "No slave found aboard the 'Cameo.' " Mr. Hayden kept the fugitive about two weeks, when one night, at a meeting of the Vigilance Committee, he informed us that his house was closely watched by a constable and policeman, and he thought it necessary to remove him at once. Accordingly, by agreement, Mr. William I. Bowditch, of Brookline, came with his span of horses to Boston, and he drove to Mr. Hayden's house. Mr. Bowditch opened the carriage door, and the fugitive, dressed in woman's clothes, got in. We then drove down Cambridge Street, over the bridge to East Cambridge, thence to Somerville, from there to Medford, and finally to Concord— arriving at about one o'clock. We drove directly to Mr. Allen's house, by agreement—he being one of the Vigilance Committee. The door was opened, when two men stepped out of the house and took in our lady. We then drove to the tavern, put up our horses and rested until three A.M., arriving at Brookline at about breakfast time.

The slave was afterwards sent to Canada, where he lived nine years. After the Emancipation Proclamation of 1863, he returned to Boston, joined a colored regiment, went South, and was killed in battle. This slave proved a true patriot by sacrificing his life for his country.

Narrative of the Gileadites

John Brown had not attained any degree of prominence when he organized the U.S. League of Gileadites, an organization of escaped slaves resisting any efforts to return them to bondage. Brown biographer Richard O. Boyer wrote of the following: "It is a crucial document in John Brown's life, one of the best things he ever wrote, more to the point than most of his words as to the actual business of fighting slavery" (page 435). It specifically outlines a program of resistance, and was signed by forty-four black men and women.

Nothing so charms the American people as personal bravery. Witness the case of Cinques, of everlasting memory, on board the "Amistad." The trial for life of one bold and to some extent successful man, for defending his rights in good earnest, would arouse more sympathy throughout the nation than the accumulated wrongs and sufferings of more than three millions of our submissive colored population. We need not mention the Greeks struggling against the oppressive

Turks, the Poles against Russia, nor the Hungarians against Austria and Russia combined, to prove this. *No jury can be found in the Northern States that would convict a man for defending his rights to the last extremity* [emphasis added]. This is well understood by Southern Congressmen, who insisted that the right of trial by jury should not be granted to the fugitive. Colored people have ten times the number of fast friends among the whites than they suppose, and would have ten times the number they now have were they but half as much earnest to secure their dearest rights as they are to ape the follies and extravagances of their white neighbors, and to indulge in idle show, in ease and in luxury. Just think of the money expended by individuals in your behalf in the past twenty years! Think of the number who have been mobbed and imprisoned on your account! Have any of you seen the Branded Hand? Do you remember the names of Lovejoy and Torrey?

Should one of your number be arrested, you must collect together as quickly as possible, so as to outnumber your adversaries who are taking an active part against you. Let no able-bodied man appear on the ground unequipped, or with his weapons exposed to view: let that be understood beforehand. Your plans must be known only to yourself, and with the understanding that all traitors must die, whenever caught and proved to be guilty. "Whosoever is fearful or afraid, let him return and part early from Mount Gilead." (Judges vii. 3; Deut. xx. 8). Give all cowards an opportunity to show it on condition of holding their peace. *Do not delay one moment after you are ready: you will lose all your resolution if you do. Let the first blow be the signal for all to engage; and when engaged do not do your work by halves, but make clean work with your enemies—and be sure you meddle not with any others.* By going about your business quietly, you will get the job disposed of before the number that an uproar would bring together can collect; and you will have the advantage of those who come out against you, for they will be wholly unprepared with either equipment or matured plans; all with them will be confusion and terror. Your enemies will be slow to attack you after you have done up the work nicely; and if they should, they will have to encounter your white friends as well as you; for you may safely calculate on a division of the whites, and may by that means get to an honorable parley.

Be firm, determined, and cool; but let it be understood that you are not to be driven to desperation without making it an awful dear job to others as well as to you. Give them to know distinctly that those who live in wooden houses should not throw fire, and that you are just as able to suffer as your white neighbors. *After effecting a rescue, if you are assailed, go into the houses of your most prominent and influential white friends with your wives; and that will effectually fasten upon them the suspicion of being connected with you, and will compel them to make a common cause with you, whether they would otherwise live up to their profession or not. This would leave them no choice in the matter.*

Some would, doubtless, prove themselves true of their own choice; others would flinch. That would be taking them at their own words. You make a tumult in the court-room where a trial is going on by burning gunpowder freely in paper packages, if you cannot think of any better way to create a momentary alarm, and might possibly give one or more of your enemies a hoist. But in such a case the prisoner will need to take the hint at once and bestir himself; and so should his friends improve the opportunity for a general rush.

A lasso might possibly be applied to a slave-catcher for once with good effect. Hold on to your weapons, and never be persuaded to leave them, part with them, or have them far away from you. *Stand by one another, and by your friends, while a drop of blood remains; and be hanged, if you must, but tell no tales out of school. Make no confession.*

CANADA

As early as 1820, Charles Stuart, secretary of the Canadian Anti-Slavery Society, set aside some town lots for the accommodation of escaped slaves. During the same year the Underground Railroad is reported to have established definite routes into Canada from all parts of the United States.

At first the number of slaves entering Canada was small but the number increased with each decade, reaching the greatest volume after the passage of the Fugitive Slave Law of 1850. Historians differ on the number of fugitive slaves who entered Canada through the Underground Railroad; the figures range from twenty-five to forty thousand. Siebert concluded that the portion of Canada most easily reached by fugitives was the lakebound region lying between New York on the east and Michigan on the west, and presenting a long inviting coastline to northern Ohio, northwestern Pennsylvania, and western New York (see Siebert, *The Underground Railroad,* page 195). Lower Canada was often reached through the New England states and by way of the coastline routes.

The Reverend William Mitchell estimated that no less than twelve hundred refugees reached the Toronto area every year. Levi Coffin reported that there were forty thousand in the whole of Canada in 1844. No less than three thousand reached there within three months after the Fugitive Slave Law of 1850 was passed.

Historian Robin Winks wrote in his book on blacks in Canada (page 144):

262

When the early fugitive Negro arrived in Upper Canada, he generally stopped quite near the border. Without funds, he could not move deeply into the interior; as an exile, he wished to remain close to the frontier for an eventual return; if a farmer, as most were, he preferred those near regions which seemed less dramatically different to the soils that he knew best. Small knots of Negroes settled at Welland and St. Catharines, back from the Niagara River; at Colchester, Windsor, and Amherstburg, opposite Detroit, near London, Chatham, and Dresden, in the center of the long peninsula of fertile lands that dipped south against Lake Erie almost to the latitude of New York City; and more slowly in Toronto, Oro, and in the Queen's Bush. Later arrivals were naturally attracted to places where Negroes had already established themselves. The fugitive Negro sought out his own kind increasingly as time passed, scorning the descendants of the Loyalist and slave Negroes in the Canadas, who themselves preferred to remain apart from the new arrivals.

Amherstburg, adjacent to Fort Malden, was the most important of these early settlements, and in the 1820s fugitive slaves helped make it the center of a modest but flourishing Canadian tobacco culture.

Others came in groups and organized settlements. The most successful in terms of its wealth, its population of two hundred families, and its general organization was Kent County. It was under the management of the Elgin Association, which had been founded by the Reverend William King. One thousand acres were acquired and sold to individual families in fifty-acre plots at $2.50 per acre. Another colony at Dawn was founded by Hiram Wilson, one of the seventy agents commissioned by the American Anti-Slavery Society to work among fugitive slaves. William King established another important center at North Buxton in 1850. Descendants of former slaves who were the charter residents of this community still reside in North and South Buxton.

Winks observed (page 248):

Few fugitives attempted to deny that they encountered substantial prejudice. In the 1850s city directories began to designate those residences and businesses owned by Negroes. Blacks were expelled from camp meetings, and those churchmen who—like Cronym in London—wished to help educate the fugitive, now argued that separate schools were needed because of white opposition. Dresden was called "Nigger Hole" by those who had opposed the Dawn settlement; racial jokes increased in the press; Negroes who, a decade or two earlier, had been able to employ whites to work for them no longer could do so.

Migration among fugitive slaves reached its peak in the 1840s and 1850s with blacks settling in Colchester, Elgin, Dresden, Dawn, Windsor, Sandwich, Bush, Wilberforce, Hamilton, St. Catherines, Chatham, Riley, Auberton, London, Malden, Confield, Amherstburg, Buxton, and Toronto. Among the noted and worthy Underground agents in Toronto was Dr. Alexander Ross, who made many daring excursions into the deep South rescuing slaves.

Nova Scotia, with less than one-tenth of the population of the country, today has approximately twelve percent of the black population. This is because one of the terminals of the Underground Railway was in the Nova Scotia county of Guysborough. Lincolnville, Tracadie, Milford Haven, and Boylston, in that county, are still full of black residents who are able to trace their roots to escapees on the Underground Railroad, and earlier black Loyalists.

BIBLIOGRAPHICAL ESSAY

In preparing this book, I have relied on primary and secondary sources, including biographies, memoirs, slave narratives, diaries, letters, and scrapbooks.

There is a vast amount of information in the many antislavery newspapers of the period, including *The Liberator, The National Anti-Slavery Standard, The Colored American, The Anti-Slavery Advocate, The Pennsylvania Freedmen, The Emancipator, The National Era, The North Star, The Philanthropist, The Herald of Freedom, The Provincial Freeman,* and *The Voice of the Fugitive.* Many of these periodicals provide first-hand accounts of fugitive slaves and their plights. Particularly helpful was a compilation by Samuel May of newspaper accounts of recaptured slaves entitled *The Fugitive Slave Law and Its Victims,* New York, 1861.

Of obvious importance were the many narratives by slaves and those who helped in the abolitionist movement: Linda Brent, *Incidents in the Life of a Slave Girl,* Boston, 1861; *Narrative of William Wells Brown,* Boston 1847; *Narrative of the Life and Adventures of Henry Bibb,* New York, 1849; *Frederick Douglass, My Bondage and My Freedom,* New York, 1855; *The Life of Josiah Henson,* Boston, 1849; *Narrative of Thomas Smallwood,* Toronto, 1851; *Narrative of the Suffering of Lewis Clark,* Boston, 1845; *Narrative of William Hayden,* Cincinnati, 1846; *The Rev. J. W. Loguen, as a Slave and as a Freeman,* Syracuse, 1859; *Running a Thousand Miles for Freedom or The Escape of William and Ellen Craft from*

265

Slavery, London, 1860; *Memoirs of Rev. Elijah P. Lovejoy*, New York, 1838; *Some Recollections of Our Anti-Slavery Conflict*, Boston, 1869; *Samuel Ringgold Ward, The Autobiography of a Fugitive Negro*, London, 1855; *James Pennington, The Fugitive Blacksmith*, London, 1849.

The classic collection of narratives compiled by William Still remains the most important source of information on the history and traditions of the Underground Railroad.

Suggested Readings

Aptheker, Herbert. *A Documentary History of the Negro People.* Secaucus, NJ: Citadel Press, 1973.

Bearse, Austin. *Reminiscences of a Fugitive—Slave Law Days.* Boston: Warren Richardson, 1880.

Billington, Ray Allen, ed. *The Journal of Charlotte Forten.* New York: Dryden Press, 1953.

Blackett, R. J. M. *Building an Antislavery Wall.* Baton Rouge, LA: Louisiana State University Press, 1983.

Blassingame, John W., ed. *Slave Testimony.* Baton Rouge, LA: Louisiana State University Press, 1977.

Blegen, Theodore Christian. *Minnesota: A History of the State.* Minneapolis: University of Minnesota Press, 1963.

Blockson, Charles L. "Escape from Slavery: The Underground Railroad," *National Geographic*, July 1984, pp. 3–39.

Boyer, Richard O. *The Legend of John Brown.* New York: Alfred A. Knopf, 1973.

Bradford, Sarah H. *Harriet, the Moses of Her People.* New York: J. J. Little, 1901.

Breyfogle, William. *Make Free: The Story of the Underground Railroad.* Philadelphia: J. B. Lippincott Company, 1958.

Brown, John. *The Sword and the Word.* South Brunswick, NJ, and New York: A. S. Barnes and Company, 1970.

Buckmaster, Henrietta. *Let My People Go.* New York: Harper & Brothers, 1941.

Chace, Elizabeth Buffum, and Lovell, Lucy Buffum. *Two Quaker Sisters: Diaries of Elizabeth Chace and Lucy B. Lovell.* New York: Liveright, 1937.

Chamerovze, L. A. *A Narrative of the Life, Sufferings and Escape of John Brown*. J. G. K. Traui & Co., 1859.

Child, Lydia Maria. *Isaac T. Hopper*. Boston: J. P. Jewett & Co., 1853.

Cockrum, William Monroe. *History of the Underground Railroad As It Was Conducted by the Anti-Slavery League*. Oakland City, IN: J. W. Cockrum Printing Company, 1915.

Coffin, Levi. *Reminiscences*. Cincinnati: Robert Clarke & Co., 1876.

Commonwealth. July 17, 1863. Collection of interviews by Benjamin Drew.

Conrad, Earl. *Harriet Tubman*. Washington, DC: Associated Publishers, 1942.

Cook, Herman, "An Iowa Fugitive Slave Case," *Annals* (3) 2:531–539 (October 1896).

Cunard, Nancy. *Negro: An Anthology*. Edited by Hugh Ford. New York: Frederick Ungar Publishing, 1970.

Davidson, John Nelson. *Negro Slavery and the Underground Railroad in Wisconsin*. Milwaukee: Parkman Club, 1891.

Douglass, Frederick. *Life and Times*. Hartford, CT: Hartford Park Publishing Company, 1882.

Drayton, Daniel. *Personal Memoir*. Boston: Bela Marsh, 1855.

Drew, Benjamin. *A North-Side View of Slavery: The Refugee: Or, The Narratives of Fugitive Slaves in Canada*. Boston: J. P. Jewett & Co., 1856.

Dumond, Dwight Lowell. *Anti-Slavery: The Crusade for Freedom in America*. Ann Arbor, MI: University of Michigan Press, 1961.

Fairbank, Calvin. *Rev. Calvin Fairbank During Slavery Times*. Chicago Patriotic Publishing Co., 1890.

Fairchild, James Harris. *The Underground Railroad*. Cleveland: Western Historical Society, 1895.

Foner, Philip. *The Making of Black America*. Westport, CT: Greenwood Press, 1983.

Franklin, John Hope. *From Slavery to Freedom*. New York: Alfred A. Knopf, 1967.

Freemen's Record. March 1865.

Furnas, J. C. *Goodbye to Uncle Tom*. New York: W. Sloane Associates, 1956.

Gallwey, Sidney. Letter to Charles L. Blockson pertaining to the Underground Railroad in Rochester, NY, August 5, 1984.

————. *Underground Railroad in Tompkins County*. Ithaca, NY: DeWitt Historical Society, 1963.

Gara, Larry. *The Liberty Line: The Legend of the Underground Railroad*. Lexington, KY: University of Kentucky Press, 1961.

Genovese, Eugene. *Roll Jordan, Roll, The World the Slaves Made*. New York: Pantheon Books, 1974.

Giddings, Paula. *When and Where I Enter: The Impact of Black Women on Race and Sex in America*. New York: William Morrow, 1984.

Grimes, William. *Life of William Grimes: The Runaway Slave*. New Haven: W. Grimes, 1855.

Harding, Vincent. *There Is a River: The Black Struggle for Freedom in America*. New York: Vintage Books, 1981.

Haviland, Laura S. *A Woman's Life Work*. Chicago: C. V. Waite, 1881.

Higginbotham, Leon, A., Jr. *In the Matter of Color*. New York: Oxford University Press, 1978.

Hill, Daniel G. *The Freedom Seekers: Blacks in Early Canada*. Agincourt, Canada: Book Society of Canada, 1981.

Hinton, Richard S. *John Brown and His Men,* New York: Funk & Wagnalls Co., 1904.

Holland, Frederic. *Frederick Douglass: The Colored Orator*. New York: Funk & Wagnals, 1895.

Johnson, Homer U. *From Dixie to Canada: Romances and Realities of the Underground Railroad*. Orwell, OH: H. U. Johnson, 1896.

Johnson, William H. *Autobiography of Dr. William Henry Johnson*. Albany, NY: Argus Co., 1900.

Jones, Thomas H. *Experience Narrative of Uncle Tom Jones, Who Was for Forty Years a Slave*. Boston, 1862.

Katz, Jonathan. *Resistance at Christiana: The Fugitive Slave Rebellion, Christiana, Pennsylvania, September 11, 1851*. New York: Thomas Y. Crowell Co., 1974.

Lane, Lunsford. *The Narrative of Lunsford Lane, Formerly of North Carolina. . . .* Boston: Hewes & Watson, 1848.

Lawrence, George A. *A Pioneer of Freedom*. Galesburg, IL: The Wagner Printing Co., 1913.

Littlefield, Daniel. *African and Seminoles*. Westport, CT: Greenwood Press, 1977.

Litwack, Leon. *North of Slavery: The Negroes in the Free States*. Chicago: University of Chicago Press, 1961.

Logan, Rayford W., and Winston, Michael R., eds. *Dictionary of American Negro Biography*.

Loguen, J. W. *The Rev. J. W. Loguen, as a Slave and as a Freeman*. Syracuse, NY: J. G. K. Truair & Co., 1859.

Lumpkin, Katherine DuPre. "The General Plan Was Freedom: A Negro Secret Order on the Underground Railroad." *Phylon* (Spring 1967). Atlanta GA: Atlanta University. pp. 63–76.

Mars, James. *Life of James Mars: A Slave Born and Sold in Connecticut*. Hartford, CT: Press of Case, Lockwood & Co., 1865.

May, Samuel. *The Fugitive Slave Law and Its Victims*. New York: American Anti-Slavery Society, 1861.

McDougall, Marion Gleason. *Fugitive Slaves (1619–1865)*. Boston: Ginn & Co., 1891.

McGowan, James A. *The Life and Letters of Thomas Garrett, Station Master on the Underground Railroad*. Moylan, PA: Whimsie Press, 1977.

Merrill, Arch. *The Underground, Freedom's Road*. New York: American Book Stratford Press, 1963.

Mitchell, William M. *The Underground Railroad*. London: W. Tweedie, 1860.

Muelder, Hermann R. *Fighters for Freedom*. New York: Columbia University, 1959.

Munro, John A. "The Negro in Delaware." *South Atlantic Quarterly*, LXI (1957), p. 436.

Mutunhu, Tendai. "Tompkins County: An Underground Railroad Transit in Central New York." *Afro-American In New York Life and History*, Vol. 3, No. 2 (July 1979), p. 27.

Nell, William C. *Colored Patriots of the American Revolution*. Boston: R. F. Wallcut, 1855.

New Jersey Writers Project. *Stories of New Jersey*. Newark, NJ: New Jersey State Library, 1811.

Nicholas, Charles H. *Many Thousand Gone: The Ex-Slaves' Account of Their Bondage and Freedom*. Leiden: Brill, 1963.

Northrup, Solomon. *Twelve Years a Slave, Narrative of Northup . . .* Wilson, N.Y.

Olmsted, Frederick Law. *A Journey in Back Country*. New York: Mason Brothers, 1860.

Pettit, Eber M. *Sketches in the History of the Underground Railroad*. Fredonia, NY: W. McKinstry & Son, 1879.

Pickard, Kate. *The Kidnapped and the Ransomed, Being the Personal Recollections of Peter Still and his Wife "Vini."* Fredonia, NY: W. McKinstry & Son, 1856.

Preston, E. Delorus, Jr. "Genesis of the Underground Railroad," *Journal of Negro History,* Vol. 18 (1933), pp. 144–170.

―――――. "The Underground Railroad in Northwest Ohio," *Journal of Negro History,* Vol. 17 (1932), pp. 414–416.

Price, Clement Alexander, ed. *Freedom Not Far Distant: A Documentary History of African Americans in New Jersey.* Newark, NJ: New Jersey Historical Society, 1980.

Proceedings of the American Antiquarian Society, Vol. 45 (April 17, 1935).

Quarles, Benjamin. *Black Abolitionists.* New York: Oxford University Press, 1969.

Redpath, James. *The Public Life of Captain John Brown.* Boston: Thayer and Eldreidge, 1860.

Robbins, Arlie C. *Legacy to Buxton.* North Buxton, Ont.: Oxford University Press, 1969.

Roper, Moses. *The Narrative of the Adventures of Escape of Moses Roper, from American Slavery.*

Ross, Alexander M. *Recollections and Experiences of an Abolitionist.* Toronto: Rowell and Hutchinson, 1875.

Scott, Emma Julia. "The Underground Railroad." Woodford County (IL) Historical Society paper presented August 30, 1934.

Siebert, Wilbur H. *Mysteries of Ohio's Underground Railroad,* Columbus, OH: Long's College Bookstore, Co., 1951.

―――――. *The Underground Railroad: From Slavery to Freedom.* New York: Macmillan Company, 1898.

―――――. "The Underground Railroad in Massachusetts," *Proceedings of the American Antiquarian Society,* Vol. 45 (April 17, 1935).

―――――. *Vermont's Anti-Slavery and Underground Railroad Record.*

Simmons, William J. *Men of Mark: Eminent, Progressive and Rising.* Cleveland: M. Rewell & Co. 1887.

Smedley, Robert C. *History of the Underground Railroad in Chester and the Neighboring Counties of Pennsylvania.* Lancaster, PA: Office of the Journal, 1883.

Stampp, Kenneth M. *The Peculiar Institution.* New York: Random House of Canada Limited, 1956.

Stavis, Barrie. *John Brown: The Sword and the Word.* New York: A. S. Barnes, 1970.

Sterling, Dorothy. *We Are Your Sisters: Black Women in the Nineteenth Century*. New York: W. W. Norton, 1984.

Stevens, Charles E. *Anthony Burns, A History*. Boston: John P. Jewett & Co., 1856.

Still, William. *Underground Railroad Records*. Philadelphia: W. Still, 1872.

Stowe, Harriet Beecher. *Key to Uncle Tom's Cabin*. Cleveland: Jewett, Proctor & Worthington, 1853.

Strother, Horatio T. *The Underground Railroad in Connecticut*. Middletown, CT: Wesleyan University Press, 1962.

Thompson, George. *Prison Life and Reflections*. New York: S. W. Benedict, 1848.

Villard, Oswald Garrison. *John Brown*. Boston: Houghton Mifflin Co., 1910.

Wade, Richard C. *Slavery in the Cities*. New York: Oxford University Press, 1964.

Walls, William J. *The African Methodist Episcopal Zion Church: Reality of the Black Church*. Charlotte, NC: A. M. E. Zion Publishing House, 1974.

Weld, Theodore D. *American Slavery As It Is*. New York: American Anti-Slavery Society, 1839.

Wilson, Henry. *History of the Rise and Fall of the Slave Power in America,* 3 vols. Boston: J. R. Osgood and Co., 1872–77.

Winks, Robin W. *The Blacks in Canada: A History*. New Haven: Yale University Press, 1971.

Wood, Peter. *Black Majority*. New York: Alfred A. Knopf, 1974.

Woolman, John. *Some Consideration in the Keeping of Negroes, 1754*. Philadelphia: James Chattin, 1754.

INDEX